Yeats and the Visual Arts

Yeats and the Visual Arts

RUTGERS UNIVERSITY PRESS

Elizabeth Bergmann Loizeaux

New Brunswick and London

Publication of this book has been aided by a publication grant from the National Endowment for the Humanities and a book subsidy award from the General Research Board, The Graduate School, University of Maryland.

Manufactured in the United States of America

Library of Congress Cataloging-in-Publication Data

Loizeaux, Elizabeth Bergmann.
Yeats and the visual arts.

Includes index.
1. Yeats, W. B. (William Butler), 1865–1939—Knowledge —Art. 2. Art in literature. I. Title.
PR5908-A35L6 1986 821'.8 85-30274
ISBN 0-8135-1175-5

British Cataloguing-in-Publication Information Available

For my parents,
Carl and Betsy Bergmann

Contents

Color Illustrations

Following Page 116

Black and White Illustrations

Acknowledgments

I would like to thank the following people and institutions who helped make this book possible:

George Bornstein for getting the project underway and supporting it throughout;

Richard J. Finneran, David R. Clark, and Annabel Patterson for reading the manuscript at various stages and offering encouragement;

Colin White for giving of his expertise on Edmund Dulac;

William O'Donnell, William M. Murphy, George Mills Harper, Paul Delaney, John Kelly, and Jon Stallworthy for responding quickly and generously to requests for information;

Anne Yeats and Michael Yeats for answering questions and permitting access to Yeats materials;

The National Endowment for the Humanities, the General Research Board of the University of Maryland, and the University of Maryland Department of English for granting financial support;

The staffs of the Tate Gallery, the British Library, the Humanities Research Center in Austin, the National Gallery of Ireland, and the National Library of Ireland.

I owe special gratitude to Neil Fraistat and RoseAnn Fraistat for reading the manuscript so carefully and giving so generously of their time and support; to John Auchard, Ted Leinwand, and Joan Goldberg for their encouragement and sympathy, and to Jan Liss for her help with photographs.

My largest debt is to my husband Bill, without whose love this book could not have been written.

Abbreviations

Au	*Autobiographies.* London: Macmillan, 1955.
AV-A	*A Critical Edition of Yeats's "A Vision" (1925).* Ed. George Mills Harper and Walter Kelly Hood. London: Macmillan, 1978.
AV-B	*A Vision.* London: Macmillan, 1962.
E&I	*Essays and Introductions.* London and New York: Macmillan, 1961.
Ex	*Explorations.* Selected by Mrs. W. B. Yeats. London: Macmillan, 1962; New York: Macmillan, 1963.
L	*The Letters of W. B. Yeats.* Ed. Allan Wade. London: Rupert Hart-Davis, 1954; New York: Macmillan, 1955.
LDW	*Letters on Poetry from W. B. Yeats to Dorothy Wellesley.* Introduction by Kathleen Raine. London and New York: Oxford University Press, 1964.
LTSM	*W. B. Yeats and T. Sturge Moore: Their Correspondence, 1901–1937.* Ed. Ursula Bridge. London: Routledge and Kegan Paul; New York: Oxford University Press, 1953.
LTWBY	*Letters to W. B. Yeats.* Ed. Richard J. Finneran, George Mills Harper, and William M. Murphy. London: Macmillan; New York: Columbia University Press, 1977.
Mem	*Memoirs.* Ed. Denis Donoghue. London: Macmillan, 1972; New York: Macmillan, 1973.
Myth	*Mythologies.* London and New York: Macmillan, 1959.
OBMV	*The Oxford Book of Modern Verse, 1892–1935.* Chosen by W. B. Yeats. Oxford: Clarendon Press, 1936.
OTB	*On the Boiler.* Dublin: Cuala Press, 1939.
UP1	*Uncollected Prose by W. B. Yeats.* Vol. 1. Ed. John P. Frayne. London: Macmillan; New York: Columbia University Press, 1970.
UP2	*Uncollected Prose by W. B. Yeats.* Vol. 2. Ed. John P. Frayne and Colton Johnson. London: Macmillan, 1975; New York: Columbia University Press, 1976.

VP *The Variorum Edition of the Poems of W. B. Yeats*. Ed. Peter Allt and Russell K. Alspach. New York: Macmillan, 1957; corrected third printing, 1966.

VPl *The Variorum Edition of the Plays of W. B. Yeats*. Ed. Russell K. Alspach. London and New York: Macmillan, 1966; corrected second printing, 1966.

YL O'Shea, Edward. *A Descriptive Catalog of W. B. Yeats's Library*. New York and London: Garland, 1985.

Yeats and the Visual Arts

Introduction

"I would have all the arts draw together," Yeats wrote in the 1937 introduction to *Essays and Introductions,* "recover their ancient association, the painter painting what the poet has written, the musician setting the poet's words to simple airs, that the horse-man and the engine-driver may sing them at their work" (*E&I* ix). Yeats's desire for such communion, particularly between literature and the visual arts, grew naturally out of personal circumstance and the lessons he learned from those around him. He was born a painter's son and trained for a time in his father's art. From an early age, he lived among those who took the visual arts as their life's work: painters, sculptors, craftsmen, collectors, art critics, art historians, museum curators. John Butler Yeats was for a while a follower of the Pre-Raphaelites, and his son espoused not only their vision of art allied to spirit and imagination, but the union of the arts—especially poetry and painting—that they and their works proclaimed. Yeats knew Dante Gabriel Rossetti's paintings and related sonnets, John Everett Millais's paintings on romantic poems, the illuminated books of their predecessor and hero William Blake; and he heard William Morris praise an idealized medieval world where artists of all kinds worked together. These visions of "the arts" affected in important ways Yeats's theory and practice as poet and dramatist.

Out of such alliances between literature and the visual arts developed Yeats's practice of discussing poetry, especially his own, by analogy to painting and sculpture: "I began my own life as an art student and I am a painter's son, so it is natural to me to see such analogies."[1] Yeats's mind operated essentially by association, linking image to image, idea to idea, building up conceptual structures whose rich complexities are among the chief pleasures of his poetry and prose. Except in his work as playwright and producer, Yeats rarely analyzed the connections between literature and the visual arts. Yet he linked them constantly and persistently, creating a web of associations that tied his art to painting and sculpture.

These analogies among the arts also aided the lifelong search for unity that motivated Yeats's thought and work. He attended closely to Blake's belief that, as Hazard Adams phrases it, "man achieves the greatest imaginative vision when he finally apprehends unity by seeing that all things are analogies of all other things."[2] The "Dove or Swan" section of *A Vision* reveals the important role the particular analogy between literature and the visual arts played in Yeats's apprehension of unity.

Although visual sources of Yeats's images have been a constant interest to his readers and critics since T. R. Henn's *The Lonely Tower* (1950), there has been little wider-ranging inquiry into Yeats's relationship to the visual arts. This book will examine Yeats's interests in particular artists and works of art, and will show how they affected the theory and practice of his poetry and plays. I propose two main ideas. First, Yeats's taste in the arts developed, as he indicated, "in the midst of the last phase of Pre-Raphaelitism" (*E&I* 346). Despite his widening knowledge of other schools, Pre-Raphaelite principles, filtered through late-century aestheticism, always underlay his attitudes toward art. Second, the analogies between literature and the visual arts, which Yeats used so often, apply to his own art; they can help us understand not only the relation his work bore to the visual arts, but the development of his poetry and the poetry itself. I argue that the poem-as-picture analogy that describes the major characteristics of his early work gave way to the poem-as-sculpture in the later verse, and that Yeats's experiments producing plays largely effected the transition. Implicit in this argument is the belief that in the study of interart connections we cannot treat the visual arts as one: sculpture differs from painting in important ways that distinguish their analogies to literature.

I intend this study to be suggestive rather than inclusive. Much, therefore, lies outside of its scope. I have touched on, but not treated, Yeats's knowledge of Eastern art. Nor have I provided detailed accounts of many of his interests in Western art or of his numerous relationships with living artists and members of the art world. Where I have found it useful, I have drawn on the theoretical debate about interart relationships, but have not tried to offer a theory of those relationships or an analysis of how Yeats's ideas and practice affect in large ways our formulation of the debate. All of these areas suggest interesting possibilities for future study.

The seven chapters that comprise this book follow, chronologically, Yeats's career. Chapter 1 sets him in the context of late-century Pre-Raphaelitism, examines his responses to the visual arts, and shows him adopting, rather than making, opinion. Chapter 2 looks at Yeats's unsuccessful experiments, during the 1880s, with poems on pictures and, using his own description of his early verse as "poetry of vision," explores the relationships between poetry and the visual arts implicit in his thinking. Chapter 3 views the early poetry in light of those implications. By drawing analogies between three works of art that Yeats admired and three poems characteristic of the early stages of his poetic development through the 1890s, it examines the relation of his poems to vision, the transformation of symbols in painting to symbols in poetry, and Yeats's use of poetic space. Chapter 4 charts Yeats's experiments uniting poetry and the visual arts in the production of plays. It shows how the model he took for stage presentation changed, under the pressure of experience, from painting to sculpture. Chapter 5 looks at Yeats's later knowledge and conception of the visual arts, especially as revealed by his most sustained commentary on them, the "Dove or Swan" section of *A Vision*. Chapter 6 examines the late poetry's explicit use of the visual arts as subjects for poems, as symbols, and as players in an aesthetic debate about "monuments." Chapter 7, taking its cue from Yeats's own statements and the observations of critics, discusses the sculptural in Yeats's later poems.

Despite his interest in the visual arts and his practice of drawing analogies between them and his own art, Yeats never went as far as Ezra Pound, T. E. Hulme, Stéphane Mallarmé, and other moderns who, as Frank Kermode observed, "all obscurely wished that poetry could be written with something other than words."[3] For Yeats always, "Words alone are certain good" (*VP* 65). Words can, and do, portray like painting and sculpture. But, Jan Mukařovský reminds us—in a comment about the pictorial analogy that also applies, especially for Yeats, to the sculptural—"a word remains a word and by copying painting literature attains only the discovery of a new possibility . . . of the artistic exploration of the word."[4] The purpose of this book is not to wish Yeats's words into paint or stone, but to reveal how, by seeing and using the relationships of literature to the visual arts, he expanded and explored the possibilities of verbal expression.

1

Yeats and the Pre-Raphaelites

A study of Yeats and the visual arts must begin with the Pre-Raphaelites. Theirs were the visual arts with which he grew up and to which he most often turned during the 1880s and 1890s when his own art and life were beginning to find shape. "I had learned to think in the midst of the last phase of Pre-Raphaelitism," he later recalled (*E&I* 346). Yeats's relation to the Pre-Raphaelites has been most often discussed in terms of the poetry: his attraction to Rossetti's intensity, his debt to the simplicity and stateliness of Morris's late verse, his absorption in the Pre-Raphaelite world of autumnal languor.[1] But for Yeats himself, the connection was as much, if not more, a matter of the visual arts.

Yeats's letters and essays of the late 1880s and the 1890s and his later autobiographical account of his youth are filled with references to Pre-Raphaelite painting and to the works of its offspring, the Arts and Crafts Movement. They make clear that defining his relation to Pre-Raphaelite art became a way of defining himself as both man and poet. The visual arts of the Pre-Raphaelites supplied Yeats with rationales for renouncing his father, for identifying friends, and for judging other artists. Selecting certain Pre-Raphaelites for admiration, leaving others aside, examining the works he loved, and identifying their strengths and weaknesses became, more importantly, a method for determining his own poetic course. The phenomenon of using another's art as a way of understanding one's own is not in itself strange: as a psychological maneuver it provided Yeats the distance necessary to give and take self-criticism, and much of his analysis of other writers has been correctly read as commentary on his own poetic position.[2] What is unusual are the frequency and ease with which he would turn to the visual arts instead of poetry for this purpose.

To understand the relation between Yeats's attitudes toward Pre-Raphaelite art and his early poetry, it is necessary to examine first his Pre-Raphaelitism during the 1880s and 1890s. Although Yeats's comments on the Pre-Raphaelites are scattered throughout his letters, essays, and *Autobiographies,* they reveal a consistent set of perceptions about the art he so admired. By more recent accounts of the Pre-Raphaelite movement, Yeats's ideas may seem quirky or simply wrong. They were, however, bred by attitudes current at the time. Yet, if Yeats appears more often as a supporter and amplifier of shared opinion about the Pre-Raphaelites than as an innovative thinker, he was never a slavish follower. Pre-Raphaelitism as it was seen at the end of the nineteenth century suited his needs and interests, and his response to it inevitably bore the marks of his own temperament.

Pre-Raphaelitism began in 1848 when three young painters, William Holman Hunt, Dante Gabriel Rossetti, John Everett Millais, and four of their friends founded the Pre-Raphaelite Brotherhood to overthrow the grand manner of the Royal Academy and its most illustrious president, "Sir Sloshua" Reynolds. In opposition to the "conventional pyramidic composition," the dramatic contrasts of light and dark, and the "superficial bravura" of the "free, open brushwork" characteristic of the Raphael-inspired Academy pictures, they emulated the clean line, pure color, and fine painting of the early Italians—Giotto, Piero della Francesca, Fra Angelico.[3] They advocated a "return to nature" as a way of assuring "emotional sincerity" and checking mere displays of technical virtuosity. Yet they did not intend simply to record what they saw, despite their often laborious efforts to achieve literal accuracy.[4] Their realism was to serve the expression of the spiritual and emotional, "small actualities made vocal of lofty meanings," their journal, *The Germ*, explained.[5] Such ideals were carried on for the Pre-Raphaelites by Rossetti's disciples William Morris and Edward Burne-Jones and by the Arts and Crafts Movement they began.

Yeats learned of the Pre-Raphaelites from his father, who, as object of both adoration and rebellion, deeply affected his son's ideas about art. J. B. Yeats had abandoned a legal career to become a painter and had spent the first years of his new life in pursuit of Pre-Raphaelite principles. In 1869, when Yeats was four, J. B. Yeats formed with John Nettleship, Edwin Ellis, and Sydney Hall (soon replaced by George Wilson) the "brotherhood," which they claimed was nondoctrinal, but whose name nevertheless derived from the Pre-Raphaelites.[6] The group possessed a few tenuous ties to the main movement: Burne-Jones knew Nettleship well enough to dub him "His Nettleship" for his crankiness; Rossetti admired J. B. Yeats's painting *Pippa* (fig. 1) and—according to J. B. Yeats—proclaimed Nettleship's *God Creating Evil* "'the most sublime conception in ancient or modern art.'"[7]

The London intellectual world Yeats entered in 1887 at the age of twenty-two encouraged the love of Pre-Raphaelite art his father had inspired in him. Following Rossetti's death in 1882, there appeared a wave of exhibitions and publications on the Pre-Raphaelites. An edition of Dante Gabriel Rossetti's *Collected Works* in 1886 initiated William Michael Rossetti's career as his brother's literary executor. During the next fifteen years (1886–1901), he published numerous volumes of Rossetti's letters and notes, along with other Pre-Raphaelite papers, including the diary of the painter Ford Madox Brown, an unofficial member of the Brotherhood. In addition, biographical and critical appraisals crowded through the presses.[8] Yeats acquired the two most important studies, both considered standard until recently (*YL* 16, 166): Percy H. Bate's *The English Pre-Raphaelite Painters* (1899) and H. C. Marillier's *Dante Gabriel Rossetti: An Illustrated Memorial of His Art and Life* (1899).

The 1880s and 1890s, furthermore, saw the proliferation of art jour-

Figure 1. John Butler Yeats, *Pippa Passes*, 1871.
The National Gallery of Ireland, Dublin.

nals, such as *The Studio, The Dome,* and *The Pageant,* sympathetic to Pre-Raphaelitism and inspired by the later Pre-Raphaelite movement's emphasis on finely designed publications. They provided a forum for the discussion of Pre-Raphaelite issues, and their high-quality reproductions kept the Pre-Raphaelite works before the public eye.[9] Yeats knew these journals well, publishing six poems and six essays in *The Dome* between 1897 and 1900.[10]

The institutional sector of the art world also supported the Pre-Raphaelites. In 1877 the opening of the Grovesnor Gallery provided a respectable showplace for rebels who did not wish to exhibit at the Royal Academy. By the end of the next decade, London's museums were gathering Pre-Raphaelite works. Before 1900 the National Gallery, which Yeats often visited, had acquired Rossetti's *Annunciation* (fig. I) and two other paintings, eleven works by Millais including *Ophelia,* Brown's *Jesus Washing Peter's Feet* (fig. 16) and a series of his drawings, plus numerous other works by the Pre-Raphaelites and their followers.[11]

Yeats's immediate intellectual circle confirmed the importance of Pre-Raphaelitism and played a major role in promoting it during the 1890s. Oscar Wilde, the movement's most important spokesman, praised the Pre-Raphaelite revolution and publicized its decorative work, especially "all that marvel of design that comes from the hand of Edward Burne-Jones."[12] Yeats's friend, Arthur Symons, echoed Wilde's enthusiasm. Symon's journal, *The Savoy,* in which Yeats published eight poems and a short story in 1896,[13] frequently discussed the works of Brown, Rossetti, Burne-Jones, and Morris. Two other friends, Lionel Johnson and Ernest Dowson, also praised the Pre-Raphaelites. Yeats later remembered that a picture by the Pre-Raphaelite follower Simeon Solomon hung on Johnson's wall and contributed to the young poet's judgment that Johnson would make a good friend (*Au* 305). Dowson's letters constantly reveal his admiration for Pre-Raphaelite art, both in their overt praise—he called a room designed by Morris "excellent"—and in their use of the Pre-Raphaelites as standards of judgment—he praised, for example, a portrait by Charles Shannon because he found in it "the mystique of Rossetti."[14]

The enthusiasm of friends helped keep Yeats's Pre-Raphaelitism alive, but, paradoxically, his father's growing disinterest in the Pre-Raphaelites did perhaps as much. The initial admiration for Pre-Raphaelitism, which had motivated J. B. Yeats and the other members of their brotherhood, had waned as they matured and went separate ways. J. T. Nettleship, in Yeats's phrase, "turned lion-painter," and George Wilson, slipping into an easy, sentimental style, began to paint "with phlegm and melancholy" the landscapes of Aberdeen (*Au* 44, 46). J. B. Yeats developed an interest in

Figure 2. William Butler Yeats, *Coole Library,* pastel, c. 1903. Courtesy of Michael B. Yeats and Anne Yeats.

such French painters as Corot and gave up Pre-Raphaelite-inspired pictures to pursue portrait painting, which offered the possibility of an income and for which he had a greater talent.[15] Yeats associated his father's new focus with the enthusiasm for French painting, which he heard about—with increasing disaffection—at the Metropolitan School of Art (*Au* 115). Although J. B. Yeats does not seem to have been particularly taken with Impressionism and was never a sentimental or popular painter, Yeats aligned him with the Impressionists, with the painters of French peasant life, and with their popular exponents, Jules Bastien-Lepage and Carolus Duran.[16] The last two often appear in Yeats's writing in tandem with T. H. Huxley and John Tyndall, representatives of "Victorian science"—the source, Yeats thought, of his father's misguided philosophy of art (*Au* 82).

Pre-Raphaelitism for the young Yeats thus became an expression of filial rebellion, and that personal motive contributed to his love for the art his father had left behind. As Richard Ellmann has pointed out, Yeats found it difficult to establish an identity separate from that of J. B. Yeats, in part because he admired his father so immensely. As a lawyer turned

Figure 3. John Butler Yeats, *W. B. Yeats,* n.d.
The National Gallery of Ireland, Dublin.

artist and as an artist who never did manage to make a living from his work, J. B. Yeats stood against the prescribed patterns of Victorian life and art—a stance his son could not oppose.[17] But Yeats's endorsement of Pre-Raphaelitism allowed him to define a position of his own without entirely condemning his father. By holding to Pre-Raphaelitism, Yeats declared himself against J. B. Yeats and the new French school while simultaneously affirming his allegiance to his father's earlier Pre-Raphaelite self.

Yeats's own efforts in the visual arts—which are few, and which he seems to have given up in the early 1900s—suggest the power of both J. B. Yeats's influence and Yeats's desire to go his own way. *Head of a Young Man* (fig. II), painted in 1887, supports the *Autobiographies*' claim that "I could only imitate my father" (*Au* 83). The delicate watercolor portrait is reminiscent of J. B. Yeats's work, but its clear yellow and red ally it to the Pre-Raphaelites. By the turn of the century when Yeats made two pastel sketches of Coole (fig. 2), J. B. Yeats's artistic influence seems to have faded. These works, empty of human figures, evoke the mood of place rather than reveal the psychology of a sitter as J. B. Yeats's portraits do (figs. 3, 4). In them, James White has found the influence of Turner, whom Yeats's generation admired, as we will see, in the name of Pre-Raphaelitism.[18]

Figure 5. Dante Gabriel Rossetti, *The Girlhood of Mary Virgin*, 1849. Tate Gallery, London.

painters who found inspiration in their own poems as well as in those by others.

Yeats first saw the literary side of Pre-Raphaelitism in his father's work. In his early days as a painter, J. B. Yeats had favored literary subjects, illustrating a scene from Browning's *In a Gondola* and—as Christina and Dante Gabriel Rossetti had—"Pippa Passes" (fig. 1).[21] He furthermore told his son about the poet-painters Blake and Rossetti and

Figure 6. Dante Gabriel Rossetti, *Proserpine,* 1874.
Tate Gallery, London.

Figure 7. Cupboard, designed by Phillip Webb, decorated by Edward Burne-Jones, 1857. Ashmolean Museum, Oxford. Given by Burne-Jones to William and Jane Morris as a wedding present.

gave him their books to read (*Au* 114). Years later Yeats recalled with special vividness his "perpetual bewilderment" when J. B. Yeats abandoned pictures on subjects from "poetic tradition" (*Au* 115).

Both the original Brotherhood and that of J. B. Yeats were particularly drawn to the romantics, whose poems "most moved" Yeats and who had first inspired the Pre-Raphaelites to ally art and literature. Early-nineteenth-century periodicals, such as *Annals of the Fine Arts,* which published Keats's "Ode on a Grecian Urn," show the romantic age ignoring Gotthold Lessing's famous protest, in his 1766 *Laocoön,* against the intermingling of the arts.[22] The Pre-Raphaelites perpetuated the romantics' belief in the familial relations among the sister arts and illustrated one such relation in the tribute their paintings paid to the romantic poets. Hunt and Millais discovered the little-known poet Keats,[23] whose works became favorite subjects for paintings and drawings, among them Millais's *Isabella* and Hunt's *The Eve of St. Agnes.* J. B. Yeats and his friends shared the Pre-Raphaelite interest in romantic poetry. George Wilson, for example, painted the Shelley-inspired *Asia* and *Alastor* and illustrated Keats's "La Belle Dame sans Merci."[24] J. B. Yeats, in turn, transmitted the romantic/Pre-Raphaelite association to his son, sometimes by such unintentional but effective means as giving Yeats the volume of Shelley's poems whose margins he had decorated with pencil sketches of typical Pre-Raphaelite faces.[25]

The Pre-Raphaelites also perpetuated the romantic enthusiasm for Dante, Shakespeare, and Chaucer, by finding in them subjects for paintings that Yeats admired. As a youth he had been enchanted in Morris's house by a cupboard (fig. 7) designed by Phillip Webb and decorated by Burne-Jones with scenes from "The Prioress' Tale," a story his father had read him as a child (*Au* 140, 47). The Pre-Raphaelites' depictions of Dante, a favorite author with Rossetti, impressed Yeats even more. When, at the age of fifteen or sixteen, he saw Rossetti's *Dante's Dream* (fig. IV) in Liverpool, "its colour, its people, its romantic architecture" so affected him that the painting "blotted all other pictures away."[26]

The visual qualities that attracted Yeats in Pre-Raphaelite art were those he could easily associate with poetry: color and pattern. The first could be an element of poetic description. The second functioned like rhythm in poetry. Yeats constantly isolated color as the focus of his discussions of art, and he transferred both qualities to his own poetry, as we will see in chapter 3.[27]

Yeats's natural sensitivity to color was reinforced early on by the talk of its importance he heard among his father's friends. Like the Pre-Raphaelites, they praised the primary colors, as Yeats recalled thirty years later when standing before the Rossettis and Millais in the Tate (*E&I* 346). When the Yeats family moved in 1879 to Bedford Park—a new London neighborhood designed by Pre-Raphaelite sympathizers as a haven for artists, writers, and composers[28]—Yeats also learned from others to scorn the fireplace tiles, which "seemed to have been shaken out of a muddy kaleidoscope," and to love the clear, brilliant colors of the Pre-Raphaelites (*Au* 43). The reds and golds that so affected Yeats in *Dante's Dream* became favorites, but the deep blue prevalent in Pre-Raphaelite art especially attracted him (figs. I, VI). That color dominated his memory of the art of Bedford Park: he vividly recalled the peacock blue of the doors, the dining table, the woodwork, and the dresses of the dancing teachers and their mother (*Au* 43–44). It is the color of the background in Frank Potter's *Dormouse* (fig. III) and the only feature of that picture Yeats remembered when writing *Reveries over Childhood and Youth* in 1914, even though the painting had hung in the Yeats home for many years (*Au* 46; *E&I* 346).

From the beginning Yeats associated pattern, the repetition of form, with Pre-Raphaelite art in general and with its connection to literature: "I longed," he recalled, "for pattern, for Pre-Raphaelitism, for an art allied to poetry" (*Au* 81). Yeats found pattern attractive theoretically because it was a mark of nonmimetic art, a signal of the ordering process. As a child he was surrounded with the most obvious Pre-Raphaelite use of pattern, the repeated motifs of the wallpapers and tapestries of the Arts and Crafts Movement. But he found it in more subtle form in the careful harmony of shapes in Pre-Raphaelite painting: in the arrangement of vertical and horizontal forms in *Girlhood of Mary Virgin* or the measured balance of light and dark in *Dante's Dream*. Yeats recognized that line—the creator of clear, distinct shapes—gave pattern its energy and force and saved it from softness and sentimentality. Blake had articulated the belief in the "firm and determinate outline," which Yeats saw carried out in the Pre-Raphaelite paintings and crafts. He frequently quoted Blake's dicta on line and did so at length in his essay on Blake's illustrations to Dante (*E&I* 120).

The emphasis on the imaginative, spiritual, and literary aspects of Pre-Raphaelite art necessarily limited the cast of artists Yeats and his friends admired. Of the 1848 Brotherhood's seven members,[29] Yeats unreservedly praised only one—Dante Gabriel Rossetti. For John Everett Millais and the Pre-Raphaelites' close associate Ford Madox Brown, he had early affection; but despite their literary subjects, the appeal soon waned as Yeats discovered the Victorian moralism of their art and as Millais became more and more absorbed by the Academy establishment.[30] Yeats rarely mentioned Hunt, and then only disparagingly, and he seemed unaware of Collinson, Stephens and Woolner.[31]

To Yeats and his generation, Rossetti, Edward Burne-Jones, and

William Morris represented the Pre-Raphaelite movement.[32] Because Rossetti had been John Butler Yeats's Pre-Raphaelite idol, Yeats had learned in childhood to see him as the movement's head. His father's brotherhood had been "agog" about Rossetti,[33] and J. B. Yeats in particular had loved finding "in any stray model either the red hair or the curled lips or the columnar throat of the Rossetti woman."[34] Rossetti, in turn, admired J. B. Yeats's work and several times invited him to call. Whether out of lack of confidence or fear of the master, J. B. Yeats neglected the offers. He later said with regret, "Meeting a man like Rossetti must have been like sitting down to a great banquet in a King's hall."[35]

Such homage was echoed by others during the 1880s and 1890s. Articles and books on Rossetti proliferated, far out-numbering those on other Pre-Raphaelite figures.[36] Increasingly, aestheticism became identified with Pre-Raphaelitism in general and Rossettiism in particular.[37] Rossetti provided the specific inspiration for Yeats's immediate intellectual circle. Of the Rhymers Yeats later recalled, "Rossetti was a subconscious influence, and perhaps the most powerful of all" (*Au* 302).

The conscious influence was Pater. Indebted to Rossetti for the discussions of painting in *The Renaissance*,[38] Pater in turn encouraged, by his general stance toward art, admiration for Rossetti. The Rhymers' interpretation of that stance, however, promoted a Rossettiism more sensual and exotic than Pater's own. Their misreading of the conclusion to *The Renaissance* as a call to aestheticism led to the cultivation of the senses' delight in both art and life. With a passionate destructiveness that Pater had not forseen, Yeats and his friends tried to burn with the "hard gem-like flame." In Rossetti they found a spiritualized sensuousness that imaged their creed. For them, the later paintings, such as *Venus Verticordia* (1864–1868) and *Monna Vanna* (1866, retouched 1873),[39] represented life at its most intense and, hence, art at its most beautiful (fig. VII). The women's expressions of rapture and the sensuous details pictured the refined senses' ecstasy.[40]

Yeats helped encourage the view of Rossetti as a painter of the passionate and spiritual. In a 1902 essay on William Morris, he summed it up: "Rossetti, drunken with natural beauty, saw the supernatural beauty, the impossible beauty, in his frenzy" (*E&I* 64). Furthermore, Yeats helped establish Rossetti as a proponent of "art for art's sake." Despite the moral content of works such as *Found*, Yeats and his friends saw in the paintings a delight in form without regard for "meaning." While he may have been attracted to the religious ideas he found in Rossetti's paintings, Yeats followed his age in emphasizing that Rossetti "loved form and colour for themselves and apart from what they represent."[41]

William Morris and Edward Burne-Jones had been Rossetti's pupils and were now, for Yeats and his circle, Rossetti's living representatives. In

Figure 8. Dante Gabriel Rossetti, *The Maids of Elfen-Mere,* wood engraving by Dalziel Brothers for William Allingham's *The Music Master, A Love Story And Two Series of Day and Night Songs,* 1855. Department of Rare Books and Special Collections, The University of Michigan Library, Ann Arbor.

Figure 9. Edward Burne-Jones, *The Golden Stairs*, 1880.
Tate Gallery, London.

Figure 10. William Morris, *The Orchard,* tapestry, 1890. Courtesy of the Board of Trustees of the Victoria and Albert Museum, London.

1857, spurred on by the discovery of the illustration to William Allingham's "The Maids of Elfen-Mere" (fig. 8) that Yeats later praised (*UP* 1:209), Morris and Burne-Jones had sought out Rossetti, and together they formed another brotherhood which led to Burne-Jones's apprenticeship under Rossetti and to Morris's discovery of his talent for the decorative arts.

Although Yeats praised both, Morris inspired his greater admiration. Burne-Jones's art was, for Yeats, too calm and ethereal. Yeats liked the "peculiar kind of subtle expression and pensive grace" that he found in Burne-Jones's cartoons for a stained glass window, shown at the 1890 Arts and Crafts Exhibition that he reviewed, but he preferred the earlier, more vigorous designs (fig. 9) "done when Burne-Jones was young, and

his manner almost indistinguishable from that of Rossetti" (*UP* 1 : 184). Furthermore, despite his literary subjects, Burne-Jones was not a poet-painter, unlike Rossetti and Morris.

The strength of Morris's personality, his ability to combine art and poetry, and his attempt to bring the magic of fine design into everyday life inspired Yeats to call him a "man of genius" (*UP* 1 : 183). Yeats always admired Morris's decorative arts—whose pattern he associated with the rhythm of poetry—more than his paintings (figs. VI, 10). The Arts and Crafts Movement, which Morris had helped set in motion, first enchanted Yeats at the age of fourteen when the Yeats family moved to Bedford Park. His response to this Pre-Raphaelite-inspired garden community shows that even when not explicitly literary, the work of the Arts and

Crafts Movement transported Yeats to a world he connected with literature. The church and houses designed by Norman Shaw, the little shops with old-fashioned signs carefully painted by artists, the wallpapers designed by Morris all evoked a world suffused with literary associations. "We went to live in a house like those we had seen in pictures," Yeats later remembered, "and even met people dressed like people in the storybooks" (*Au* 43). He sat at a table where he imagined "Sinbad the sailor might have sat," and he admired the sisters of a Bedford Park painter because they wore "dresses so simply cut that they seemed a part of every story" (*Au* 44).

Morris's Arts and Crafts Movement attracted Yeats not only because its products evoked the world of literature, but because it philosophically supported the connection between visual art and poetry. Morris had found his inspiration in the Middle Ages, where he imagined the arts worked together, painters painting pictures of what poets wrote, poets taking subjects from paintings, craftsmen joining in the work of designing and decorating buildings and their furnishings. The "melancholy beauty of 'The Earthly Paradise'" cast its spell, Yeats thought, over Morris's own art and over the entire Arts and Crafts Movement (*UP* 1:184).

Yeats further emphasized the literary connections of Morris's decorative arts by finding in them the same impulse that had stirred the romantic poets:

> The movement most characteristic of the literature and art and to some small extent of the thoughts, too, of our century has been romanticism. . . . It marked the regained freedom of the spirit and imagination of man in literature. Since then painting in its turn has flung aside the old conventions. The arts of decoration are now [1890] making the same struggle. They have been making it for some years under the leadership of William Morris. (*UP* 1:183)

The line of descent Yeats traces here reveals not only his view of Pre-Raphaelitism as an art of spirit and imagination and his desire to associate literature with art, but his implicit assumption that visual artists can pick up and carry on a revolution begun by poets.

The admiration of Yeats and his friends for the spirit and imagination of Rossetti, Morris, and Burne-Jones was bound, as many of Yeats's already-quoted comments on them imply, to a fascination with the women featured so prominently in Pre-Raphaelite art. Yeats carried this ideal of woman into his life—casting Maud Gonne as an Irish incarnation of the Pre-Raphaelite beauty—and into his art. Rossetti provided the most striking images of Pre-Raphaelite women, and it is his work that Yeats mentions most often. J. B. Yeats, seeking models with the long throats and

Figure 11. Dante Gabriel Rossetti, *Sibylla Palmifera (Venus Palmifera)*, 1866–1870. Lady Lever Art Gallery, Port Sunlight.

auburn hair of those pictured by Rossetti, had set the precedent for his son's admiration.[42] The Rhymers perpetuated the infatuation, as Yeats recalled: "Woman herself was still in our eyes . . . romantic and mysterious, still the priestess of her shrine, our emotions remembering the *Lilith* and the *Sibylla Palmifera* of Rossetti" (*Au* 302). The distinguishing characteristic of the Rossetti woman was, as the Rhymers' choice of paintings suggests, her dual nature.[43] Rossetti tells us in accompanying poems that *Sibylla Palmifera* represents "Soul's Beauty" and *Lilith*, "Body's Beauty," although both obviously contain traits of the other (fig. 11). These women

Figure 12. Dante Gabriel Rossetti, *Astarte Syriaca (Venus Syriaca)*, 1877. Manchester City Art Galleries.

were simultaneously sensual and spiritual, as Yeats acknowledged when he explained that if Rossetti "painted a woman's face he painted it in some moment of intensity when the ecstasy of the lover and of the saint are alike, and desire becomes wisdom without ceasing to be desire" (*E&I* 53). Rossetti's women were also alluring, but unattainable, meant to tantalize but always frustrate.

While Yeats maintained this seductive image of female beauty—and in Manchester went with Maud Gonne to see its most sultry manifestation, *Astarte Syriaca* (fig. 12)[44]—he occasionally longed for a homier, more comfortable version, and he found it in Morris's work. Yeats derived his idea of Morris's women mainly from Morris's writings, but Rossetti's atypical *The Bride* (fig. 13) in particular, and Burne-Jones's "knights and ladies" in general, provided the visual depiction. Yeats thought of Morris's "good women," he said, "as like 'The Bride' in whose face Rossetti saw and painted for once the abundance of earth and not the half-hidden light of his star" (*E&I* 56). Morris's women live in harmony with his dream world of natural abundance. Like Burne-Jones's figures, they are "never, no, not once in forty volumes, put out of temper" (*AU* 143). "They are good housewives; they sit often at the embroidery frame, and they have wisdom in flocks and herds and they are before all fruitful mothers" (*E&I* 57). The calm domesticity, the consummation of sensuality in fruitful motherhood provided respite from the exotic and passionate appeal of Rossetti's untouchable heroines who most attracted Yeats.

With sensibilities firmly founded in Pre-Raphaelitism, Yeats and his friends also admired other artists whose work showed the qualities of spirit and imagination they found in Rossetti, Morris, and Burne-Jones. Their gallery included Gustave Moreau,[45] Puvis de Chavannes,[46] George Frederic Watts,[47] James McNeill Whistler,[48] Aubrey Beardsley,[49] Edward Calvert, Samuel Palmer, and J. M. W. Turner,[50] but the most important to Yeats was William Blake.

During the 1880s and 1890s, Yeats took Blake as his "particular study" (*E&I* vii), founding his ideas about Blake on the paintings and prints as well as on the poetry.[51] In his rooms at Woburn Buildings, Yeats surrounded himself with Blake's art: on the walls hung the first seven engraved illustrations to the *Divine Comedy* (a gift from the children of Blake's patron, John Linnell [*Au* 162]) and a reproduction of *The Ancient of Days*.[52] Discussions of Blake's art so pervade Yeats's essays of the 1890s that when he assembled them for publication in 1902, he titled the volume *Ideas of Good and Evil,* a phrase from Blake, and wrote to the publisher, "what do you think of giving his Francesca and Paolo as a frontispiece?" (*L* 377).

Figure 13. Dante Gabriel Rossetti, *The Beloved (The Bride)*, 1865–1866. Tate Gallery, London.

Although Yeats wrote more extensively on Blake than on any other artist, including Rossetti, he viewed Blake through the glass of Pre-Raphaelitism, not vice versa. In Blake's nonmimetic, literary art, Yeats saw the forerunner of the Pre-Raphaelite movement. Although Blake explicitly rejected narrative and allegorical painting, his pictures work in complex ways with both his own and others' texts. They often, in themselves, suggest a narrative, and when seen in a series create, in Harold

Bloom's phrase, "visionary cinema,"[53] a story that develops from frame to frame. Yeats also found in Blake the union of the physical and spiritual he admired so much in the Pre-Raphaelites' women, and a confirmation of passion's ability to effect that union. Illustrating Blake's ideas by reference to "certain drawings to *Vala*," Yeats explained: "The sensations of this 'foolish body' . . . were in themselves but half-living things, 'vegetative' things, but passion, that 'eternal glory,' made them a part of the body of God" (*E&I* 113).

Yeats liked Blake's pictures best when they possessed the qualities of the Pre-Raphaelite works he admired, and tempered his praise when they did not. In "William Blake and His Illustrations to the *Divine Comedy*," Yeats's most detailed account of Blake's paintings and engravings, he commented with regret that Blake, in his desire for "severe art," rejected those artists who "dwell over-fondly upon any softness of hair or flesh."[54] Yeats clearly liked at least one such artist, Rossetti. He also claimed that Blake "forgot how he who wraps the vision in light and shadows, in iridescent or glowing colour"—as the Pre-Raphaelites had—may also create "powerfully charged" art.[55]

Yeats owes his view of Blake not only to his own Pre-Raphaelite sensibilities but to the Pre-Raphaelites themselves, especially Dante Gabriel Rossetti and his brother William Michael. They had looked to the little-known Blake as mentor and had brought his work to a wider audience through their talk and publications.[56] Around 1881 Yeats, marveling at the "wonderful and mysterious pictures,"[57] read William Gilchrist's *Life of William Blake, "Pictor Ignotus"* (1863), which had been rewritten and completed by the Rossettis after Gilchrist's sudden death in 1861.[58] Dante Gabriel Rossetti did most of the revising, remaking Blake in his own image—"a Pre-Raphaelite artist-poet, medieval, sensuous and spiritual."[59] From this and other works on Blake by the Rossettis, Yeats derived many of the specific facts and opinions that informed his treatment of Blake's art.[60] He often repeated, for example, their view that the illustrations to *Job* and to the *Divine Comedy* (figs. 14, 15) were Blake's greatest achievements.[61] His interest in these particular works shows not only his adherence to the judgments of the Pre-Raphaelites but, again, his attraction to literary subjects, especially those the Pre-Raphaelites and their followers had also painted.[62]

Among the members of Yeats's circle, praise for Blake and the association of Blake and the Pre-Raphaelites were common. The Rhymers' master, Pater, knew Blake's work well and, as the references scattered through his writings show, assumed his audience shared both his knowledge and his view of Blake as a precursor to Rossetti.[63] Pater's student, Lionel Johnson, included Blake and Christina Rossetti among his youthful

Figure 14. William Blake, *The Creation* from *Illustrations of the Book of Job*, 1825. Rare Book and Special Collections Division, Library of Congress, Washington, D.C. Yeats owned an original print of this illustration.

Figure 15. William Blake, *Paolo and Francesca (Whirlwind of Lovers)* from *Illustrations to Dante's "Divine Comedy,"* 1827. Lessing J. Rosenwald Collection, Library of Congress, Washington, D.C. A reproduction of this plate accompanied the first part of Yeats's essay "William Blake and His Illustrations to the *Divine Comedy*" in *The Savoy*, July 1896. Yeats also owned an original print of this illustration.

"treasures."[64] Arthur Symons, the most serious Blake critic among them beside Yeats (whose interest in Blake animated Symons's own), published *William Blake* in 1907. Its preface humbly acknowledged, "Things have been written about Blake by Rossetti which no one will ever surpass."[65]

The image of Blake as a Pre-Raphaelite poet-painter was first instilled in Yeats by the father who gave him both Rossetti and Blake to read (*Au* 114). J. B. Yeats's brotherhood had taken a "passionate interest" in Blake,[66] and Yeats in turn admired those works of the brotherhood which showed Blake's influence. In 1890 Yeats began preparing an essay on J. T. Nettleship's "Blake drawings" and arranged for their publication. But the project came to nothing, the *Autobiographies* recounts, because it elicited from the publishers the same response that had often greeted the Pre-Raphaelites: "an obsequious caw in the Huxley, Tyndall, Carolus Duran, Bastien-Lepage rookery."[67]

It was Edwin Ellis, a member of J. B. Yeats's brotherhood, with whom Yeats collaborated on the three-volume edition and explanation of Blake's works, begun in 1889 and published in 1893. The emphasis here and in the essays on Blake reveals what made him Yeats's "particular study": Blake's attempt to create a symbolic system. Yeats observed, "He was a man crying out for a mythology, and trying to make one because he could not find one to his hand" (*E&I* 114). Although Pre-Raphaelite art contains symbols, they are discrete—a rose, a lily—and borrowed from a rich tradition, but not among themselves forming a coherent symbology. Unlike the Pre-Raphaelites, Blake was a visionary, one who, as Northrop Frye explains, "creates, or dwells in, a higher spiritual world in which the objects of perception in this one have become transfigured and charged with a new intensity of symbolism."[68] The Pre-Raphaelites, on the other hand, dwell in this world and transform it by adding symbols and literary allusions. Larger significance is worked into, rather than being inherent in, their vision.

Yeats admired the ambitiousness of Blake's project to create a mythology, but believed that the inclusiveness of Blake's symbolic vision hindered his effort to defeat the "classicisms" of Reynolds, of art tied to materiality. The Pre-Raphaelites, he thought, succeeded better because their vision was more limited. Focusing on the artistic issue, they used their symbols to combat materialistic art, not to explore a larger system their work set out and built on. "Blake made, in a blind, hopeless way," Yeats explained, "something of the same protest made afterwards by the Pre-Raphaelites with more success. They saw nothing but an artistic issue and were at peace; whereas he saw in every issue the whole contest of light and darkness and found no peace."[69] Looking at the Pre-Raphaelites today we might doubt the success Yeats claimed for them—their art seems, above all, materialistic. Yeats's comment, however, reveals not only his participation in the late nineteenth century's view of the Pre-Raphaelites as the victors in the battle for spirit and imagination, but his perceptive understanding of their limitation. It also makes clear that Yeats would side with Blake if he were made to choose.

As his response to Blake suggests, Yeats studied the artists he admired for what they could tell him or confirm about the conduct of his own life and art. At times his comments on Blake and the Pre-Raphaelites can be taken as those of a sympathetic observer of art; more often, they betray the urgency of self-assessment.[70] Even though some of the Pre-Raphaelites were dead, and none, except Morris, ever became friends, Yeats gathered these artists around him, discovering or creating ties to them—imagining himself content painting the Oxford Union with Burne-

Jones and Morris under Rossetti's direction, finding in Burne-Jones evidence of a shared passion for Ireland, and claiming Irish ancestry for Blake.[71] For support Yeats relied on them and on those committed to their art—the Rhymers were "all" Pre-Raphaelite, Yeats reminds us (*Au* 168). They provided the community, real or imagined, that countered the sense of isolation caused by temperament and a view of the artist in lonely pursuit of the ideal, part of the legacy from the romantic poets and the Pre-Raphaelites themselves.[72]

As he formulated his poetic theory, then, it is not surprising that Yeats turned for guidance not only to the poets he most admired, but to these artists. Furthermore, as he tried to unify thoughts that seemed diverse and scattered, connections between the visual arts so important to him and his own craft took on added importance. Yeats was justified in cultivating those connections by the Pre-Raphaelites' belief in unity of the arts, but he was inspired by the desire to make his thoughts and art whole. As with other aspects of Yeats's thought and practice during the 1880s and 1890s, the connections that he explored between art and poetry set a foundation for the rest of his career. We turn to the nature and implications of these relationships in the next two chapters.

2

Poems and Pictures

Yeats's Early Poetic Theory

Yeats's attempts during the 1880s and 1890s to hammer his thoughts into unity (*Ex* 263) included constructing relations between his poetry and the visual arts he loved. At times his attempts took the form of programmatic statements about "the arts," aimed at those who had not adopted the medieval ideal of unity of the arts espoused by the Pre-Raphaelites.[1] Most often, however, he groped intuitively for coherence on a more personal level. The essays and letters reveal no conscious plan for uniting poetry with the visual arts, largely because his sense of their interrelation was so deeply embedded that he rarely conceived of them as separate. He assumed their association. What the writings of the 1890s do show is the almost subterranean process by which Yeats explored how, for him, his poetry and the visual arts were to fit together. There is never a final answer—only a web of associations and an occasional conviction, which he tested in theory and practice and which experience eventually refuted or made irrelevant. The constant shifting and refining of associations fed the creative process: new juxtapositions of poetry and painting, new ways of viewing their alliance, suggested to Yeats new poetic strategies and helped him, finally, to evolve his own style.

The general idea of poetry attached to the visual arts came naturally to Yeats. It is, first, simply the other side of his love for painting and crafts associated with poetry, which we saw in the last chapter. Furthermore, the Pre-Raphaelites, especially Rossetti, wrote poems explicitly connected to the visual arts, as did their predecessor, Keats. But Yeats would have associated the visual arts with poetry even before he read Rossetti and Keats. He learned about poetry, began reading on his own, and wrote his first verses while surrounded by his father's paintings and drawings. Part of Yeats's education took place in his father's Dublin studio, where for a time he breakfasted every morning and heard J. B. Yeats read the most passionate moments of *Prometheus Unbound, Coriolanus,* and *Manfred* (*Au* 65).

Yeats's sense of the interrelation of poetry and the visual arts surfaces most tellingly in his lifelong habit of using analogies from the visual arts to discuss poetry. "Last time I was speaking here," Yeats explained to his audience during the second of three 1910 lectures on poetry, "I used a great deal of analogies from painting, and I shall begin again with an analogy from painting. I began my own life as an art student and I am a painter's son, so it is natural to me to see such analogies."[2] These comparisons are evident early in his career, as the prose of the 1880s and 1890s shows. In an 1895 letter to Olivia Shakespear, for example, he used color to describe the effect of words: "You need never seek for the half-tints, but must strive for the black and white," he advised her (*L* 257). Occasionally he used sculpture or architecture as a metaphor—as when he refused to quote selections from Samuel Ferguson's "Willy

Gilliland" and "The Welshmen of Tirawley" because "I could give no idea of a fine building by showing a carved flower from a cornice" (*UP* 1:84)—but most of his analogies came from painting.

Such analogies, combined with the self-assessment that we saw in Yeats's exploration of Pre-Raphaelite art, suggest that during the 1880s and 1890s he sought solutions to poetic problems in the aims and methods of the visual arts. Yeats's notion of exactly how the poet resembled the painter shifted and grew in complexity as he learned his craft, but the general idea persisted through the 1890s. His early experiments with writing on works of art as a way of unifying painting and poetry gave way in the 1890s to what he called poetry of vision. Before we begin to examine Yeats's poetry in detail in the next chapter, it is useful first to trace the early assumptions he made about poetics and the visual arts and to consider some of the theoretical issues raised by those assumed interconnections.

Yeats's first problem as a poet was "abstraction." Generalizations about life and art made poor poetry, he knew, and yet his head was filled with vague notions—fed by his reading of the romantics—of truth and beauty and the poet's relation to them. Family members reported that the adolescent Yeats was dreamy and abstracted. In his attempts to harness his thoughts to poetic purpose, Yeats turned to two other arts, both visual. He was content, he recalled in the *Autobiographies,* only when "my abstractions had composed themselves into picture and dramatization" (188). Drama for Yeats, of course, involved much more than the visual presentation of a play, but that was a large part of it, as we will see in chapter 4. Yeats liked productions that looked like Pre-Raphaelite paintings, and when searching in the early days of the Irish theater movement for an appropriate style of acting, he turned to them as model: "The theatre of art . . . must therefore discover grave and decorative gestures, such as delighted Rossetti and Madox Brown," he wrote in "The Theatre" in 1899 (*E&I* 170; fig. 16).

Yeats's desire for "picture" as a corrective to abstraction linked his early poetic pursuits to the visual arts even more directly than his desire for dramatization. In an unpublished poem of the 1880s he set out this bit of poetic theory:

a song should be
A painted and be[-]pictured argosy.[3]

The lines suggest that Yeats perceived the poet's task as procedurally analogous to the painter's—the ship of song was to be painted. Furthermore, he saw the results as similar—the argosy was to convey pictures.

Even with some notion of what the poet ought to do, however, Yeats

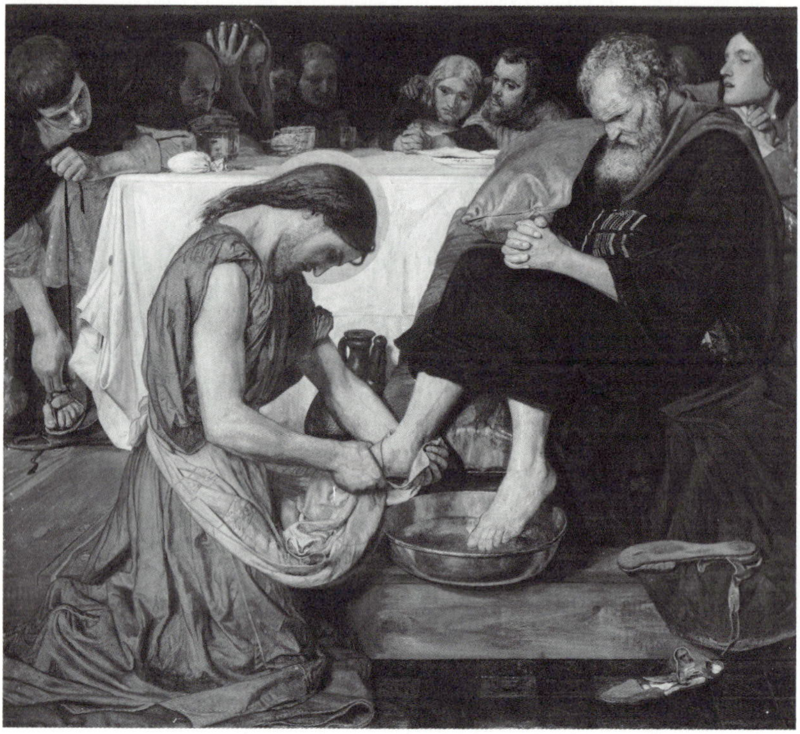

Figure 16. Ford Madox Brown, *Jesus Washing Peter's Feet,* 1852–1856. Tate Gallery, London.

faced the fundamental problem of how to proceed. Taking his cue from those whose poetry was most obviously tied to the visual arts, Rossetti and Keats, Yeats began to pursue one way of creating his painted and bepictured argosy: writing on works of art. During the 1880s, this approach produced one play and three poems that we know of. The first, *Love and Death,* an unpublished play of 1884, was based on a Pre-Raphaelite drawing by his father. There is a brief account of its plot in *Autobiographies* (74–75), and Ellmann reports that it is the worst of the dramas Yeats wrote that year.[4]

But Yeats found the technique promising enough to try it again two years later in "On Mr. Nettleship's Picture at the Royal Hibernian Academy," published by *Dublin University Review* in April 1886:

> Yonder the sickle of the moon sails on,
> But here the Lioness licks her soft cub

Figure 17. Sketch of J. T. Nettleship's *Refuge,* printed in *Royal Hibernian Academy, 1886,* the Art Supplement to the *Dublin University Review,* March 1886. General Research Division, The New York Public Library, Astor, Lenox and Tilden Foundations.

Tender and fearless on her funeral pyre;
Above, saliva dripping from his jaws,
The Lion, the world's great solitary, bends
Lowly the head of his magnificence
And roars, mad with the touch of the unknown,
Not as he shakes the forest; but a cry
Low, long and musical. A dew-drop hung
Bright on a grass blade's under side, might hear,
Nor tremble to its fall. The fire sweeps round
Re-shining in his eyes. So ever moves
The flaming circle of the outer Law,
Nor heeds the old, dim protest and the cry
The orb of the most inner living heart
Gives forth. He, the Eternal, works His will.
(*VP* 688–689)

The subject for this poem is *Refuge,* painted after J. B. Yeats's friend had turned from Pre-Raphaelitism to the depiction of lions (fig. 17).[5] Perhaps the poem is Yeats's attempt to convince himself of Nettleship's continuing worthiness as a painter; perhaps it is ironic, although his discussion of it in letters suggests not (*L* 32). In either case, Yeats considered it serious poetry since he allowed its publication at a time when he was trying to establish his reputation. The poem, carefully surveying the depicted scene, provides the visual details (the sickle of the moon, the soft cub, the dewdrop on the blade of grass) and places them in their appropriate spatial relation (yonder, here, above). Aware even while writing the poem that such inventory is limited as poetry, Yeats tried to move beyond description by glossing the painting's meaning. Yet no poetic transcendence is forthcoming, and the poem's attempt in the final five lines to reveal the painting's apocalyptic significance seems a last-ditch effort. In an 1887 letter to an unnamed correspondent, Yeats defended the musicality of the lion's roar (*L* 32), but he reprinted the poem only once.

Yeats's next experiments in the genre, "In Church" and "A Summer Evening," came to similar ends. His continued attraction to this poetic method indicates a desire to attach poetry to painting, but the generous serving of irony with which he discussed "In Church" in a letter to Katharine Tynan admits the inadequacy, for him, of writing on works of art. A Tract Society illustration, "a wretched thing of a girl in church," provided the material for the poem written in 1889 (fig. 18). It showed, Yeats explained, "how orthodox I can be."[6] The poem, however, is not entirely spoof: Yeats published both it and the illustration in *The Girl's Own Paper* (8 June 1889). Like "On Mr. Nettleship's Picture," "In Church" never gets off the ground despite its subject (*VP* 735–736), and Yeats vowed "I shall never do any more" (*L* 124).

Yeats returned to the technique much later in life and with much better results, but during the 1890s he kept his promise and even chided those who did not see the dangers he had discovered. His review of *Sight and Song* (1892), written by Katherine Bradley and Edith Cooper under the joint pseudonym Michael Field, reproved the authors for the same error he had committed only a few years earlier: "the two ladies . . . have set to work to observe and interpret a number of pictures, instead of singing out of their own hearts and setting to music their own souls" (*UP* 1 : 225). The review is as much a criticism of Yeats's own experiments as of Michael Field's. In his poems on pictures, Yeats, in a small way, had encouraged "the growing tendency"—of which he found *Sight and Song* a "new instance"—"to make the critical faculty do the work of the creative" (*UP* 1 : 225). Like Michael Field's poem on Cosmè Tura's *St. Jerome*, his own poems have "intellectual agility"—although there may be more of it in Michael Field than in Yeats—and they, too, in the end are "simply unmitigated guide-book" (*UP* 1 : 227). Yeats judged *Sight and Song* "interesting, suggestive and thoroughly unsatisfactory" (*UP* 1 : 225).

Figure 18. M. Walker, *In Church*, from *The Girl's Own Paper*, 8 June 1889.

He could criticize so confidently because in the long process of composing "The Wanderings of Oisin" (1889) he had refined his original notion of song as a painted and be-pictured argosy and developed a more satisfactory way of countering abstraction with picture. He had begun to see poetry as vision. Musing over the proofs to "Oisin" he found the last part the most satisfying because it is, he said, "a kind of vision" (*L* 87). Later, in 1913, when trying to sort out his poetic practice, he wrote to J. B. Yeats characterizing all of his early verse as poetry of vision and explaining what he meant by vision: "the intense realization of a state of ecstatic emotion symbolized in a definite imagined region" (*L* 583).

By thinking of poetry as "vision," Yeats maintained an explicit commitment to the visual, but escaped from the cul-de-sac of writing poems on pictures. When he defined poetry of vision for his father, he offered Keats as the chief example. Yeats, with his trouble coaxing abstractions into picture, admired the vividly pictorial poetry of Keats, one of those who "wrote out of the impression made by the world upon their delicate senses" (*E&I* 347). Occasionally Keats achieved his picture by writing on works of art—as Yeats had—but most often he wrote from the natural world. Yeats, nevertheless, attributed Keats's poetry in general to the influence of painting. In the *Autobiographies* he complained that J. B. Yeats would not read Keats to him as a child because, he concluded, his father cared little "for any of that most beautiful poetry which has come in modern times from the influence of painting" (*Au* 65). Yeats saw that the natural world might provide Keats's inspiration, but the painter provided the model of presentation.

While Keats's poetry was influenced by Nicolas Poussin, Claude Lorrain, and Titian,[7] to name a few, Yeats's poetry of vision, as his definition suggests, was inspired by the Pre-Raphaelites and those his generation admired in their name. "The intense realization of a state of ecstatic emotion" identifies his poetry with what Yeats and his circle saw in such Pre-Raphaelite paintings as *Sibylla Palmifera* (fig. 11) and *Lady Lilith*. It echoes Yeats's own admiration of Rossetti's women, captured in "some moment of intensity when the ecstasy of the lover and of the saint are alike" (*E&I* 53). "Ecstatic emotion" further recalls Yeats's numerous approving comments on Blake's intensity and on his view of passion: "Passions, because most living, are most holy," Yeats paraphrased in "William Blake and the Imagination" (*E&I* 113). "State"—implying either an enduring condition or, since ecstatic emotion rarely lasts, a moment frozen in time—links Yeats's poetic practice to the arrested dramatic action of Pre-Raphaelite art (fig. 16). "Intense realization" and "definite imagined region" aptly describe the dual nature of Pre-Raphaelite painting: its dream world is imagined, but clean line and brilliant color make the artistic realization of that world "intense" and "definite." "Region" suggests the landscapes of J. M. W. Turner, Samuel Palmer, and Edward Calvert, which Yeats admired in the spirit of Pre-Raphaelitism. "Symbolized" allies him with the belief in that mode of expression held by Blake and the Pre-Raphaelites.

One could begin with any of the terms in Yeats's definition as a way of approaching the relationships between his poetry of vision and the visual arts. "Vision," "symbolized," and "region," however, are the most important, and an examination of them reveals both the conscious and unconscious connections Yeats drew between the arts during the 1890s.

Yeats's comments on poetry of vision identify vision as both the source and result of poems. Despite the fact that his eyesight was poor and that he was not, by many accounts, particularly observant (see *LDW* 173), Yeats was deeply impressed by the visual in nature and especially in art, as Giorgio Melchiori and Edward Engelberg among others have demonstrated.[8] The landscapes Yeats saw in the west of Ireland informed the definite imagined regions of his poetry, as did the colors, patterns, and forms he saw in art.

But "vision" for Yeats often referred to perceptions of the mind's eye rather than perceptions of the corporeal eye.[9] From an early age Yeats's vivid imagination expressed itself in mental visions that often came to him in daydreams or in the moments between waking and sleeping. They came unannounced and could not be willed. Occult studies, however, offered methods for invoking, and thus better controlling, his visions. In the spring of 1887, when Yeats was beginning part 3 of "The Wanderings of Oisin"—the part that seemed "a kind of vision" (*L* 42)—he joined Madame Blavatsky's Theosophical Lodge in London, where members were pressing for the formation of an esoteric section dedicated to proving such phenomena as the appearance of spirits. Yeats had already been to a séance, and he eagerly participated in the experiments of the esoteric section founded in 1888.[10] For Yeats, the main object of the occult, then and later, was the revelation of wisdom, most often through vision.[11] "I believe," he declared in his famous 1901 essay "Magic," "in the practice and philosophy of what we have agreed to call magic, in what I must call the evocation of spirits, though I do not know what they are, in the power of creating magical illusions, in the visions of truth in the depths of the mind when the eyes are closed."[12] His accounts of strange smells indicating the presence of spirits suggest how magic appealed to other senses, but for Yeats the wisdom of the nonmaterial world "first speaks in images," as he explained in a phrase that characteristically fuses his art and the visual (*E&I* 95).

sions, but they also evoke visions that are accessible to the uninitiated and more open to discussion. The hazel tree may invoke for some a vision of the afterlife, but it surely evokes a vision of a landscape.

In terms of the properties of the poem itself, the difference between the re-presentation of symbolic vision and the use of symbol to call up vision is frequently one of detail. To re-create vision, Yeats described what he saw, often in elaborate detail, as in "The Wanderings of Oisin." To tap the vision-creating powers of symbol, Yeats needed only to mention or briefly describe the symbol. As he studied Blake and the occult and formulated with the Rhymers the poetic goal of simplicity, Yeats increasingly believed that the evocation of vision by symbol made for better poetry than the re-presentation of symbolic vision.[16]

The symbol in itself provided on various levels connections between poetry and the visual arts. Yeats believed, as do such modern theoreticians as Suzanne Langer, that symbolism is the common language of the arts and, for Yeats, magic: "I cannot now think symbols less than the greatest of all powers," he said in 1901, "whether they are used consciously by the masters of magic or half unconsciously by their successors, the poet, the musician and the artist."[17] Yeats meant not only that symbolists share a common method, but that they share common symbols—although he never explained how this worked with regard to music. All tapped that storehouse of symbolic images, the Great Memory. In practice, Yeats often tapped it via magic or the visual arts. The symbols in his poems he frequently adopted from esoteric lore or the paintings he loved.

History seemed to Yeats to be bearing out this fundamental unity of the arts in symbol. Poetry and the visual arts in particular were both involved in symbolist movements whose aims, as well as methods and symbols, coincided. Critics of modern poetry and painting frequently note in passing that the advent of symbolism historically effected a closer alliance between those two arts, a point Yeats implicitly asserted when he claimed in his discussion of the "coming of symbolic art," "I cannot separate art and literature in this" (*UP* 2:134).

Yeats's inability to separate art and literature in terms of symbolism extended beyond his observations of historical trends in ways that affected more directly his own poetry. The symbol resolved the opposition of abstraction and picture. It embodied the abstract (the "ecstatic emotion" that the definition of poetry of vision specifies)—an embodiment Yeats conceived of in visual terms. When he defined "symbol" in 1898 he made explicit its visual nature: "it entangles, in complex colours and forms, a part of the Divine Essence" (*E&I* 148). Thus, by providing a picture, the symbol saved Yeats from the abstraction that he believed destroyed poetry, while at the same time it allowed for the expression of the abstract.

The colors and forms Yeats had in mind when he defined "symbol" included those he had seen in paintings. A surge of expressed interest in Blake and the Pre-Raphaelites accompanied his major exploration of the symbol in a series of essays written between 1896 and 1900. "William Blake and His Illustrations to the *Divine Comedy*" (1896) approaches Blake's illustrations to Dante through his theory of symbol, which Yeats had already puzzled out with Ellis's help in "The Symbolic System" in volume 1 of *The Works of William Blake;* "A Symbolic Artist and the Coming of Symbolic Art" (1898) praises the work of the Pre-Raphaelite descendent, the painter Althea Gyles; "Symbolism in Painting" (1898) focuses on the Pre-Raphaelites, and in its original form served as the introduction to the visionary artist W. T. Horton's *A Book of Images;* and, finally, "The Symbolism of Poetry" (1900) addresses the problem in Yeats's own art.

These discussions of symbol, more than those of any other poetic problem, show Yeats turning to the visual arts for guidance. Painting, of course, provided symbols that he could use in poems, but much more important, it served as the subject in his examination of how symbols work. In "Symbolism in Painting," for example, he argued that traditional symbols—images endowed with symbolic significance by past use—help a personal symbol attain its full resonance:

> If you paint a beautiful woman and fill her face, as Rossetti filled so many faces, with an infinite love, a perfectd love, "one's eyes meet no mortal thing when they meet the light of her peaceful eyes," as Michelangelo said of Vittoria Colonna; but one's thoughts stray to mortal things, and ask, maybe, "Has her lover gone from her, or is he coming?" or "What predestinated unhappiness has made the shadow in her eyes?" If you paint the same face, and set a winged rose or a rose of gold somewhere about her, one's thoughts are of her immortal sisters, Piety and Jealousy, and of her mother, Ancestral Beauty, and of her high kinsmen, the Holy Orders, whose swords make a continual music before her face. (*E&I* 150)

Two years later, in "The Symbolism of Poetry," Yeats transferred to poetry the mechanism of perception explained here:[18] "If I say 'white' or 'purple' in an ordinary line of poetry, they evoke emotions so exclusively that I cannot say why they move me; but if I bring them into the same sentence with such obvious intellectual symbols as a cross or a crown of thorns, I think of purity and sovereignty" (*E&I* 161). As the winged rose or the rose of gold ensures that in painting a beautiful woman's face calls up more than pity, so the cross or crown of thorns in poetry endows white or purple with particular significance.

Yeats's definition of poetry of vision explains that the poem's ecstatic emotion is symbolized in a definite imagined region. The concept of the poem as region, even a symbolic one, further suggests an alliance between poetry and the visual arts by violating the distinction Gotthold Lessing had drawn in *Laocoön* (1766). Following the Pre-Raphaelites and the romantics before them, Yeats ignored Lessing's classic argument for the necessary separation of the arts.[19] Partly in response to the overabundance of descriptive poetry and the lavish praise it received, Lessing had contended that the arrangement of objects in space (which descriptive poetry tried to reproduce) belongs to the province of painting and sculpture, the relation of events in time (narrative) to the province of literature—or, by extension, that the visual arts convey their ideas and emotions in a single moment, whereas literature conveys them over time.[20] Such arguments can be, and have been, refuted on a number of grounds.[21] Yeats implicitly attacked them on one when, in conceiving of his poems as regions, he claimed for poetry a spatial quality.

Yeats rarely recognized the theoretical questions such concepts of poetry raised, but he grappled with them instinctively. If not in such terms, he understood that there is an important difference between the poem as spatial and the poem as temporal. The distinction was on his mind when he first explained, in an 1889 letter to Katharine Tynan, his concept of the poem as region: "'Oisin' is an incident or series of incidents; the 'Island of Statues' a region" (*L* 106). Yeats had felt the competing claims his distinction implies when he first proposed that "a song should be/A painted and be[-]pictured argosy." The notion of the poem as "be-pictured" (covered with pictures) was an attempt to reconcile the narrative and pictorial, as Yeats would continue to do throughout the 1890s. If a picture may be apprehended in an instant, then it is incompatible with the poem, which necessarily must be apprehended over time because it takes time to read; but pictures must be looked at one after another. Yeats had thus instinctively allowed for the temporality of literature, for perhaps even narrative—the development of a story from picture to picture.[22]

During the 1890s, Yeats's increased use of symbol automatically reduced the discrepancy between the temporal revelation of ideas and emotions in poetry and the instantaneous revelation of them in picture. The symbol embodies multiple meanings and hence saves the poet from having to set out those meanings sequentially. The brevity of the lyric, the form Yeats was best at and most often used, further helped the poem approach the instantaneous nature of picture.

Yeats's 1913 definition of his early poems as regions necessarily, and perhaps, primarily, covered many short lyrics, but when he first voiced his idea of poem as region he was thinking of long poems. "A long poem should be," he theorized to Katharine Tynan in the 1889 letter quoted above, "a region into which one should wander from the cares of life" (*L* 106). The idea was not new. The romantics, with Milton and Virgil behind them, had seen lyrics as diversions from the true poetic pursuit of the long poem and had engaged in much debate over its proper form. While Yeats claimed the concept of the poem as region for himself and attributed its inspiration to the thicket in which he spent many hours hiding from the cares of adolescent life, Keats—Yeats's example of the poet of vision influenced by painting—had earlier expressed the idea in a letter to Benjamin Bailey in 1817: "I have heard Hunt say and I may be asked—why endeavour after a long Poem? To which I should answer—Do not the Lovers of Poetry like to have a little Region to wander in where they may pick and choose, and in which the images are so numerous that many are forgotten and found new in a second Reading?"[23]

Yeats's region, however, is much more narrowly conceived than Keats's region of images. From his earliest poems on, "region" meant to Yeats a place, usually geographic. The poems written before "Oisin" may be experimental, but they are linked to each other and to Yeats's more sophisticated poetic ventures of the 1890s by their attention to landscape. Nearly all of the poems of the 1880s and 1890s are set in, or evoke, a landscape. There are the islands of "Oisin" and the "Island of Statues," Colooney and the salley gardens, Innisfree and Fergus's woods, to name a few. Louis MacNeice attributes Yeats's attachment to landscape to the powerful effect of the scenery in the west of Ireland: "Yeats's best known landscapes were Sligo and Galway and he deliberately set out to match his verse to them."[24] If such things are inherited, Yeats acquired a sensitivity to that scenery from his mother; J. B. Yeats, so well known for his talk, boasted that in their son he and Susan Pollexfen had "given tongue to the sea-cliffs."[25] Guidebooks and maps continue to direct tourists to "Yeats Country."

But Yeats was not returning to the locodescriptive tradition of the eighteenth century. As John P. Frayne suggests, Yeats apparently did not know the work of William Cowper and James Thomson, and as part of his revolt against Victorianism he rejected "irrelevant descriptions of nature" (*UP* 1:30; *OBMV* ix). Yeats renounced the descriptive poets for the same reason he hated the Impressionists and ignored Constable. They shared the sin of Wordsworth, with whom "poetry gave up the right to consider all things in the world as a dictionary of types and symbols and began to call itself a critic of life and an interpreter of things as they are" (*E&I* 192). Yeats, like Keats with his image of the Lover of Poetry wandering where he may leisurely pick and choose, wanted his region to be far from the cares of daily life, of "things as they are." More than Keats, he wanted his poems to correct Wordsworth's error. His "definite imagined regions" were not to be "interpreters," but symbols of "ecstatic emotion." While his understanding of the symbolic nature of visions—be they bodily or mental—came from studies of Blake and the occult, he attributed the belief in the symbolic potential of landscape to the direct influence of painting: "It is a natural conviction for a painter's son to believe that there may be a landscape that is symbolical of some spiritual condition and awakens a hunger such as cats feel for valerian" (*Au* 74).

Yeats could hardly have avoided landscape art, the most prominent form of painting in England in the nineteenth century. While he rarely mentioned Ruskin and seems to have known little of his art criticism firsthand, Ruskin's writings on landscape painting had helped make it a much-discussed subject, and his ideas were part of the intellectual climate in which Yeats lived.[26] Yeats had first learned about landscape, however, through J. B. Yeats. His father's friends included the landscapist George Wilson, whom Yeats knew and whose works his sisters acquired (*Au* 29). J. B. Yeats himself had, in 1876, been suddenly ambitious to improve his landscape technique and hurried to England for that purpose. Once installed, he sent for his son who years later remembered when "my father and I and a group of landscape-painters lodged at Burnham Beeches."[27] Although J. B. Yeats was primarily a portraitist—and W. B. Yeats's desire for landscape seems at some level a repudiation of his father's art—he had taught his son that mere mimesis would never do, and he had introduced him to Blake. In Blake's works, and in those of his followers, Samuel Palmer and Edward Calvert, Yeats found landscape symbolic of a spiritual condition. They provided him with visual precedents for his own experiments in symbolic region.

As we have seen, the major terms defining Yeats's poetry of the 1880s and 1890s all claim explicit and implicit alliances to the visual arts. "Vision" declares both physical and mental sight as the source and effect of poetry. "Symbol" embodies the abstract in visual form and, according to Yeats, is the common language of all arts, especially poetry and painting. "Region" insists that space, though often thought the province of the visual arts, is an essential element of poetry.

These associations fed and at times grew out of Yeats's practice of his craft. They developed slowly as he studied the work of poets and painters, learned the ways of the occult, and wrote poems. In the next chapter, by examining Yeats's poetic regions and their relations to the art he admired, we will see how Yeats's poetry of vision evolved in practice and how he grappled with the problems it raised.

3

Poetry of Vision

Yeats's Early Poetic Regions

When Yeats defined poetry of vision in 1913, he had a firm retrospective view of the symbolic nature of its regions. But when he began his poetic career in the early 1880s, he did not yet understand landscape's full potential. Most of his earliest experiments in poetic regions were idealized pastoral landscapes. Although they convey a mood and a belief in the realm of beauty, they are not explicitly symbolic. Just as the symbolic landscapes of Blake, Palmer, and Calvert to which Yeats turned in the 1890s developed from the ideal landscapes of the seventeenth-century painter Claude Lorrain, so in Yeats's work the symbolic followed the ideal.

Using Yeats's own method of discussing poetry by analogy to pictures, we can see how the relations between those two arts illuminate his poetic practice, especially the development of his symbolic method. This chapter will examine three representative works in conjunction with pictures that particularly interested Yeats when he wrote them. Yeats's early dramatic poem, "The Island of Statues" (1885), offers a pastoral region similar to Turner's *The Golden Bough*. A comparison of Yeats's poem with that painting reveals both his debt to such ideal landscapes, and the two-dimensionality and spatial vagueness of his poetic pictures. Yeats's major long poem of the period, "The Wanderings of Oisin" (1889), finds its visual analogue in Morris's tapestries whose color and pattern Yeats adapted for poetic use. Finally, we will examine Yeats's increasing use of explicitly symbolic detail in *The Wind Among the Reeds* by juxtaposing a characteristic lyric, "The Song of Wandering Aengus" (1897), with the landscapes of Blake's followers, Samuel Palmer and Edward Calvert.

One of the issues that such comparisons highlight—and the most important for the direction of Yeats's poetic career—is that of aesthetic distance. Yeats's desire for poems that would be regions in which his readers could wander implies that he wished to reduce the perceived distance between the reader and the poetic world to such an extent that the reader would feel he could enter—in an almost physical way—the world of the poem. In adopting the pictorial analogy, however, Yeats automatically established aesthetic distance. The viewer of a picture can never literally enter the pictorial world. Unlike a sculpture, which shares our three-dimensional space, a picture remains an arrangement of shapes on a two-dimensional surface. Perspective, the Renaissance invention, could, of course, give the illusion of a three-dimensional pictorial world and, hence, reduce distance.[1] But, in their pursuit of spirit and imagination, the visual artists Yeats admired distorted or rejected perspective to distinguish art from life. Although Yeats praised some pictures that employed perspective but were unrealistic in other ways, he generally associated lack of perspective with imaginative art. His own poetic pictures similarly lack the illusion of three-dimensional space and keep the reader at a distance.

Although distance thwarted one poetic goal—to provide a place for the reader to wander—it often supported half-conscious attitudes that Yeats held toward his poetic regions or subjects. It betrays his suspicion that the worlds of his early pastoral verse were not, in fact, accessible to modern man, and his intuition that the allure of the ideal—the subject of so many poems—fades when it is no longer distant and unobtainable. Distance between audience and poetic world, in other words, reflected the poet's own sense of being, or desiring to be, outside the region he pictured. Toward the end of the 1890s, Yeats became aware of distance as a poetic issue, and, as his responses to the artist W. T. Horton show, he began to formulate strategies for reducing it.

Yeats owes his pastorals directly to a poet, Spenser, but his instinctive interest in the form is part of his impulse to link poetry to the visual arts. Landscape painting as a genre derived from Virgil, in whose "delicate suggestions of scenery" and "myth of ideal rusticity," Kenneth Clark tells us, the first painters of landscape as such found their inspiration.[2] When Yeats wrote most of his pastorals in the mid-1880s, he knew of Blake's direct treatment of Virgil in the illustrations to Thornton's edition,[3] but there is no evidence that he particularly admired them. He did, however, admire and praise Turner's depiction of a scene from the *Aeneid*—*The Golden Bough*—whose visual ancestry can be traced back through Claude and a long line of ideal landscape painters to those whom Virgil first inspired. Yeats linked Turner to Pre-Raphaelitism, an alliance current as well in the public mind since Ruskin, made famous by his praise of Turner, had come to the defense of the Pre-Raphaelites. In the *Autobiographies* Yeats recalled his days in art school: "I longed for pattern, for Pre-Raphaelitism, for an art allied to poetry, and returned again and again to our National Gallery to gaze at Turner's *Golden Bough*."[4]

"The Island of Statues," Yeats's most ambitious experiment in the genre, can serve as an example of his pastoral landscapes. Despite what the title might suggest, this verse play is not a poem "on" works of art, nor is it primarily allied to sculpture. Yeats completed an advanced draft of it in August 1884,[5] while he was enrolled in the Metropolitan School of Art and his longing for nonmimetic art—specifically as represented by *The Golden Bough* (fig. V)—was especially intense. As his 1889 letter to Katharine Tynan shows, this is the first poem to which he explicitly applied the term "region": "'Oisin' is an incident or series of incidents; the 'Island of Statues' a region" (*L* 106). The poem illustrates clearly what

Yeats meant by the term: most of its approximately fifteen hundred lines describe in rich detail the landscapes his characters inhabit. The play opens with the shepherds Colin and Thernot contending for the love of the shepherdess Naschina by singing songs that compete in the extravagance of their natural description:

Colin. Come forth: the morn is fair; as from the pyre
Of sad Queen Dido shone the lapping fire
Unto the wanderer's ships, or as day fills
The brazen sky, so blaze the daffodills;
As Argive Clytemnestra saw out-burn
The flagrant signal of her lord's return,
Afar, clear-shining on the herald hills,
In vale and dell so blaze the daffodills;
As when upon her cloud-o'er-muffled steep
Oenone saw the fires of Troia leap,
And laugh'd, so, so along the bubbling rills
In lemon-tinted lines, so blaze the daffodills.
Come forth, come forth, my music flows for thee,
A quenchless grieving of love melody.
Thernot. [Sings] Now her sheep all browsing meet
By the singing waters' edge,
Tread and tread their cloven feet
On the ruddy river sedge,
For the dawn the foliage fingereth,
And the waves are leaping white,
She alone, my lady, lingereth
While the world is roll'd in light
(*VP* 645–646)

This is, as Ellmann has observed, a "picture play with Spenserian shepherds."[6] While having some fun with his contending lovers, Yeats, trying to avoid abstraction and get picture, piled up the visual details. As in Turner's *The Golden Bough,* whose subject is brought to mind by Colin's allusions to the *Aeneid,* the landscape created by the shepherds' descriptions is ideal. In Yeats's later terminology, it is a "definite imagined region." "Definite" for Yeats never connoted "realistic," although he knew from Pre-Raphaelite painting that realistic details could serve idealistic art. Nor, at this stage, did it connote even "particular." The sheep in Thernot's song browse by the water, their feet are cloven, and the river sedge is ruddy, but these are not particular sheep, nor is the river a particular one. As in Turner's painting, where the location—Lake Avernus—cannot be identified by the painting's hills and trees, the landscape is definite, but generalized.[7]

Both Yeats and Turner elevate the general to the ideal through the transforming powers of light. The action of "The Island of Statues" takes place at dawn and dusk. Whereas in later poems Yeats exploited the symbolic significance of the half-light, here he seems most interested in the glow the rising and setting sun and moon cast over his scenes. For a hundred lines in act 1, Colin and Thernot desribe a world "roll'd in light." The "blaze" of the daffodils in vale and dell, Colin tells us, reflects the "brazen sky," suffusing the landscape with the same golden light that Turner used to convey the ideality of his pastoral scene in *The Golden Bough*. There, light softens the forms of jagged hills and hard stones, removing from the landscape the harsh edge of ordinary experience.

The landscapes of both poem and painting are ideal—depictions of the Golden Age—but neither is free of the stamp of human history and imperfection. Yeats's Arcady "has experienced Clytemnestra, the 'fires of Troia' and Dido," as Edward Engelberg has pointed out.[8] The sleepers Naschina frees at the end of the poem awaken into a world of change and death, a world with which she has already reckoned. While the moon casts the shadows of Almintor and the sleepers "far across the grass" at the play's close, Naschina stands "shadowless" (*VP* 679). Similarly, Turner's celebrants dance amid the ruins of previous civilizations, and beside the tree in the foreground a fox plays with a snake.[9] Naschina's lack of shadow, the painting's ruins and snake, in their indication that even the Golden Age came after the Fall, suggest a symbolic impulse in poet and painter. For Turner, the impulse led to the "rich enigmas" of his late paintings;[10] for Yeats it led to the symbolic landscapes of his early verse.

In the epilogue to his poem, Yeats acknowledges that "the woods of Arcady are dead" (*VP* 64), leaving the poet only one recourse, as Engelberg has remarked: to keep the Golden Age "alive through poetry."[11] Turner faced the same challenge in art, yet his depiction of the Golden Age differs from Yeats's in a way that suggests he believed, while Yeats could not despite his efforts, that Arcady could be so preserved. Unlike *The Golden Bough*, Yeats's landscape in "The Island of Statues" does not achieve the quality that made the Claudian tradition famous—a sense of depth. Using Claude's formula, Turner placed the vanishing point in the center of the picture, framed the foregound with trees and ruins, and shaded the midground into the background, creating for the viewer the illusion of looking out over a vast expanse. The view, the painting implies, is limited only by the human eye's inability to see farther. Turner's use of perspective also gives the viewer the sense that he can step into the picture. Its space extends into his, making the painting's world and the viewer's world seem coextensive. The painting suggests that modern man might easily enter the better world the Golden Age represents.

Yeats's landscapes rarely give this sense. In "The Island of Statues" the relationships among the elements of the landscape are so vague that the reader cannot locate them in space. They give us a two-dimensional, not a three-dimensional, view. We know, for example, that "Over the lake the water-flowers/Drift and float" (*VP* 647), so we can place the flowers on top of the lake, but we do not know where the lake is in relation to Thernot who describes it. Is it far away, or close by? Is it to the left or right of the shepherds, or is it behind them? When we do get a spatial word that suggests a third dimension, as in the "afar" in Colin's speech above, it describes where Clytemnestra saw the "signal of her lord's return," not the landscape Colin actually sees. The simile, of course, suggests that "vale and dell" are also "afar," but the vague sense of space that word conveys is made even more nebulous by its secondhand application to the present scene. Because we cannot place the details of the landscape with any sureness in space, they tend to sit vaguely next to each other, as though on a flat surface, instead of assuming their proper places in a world with depth as well as height and breadth.

This spatial vagueness, in addition to other features of "The Island of Statues," denies the reader access to the ideal world of the poem. Its space is discontinuous with his, and he cannot easily enter into these regions. In romantic and Victorian landscape poems, there is frequently an "I" with whom the reader stands or walks through a present landscape; this device creates a sense of depth and gives the reader an entrance into the poetic scene. The young Yeats rarely gives his reader such a guide.

The reader's exclusion from the ideal world of the poem betrays Yeats's often-noted uneasiness with man's potential for reclaiming the Golden Age.[12] Turner's ideal world is at least a possibility for man; Yeats's never is, not even as a place of escape from the daily world. He might want his poem to be a region into which one can wander from the cares of life, but the poem itself undermines the goal.

Although he continued to reprint several short lyrics extracted from "The Island of Statues,"[13] Yeats soon abandoned the pastoral and eventually dropped the poem from his canon. He did not identify lack of depth as a problem, and in his next major work, "The Wanderings of Oisin," he even cultivated it. But there Yeats was beginning to experiment with the symbolic potential of landscape; although flatness kept readers out of his poetic world and subverted one goal, it helped the symbolism of the poem.

Yeats called "Wanderings of Oisin" an "incident or series of incidents" as opposed to the region of "The Island of Statues," but its dominant effect is pictorial, as critics frequently note. Yeats himself later described it as "all picture, all emotion, all association, all mythology" (*Au* 212). The poem's series of incidents are embodied in a series of pictures apprehended sequentially—Yeats's be-pictured argosy. The pictures vary in quality and tone—from the clear calm of the sea over which Niamh and Oisin ride in book 1 to the gothically dim and slimy castle in book 2. Many of the pictures bear little resemblance to the Pre-Raphaelite art that Yeats so admired at the time, yet it is the Pre-Raphaelite scenes that stand out most vividly. The least Pre-Raphaelite section, book 2, has been labeled "obscure";[14] the term applies to its pictures as well as its meaning. The more Pre-Raphaelite sections so dominate the impression of the poem as a whole that commentaries have routinely been able to call it Pre-Raphaelite without arousing objections.[15] The poem cannot be tied to any particular work of the Pre-Raphaelite movement, but Ellmann's suggestion that during the 1880s and 1890s Yeats viewed his poems as analogous to tapestries—specifically those produced by William Morris and his company—offers a fruitful starting point for examining the development of Yeats's symbolic landscapes in "The Wanderings of Oisin."[16]

Yeats began "The Wanderings of Oisin" in 1886,[17] and a year later he met William Morris who became his "chief of men" (*Au* 141; *Ex* 275; *L* 724). During 1887 and 1888 when finishing the poem, Yeats saw Morris often. The letters are full of reports of dinners and meetings at Morris's house—"pictures by Rossetti all round the room" (*L* 42)—of stories about Morris, about Jane Morris and their daughter May, and about the embroidery Yeats's sister Lilly worked for them (fig. VIII).[18] When *The Wanderings of Oisin and Other Poems* was published in 1889, Yeats twice wrote Katharine Tynan that Morris had praised the book and promised to review it (*L* 102, 106). "You write my sort of poetry," Morris reportedly exclaimed to Yeats (*Au* 146).

It is difficult to assess how much Morris's verse informed "The Wanderings of Oisin." Critics convincingly cite him, while Yeats claimed he had not read Morris's poetry for a long time.[19] Regardless of its extent, the influence of Morris's verse attests to Yeats's continued attraction to the pictorial qualities of poetry. Morris had deliberately sought out those qualities, as Yeats knew: in 1896 and again in 1922 Yeats quoted Morris's claim that Chaucer and Keats (Yeats's poet of vision) were his masters "for they make pictures" (*Au* 145; cf. *UP* 1:420). But Yeats did not have to go through Morris's poetry to get his pictures. They surrounded him in Kelmscott House, which Morris had decorated and which Yeats began visiting when in the midst of writing "Oisin."

At that time, Morris was particularly involved in reviving the ancient art of high-warp tapestry weaving and introducing the production of woven fabrics to the activities of Morris & Company.[20] Yeats would have been attracted to Morris's woven products, especially the tapestries, which frequently pictured narrative subjects (as in *The Adoration of the Magi,* begun the year Yeats met Morris),[21] or which incorporated in their designs scrolls bearing lines of poetry, often Morris's own. Morris considered tapestry "the noblest of the weaving arts."[22] Because "at its highest it is the art of painting pictures with coloured wools on a warp," he insisted that artists design his tapestries.[23] After 1883 Burne-Jones designed the figures, while Morris or his assistant, John Henry Dearle, did the decorative backgrounds and borders.[24]

The weaving images that pervade Yeats's writings of the 1880s and 1890s indicate that he was taken by Morris's tapestries and in them found a more fitting analogue for his own pictures than Turner's *The Golden Bough*. The setting for *The Countess Cathleen* (1892) further suggests that tapestries had particular relevance to "The Wanderings of Oisin." In the Countess's great hall hangs a tapestry to which Oona points:

> See you where Oisin and young Niam ride
> Wrapped in each other's arms, and where the Finians
> Follow their hounds along the fields of tapestry.
> (*VPl* 44)

Because Yeats's poems are habitually self-referential, such a passage is significant. "The Wanderings of Oisin," it suggests, is Yeats's tapestry.[25]

For Yeats's poetry, the most significant difference between *The Golden Bough* and Morris's tapestries is the latter's explicit and heightened decorativeness. The flatness, the processions of figures, the color and pattern that declare a tapestry as itself a beautiful object appealed to a Yeats so eager for nonmimetic art. That the decorative can also encourage a symbolic interpretation of a work of art made Morris's tapestries all the more fitting as analogues for Yeats's experiments with landscape's symbolic potential.[26]

Morris, unlike Turner, made little use of perspective, as can be seen in *The Orchard* (fig. 10), a typical example of his tapestries during the period of Yeats's greatest contact with him. The scene possesses a greater sense of depth than the entirely two-dimensional designs of the wallpapers and woven fabrics that Yeats admired; but like the paintings of Morris, Rossetti, and Burne-Jones, it flattens out the picture planes so that the ground tilts precariously forward and the boughs of the fruit trees and vines become a flat backdrop for the four figures. "The Wanderings of Oisin," like "The Island of Statues," similarly lacks a sense of depth. Adverbs that denote depth are rare and vague, even in scenes that seem to call for them. In part 1, Niamh and Oisin's approach at sunset to the Island of Living provided Yeats the opportunity for depicting a panoramic view of the landscape, but he did not take advantage of it. The "sound of feathery choirs" of Island birds "seemed to fall from the very flame/Of the great round sun" which "sank ever lower" (*VP* 13). Things in this landscape go up and down, but rarely recede into the distance. Oisin and Niamh, as well as the phantoms of the deer, the hound, the maid, and the youth, supposedly travel through the landscape, but the descriptions of them—the lovers "ride on," galloping "o'er" the "level" sea; the vision passes "by"—show them moving like figures in a tapestry across the landscape, not into it.

The linear arrangement of characters in both poem and tapestries makes for a curious link between the narrative and the pictorial. It recreates the experience of reading in the experience of viewing the literal picture and the images presented in the poem. We "read" the picture from one side to the other as we would read a line of verse. In Morris's tapestries, the eye's movement along the line of figures is almost always from left to right, in part because the eye, so trained and practiced in reading, automatically follows that path, in part because Morris frequently reinforced that movement by the placement of his scrolls of poetry or by the gestures of his characters. In *The Orchard,* the verse displayed across the center of the picture encourages us to view it from left to right, as do the heads of the knights turned to the right to look at the beckoning maid in *The Knights of the Round Table Summoned to the Quest by a Strange Damsel* (fig. 19).

The direction in which we read Yeats's poetic pictures is less clear, although it might be reasonable to think that when the deer, hound, maid, and youth appear, revealed one at a time by the narrative, we see them moving from left to right, each figure progressing across the picture plane as the next figure introduced enters the scene.[27] In any case, the linearity of the picture presented helps reconcile the narrative/temporal structure of the poem with the spatial structure of its pictures. Within Oisin's story, events are related according to simple chronology—first this happened, then this.[28] Its temporal structure is that of the time line, as the spatial arrangement of the figures in its pictures is the visual line.

"The Wanderings of Oisin," furthermore, displays Yeats most clearly attempting to transfer into poetry the decorative color and pattern that attracted him in Pre-Raphaelite art. The poem's landscapes are brilliant with the "soft greens and rich golds of estheticisms" that Yeats later praised at the 1890 Arts and Crafts Exhibition (*UP* 1 : 185), with the reds

Figure 19. William Morris, Edward Burne-Jones and J. H. Dearle, *The Knights of the Round Table Summoned to the Quest by a Strange Damsel,* first weaving 1893. By permission of Birmingham Museums and Art Gallery.

and yellows that Shelley had gathered in Italy (*E&I* 5) and Yeats had admired in *Dante's Dream* (*Au* 114–115), and with Yeats's favorite Pre-Raphaelite blue. As Oisin and Niamh ride toward the Island of Living, the seashells cast their colors on the scene:

> Many a shell
> That in immortal silence sleeps
> And dreams of her own melting hues,
> Her golds, her azures, and her blues,
> Pierced with soft light the shallowing deeps.
> (*VP* 13)

On the Island of Forgetfulness, the lovers stir in their sleep as richly colored nature stirs:

When the sun was on silver or gold;
When brushed with the wings of the owls, in the dimness
they love going by;
When a glow-worm was green on a grass leaf, lured from its
lair in the mould

(*VP* 53)

Even the figures in the landscape glow with color. The woodland people in book I sport robes "of yellow silk,/Trimmed round with many a crimson feather" (*VP* 15). And, of course, there is Niamh, the typical Pre-Raphaelite woman:

Her eyes were soft as dewdrops hanging
Upon the grass-blades' bending tips,
And like a sunset were her lips,
A stormy sunset o'er doomed ships.
Her hair was of a citron tincture,
And gathered in a silver cincture;
Down to her feet white vesture flowed,
And with the woven crimson glowed
Of many a figured creature strange,
And birds that on the seven seas range.
(*VP* 3–4)

Like Morris who praised "the depth of tone, the richness of colour, and exquisite gradation of tints" possible in tapestries,[29] Yeats delighted, as he said of Rossetti (*E&I* 53), in color for its own sake. A few years later, red, blue, and gold would become explicitly symbolic in Yeats's work; here they are decorative.

As Yeats transferred color from art into poetry, so he transferred pattern. The landscapes in "The Wanderings of Oisin," like those in Morris's tapestries, are characterized by the repetition of shapes and colors, by pattern. While the trees in *The Orchard* bear different fruits, they all have straight trunks of the same size supporting a similar mass of greenery and stand at regular intervals. They create a pattern of trunks and leaves. Similarly, Yeats described the shore of the Island of Forgetfulness:

And we rode on the plains of the sea's edge—the sea's edge barren and grey,
Grey sands on the green of the grasses and over the dripping trees,
Dripping and doubling landward, as though they would hasten away
Like an army of old men longing for rest from the moan of the seas.
(*VP* 48)

Every tree on the shore bends away from the sea in a repetition that gives the landscape pattern. That sense of repetition is reinforced here by Yeats's emphasis on plurality—there are plains, sands, grasses, and seas as well as trees. Such repetition occurs in the poem not only within images, but among them. There are numerous woods—the dripping trees on the Island of Forgetfulness directly echoing the trees hung with "mist-drops" through which the Fenians ride in book 1 (*VP* 2). Mist closes around the lovers or the landscape in all three books. Flowers bloom. Birds sing. There are three islands, three journies across three seas, three visions of the phantoms, which in turn repeat the chase with which the poem began. The list could go on. All of these repetitions re-create in the poem's pictures the sense of order, of pattern, so important in Pre-Raphaelite art.

More significant than these visual patterns, however, was Yeats's belief that pattern of line and form in the visual arts (repetition in space) was comparable to rhythm and repeated sounds in poetry (repetition in time).[30] This belief indicates a more radical notion of analogies between the arts than that implied by the transference of color and visual pattern from one art to another. Yeats suggests that certain properties peculiar to one art can perform the same function as properties unique to another. In his review of the 1890s Arts and Crafts Exhibition, Yeats connected Morris's patterns to rhythm and the repetition of sounds by saying that Morris's arts "murmur of the middle ages" (*UP* 1 : 183). That connection had become an explicit conviction by 1899 when he declared in "The Symbolism of Poetry":

> If certain sensitive persons listen persistently to the ticking of a watch, or gaze persistently on the monotonous flashing of a light, they fall into the hypnotic trance [in which the mind liberated from the pressure of the will is unfolded in symbols]; and rhythm is but the ticking of a watch made softer, that one must needs listen, and various, that one may not be swept beyond memory or grow weary of listening; while the patterns of the artist are but the monotonous flash woven to take the eyes in a subtler enchantment. (*E&I* 159)

In the description of the shore of the Island of Forgetfulness quoted above, the immediate repetition of phrases or words ("sea's edge—the sea's edge": "grey,/Grey"; "dripping trees,/Dripping"), the repetition of sounds (*s; gr, dr,* or *tr; m; r*), and the anapestic meter not only help the sense by conveying the sound of the dripping trees and the moan of the seas, but create aural pattern.

The statement Yeats made in "The Symbolism of Poetry" suggests not only that he was thinking of tapestries ("woven") when he compared pattern to rhythm, but that rhythm and pattern are bound to art's revelation of symbolic vision. They enchant the mind so that a symbolic vision—be it one the poet re-creates in the poem or one evoked by poetic symbol—will appear. We have seen that in "The Wanderings of Oisin" Yeats tried to re-present vision, an aim that he believed he shared with the Pre-Raphaelites, especially Morris. Morris, he thought, possessed a "vision" of the Earthly Paradise which he "obeyed," as Yeats tried to obey his vision in "Oisin," "when he tried to make first his own house . . . and then houses of other people" (*E&I* 64). Yeats knew that Morris had little use for the occult or its methods of invoking vision, but he nevertheless linked Morris (mentioning the tapestries) to Jakob Böhme and Jan van Ruysbroeck, the mystics he himself admired (*UP* 1 : 420). The sources of Morris's art, he implied, were those of his own poetry of vision.

It is unclear whether the pattern in Morris's tapestries and the rhythm in "The Wanderings of Oisin" do in fact enchant the mind to make it receptive to the symbolic visions the works re-present.[31] Pattern and rhythm do, however, encourage the viewer or reader to take the visions as symbolic. Morris, like Yeats in "The Wanderings of Oisin," was not fully a symbolist, but the two-dimensionality of the tapestries, their color and their pattern—their explicit decorativeness—exert a pressure toward the symbolic. As Kenneth Clark has pointed out about such early experiments in landscape as the fifteenth-century French tapestries in which Morris found his models, the less art functions as imitation, the more it tends to function symbolically.[32] Whereas Turner's world in *The Golden Bough* looks like ours only better, Morris's does not. Its stylized trees and flowers derive from nature, but we know that even on a good day nature does not look like that. Tourists of the eighteenth century could hold to their eye a "Claude glass" to make the view they saw resemble a painting in the Claudian tradition,[33] but no mechanical device can transform a landscape into a Morrisian picture. Morris's patterns of flowers and trees represent the order of the Earthly Paradise and its resulting calm not possible in this chaotic fallen world. Yeats clearly understood this symbolic function of Morris's pictures and recognized the roles pattern in art and rhythm in poetry play in leading art away from the mimetic and toward the symbolic: "pattern and rhythm are the road to open symbolism," he declared in 1898 in "A Symbolic Artist and the Coming of Symbolic Art" (*UP* 2 : 133). He thought, taking the argument one step further, that pattern could turn the work of art itself, the artifact, into a symbol: "he who wraps the vision in lights and shadows, in iridescent or glowing color, . . . until form be half lost in pattern," he wrote defending those qualities he admired in the Pre-Raphaelites against Blake's dictates for "severe" art, "may compel the canvas or paper to become itself a symbol of some not indefinite because unsearchable essence."[34]

The decorativeness of "The Wanderings of Oisin"—its flatness, its color, its pattern—like that of Morris's tapestries, pushes the poem toward the symbolic. We cannot take any of the landscapes, even the woods through which the Fenians ride at the beginning of the poem, as representations of a real place: they are too patterned, too colored, too decorative. They must represent something else. Like Morris, Oisin seeks to discover a paradisal world. The landscapes of the three islands reflect the perfection of the kind of life lived on them, of joy, of victory, and of repose. But, unlike Morris's, the landscapes of "Oisin" also suggest the inadequacy of such perfection for mortal man. In book 1 the profusion of flowers and bees, tangling creepers and dewdrops in the forest on the Island of the Living, like Morris's Earthly Paradise, promise the pleasures of life on earth, only more abundant and ordered. But those woods are "dark" and the "trees made sudden cavern-glooms/By roots that joined above our plumes" (*VP* 16). Oisin perceives the dim underside of the joy the island people celebrate, and his sorrow pervades the song of "human joy" he sings. By isolating a quality of heaven (joy, victory, repose), each island magnifies the dual nature of mortal life signaled by the woods of the Fenians. There, the bees in the fragrant blossoms suggest the fullness and delights of earthly life, but "mist-drops" hang on the trees, miming the Fenians' tears for their dead comrades (*VP* 2).

Niamh occupies the center of these landscapes, her nature reflecting theirs. She is clearly a Pre-Raphaelite descendent, as her first appearance, quoted above, shows.[35] Like Rossetti's women, Niamh is both sensual and spiritual; but unlike them, she is attainable. "The Wanderings of Oisin," on one level, tests Yeats's fantasy of actually "acquiring" one of those Rossetti women, so attractive but so untouchable, that he said filled his thoughts. The lesson we learn from Oisin, although he himself does not recognize it, is that the women of heaven, just like its landscapes, are always more desirable from a distance. Oisin does not think twice about abandoning his mortal friends for the beauties Niamh and her world offer, but once he possesses them, he feels the tug of mortality and longs for the good old days among the Fenians, and just as easily abandons Niamh for them. When he finds these days gone, he suddenly feels lonely and again desires Niamh, to whom he can never return because he has touched earth. Despite his disappointments, at the end of the poem Oisin continues to long for a distant ideal world, this time the realm beyond life where he is sure the Fenians dwell. It may be his pagan heaven or it may be St. Patrick's hell, but in either case it is a place where loneliness will, he believes, cease in the company of old friends.

The poem's pictures reflect the lure of the unattainable. Their heightened color, insistent pattern, and flatness deny the reader access to the poetic world just as the decorativeness of Morris's tapestries keeps viewers out of the pictorial world. This suggests that despite his desire for regions into which one could wander or his desire for Pre-Raphaelite women, Yeats knew (as did, perhaps, Morris) that attainment would slake desire, and he preferred to see them from afar. The structure of the poem reinforces the sense of distance. As Oisin describes his past adventures to St. Patrick, the reader stands with them, looking at a picture of "back then." St. Patrick's interruptions and Oisin's direct addresses to him constantly remind us that we are here, the world of the three islands there.

The world of "The Wanderings of Oisin," however, remains shut off in a way that, perhaps, Morris's woven visions of the Earthly Paradise do not. Yeats said in 1896 that Morris "more than any man of modern days tried to change the life of his time into the life of his dream," suggesting that Morris shared his goal of a world of art in which man could wander (*UP* 1:419). In the decorative arts Morris did that by designing not just a tapestry or a rug, but a whole room. The viewer of such art would hence be surrounded by Morris's visions of Earthly Paradise—on the floor, the walls, the wardrobes, the sideboards. While the individual pictures that decorated a room might themselves be flat and inaccessible, the viewer, nevertheless, stood in the midst of them. The numerous pictures Yeats presents in "The Wanderings of Oisin" do not have the same effect, perhaps because the distinction Lessing had pointed out precludes it. The narrative/temporal nature of the poem means that its images are revealed in succession, as we have seen. That, combined with the flatness of the pictures, seems to prevent them from ever surrounding the reader. Like the phantoms, they pass by, separate, in another realm.

The symbolism of "The Wanderings of Oisin" is tentative and mixed with considerable allegory, as Michael J. Sidnell's and Daniel Albright's readings of it have suggested.[36] Yeats himself was unsure of it and of its effect on his readers: "In the second part of 'Oisin' under disguise of symbolism I have said several things to which I only have the key. The romance is for my readers. They must not even know there is a symbol anywhere. They will not find out. If they did, it would spoil the art. Yet the whole poem is full of symbols—if it be full of aught but clouds" (*L* 88). But with his discovery that the last part of "Oisin" was "a kind of vision" and with his growing confidence in the symbolic method encouraged by the Blake studies he began in 1889, Yeats set out to write the symbolic poems to which his definition of poetry of vision properly applies.

Although the flatness of "Oisin"'s poetic world may have aided its budding symbolism and reflected a suspicion that the unattained is more desirable, Yeats was uncomfortable with his early landscapes. In an important letter to Katharine Tynan written shortly after he had read the proofs for "The Wanderings of Oisin," he wrote: "The want of your poetry is, I think, the want also of my own. We both of us need to substitute more and more the landscapes of nature for the landscapes of art. . . . We should make poems on the familiar landscapes we love, not the strange and rare and glittering scenes we wonder at" (*L* 99).

Yeats was not, as we will see, rejecting poetry's alliance with art, but he sensed that his earlier landscapes offered worlds separate from both poet and reader—they were strange and inspired wonder, not love—and he sought to overcome the distance by turning to the more familiar. He further realized that in seeking the strange, he had seen his subjects secondhand. His landscapes were those of art, of nature as it appeared to another, not as it appeared to him. The solution to both problems was to exchange Arcadia and the strange islands of "Oisin" for Ireland. "When I first wrote," he recalled in 1908, "I went here and there for my subjects . . . but presently I convinced myself . . . that I should never go for the scenery of a poem to any country but my own" (*VP* 843–844).

The beginning of Yeats's conviction can be seen in "Oisin" whose subjects are Irish, whose framing story is set somewhere in Ireland, and whose inner story begins and ends near Lough Laen and Knockfefin (*VP* 2, 59). After "Oisin," the scenery became predominantly Irish, the setting often a specific place, as in "The Lake Isle of Innisfree," the exemplary poem with which Yeats closed his letter of advice to Katharine Tynan. Yeats indicated the direction of his own poetry when he praised Tynan's *Ballads and Lyrics* in 1892: "The landscapes are no more taken from the tapestry-like scenery of Rossetti and his imitators, but from her own Clondalkin fields, and from the grey Dublin hills" (*UP* 2:512).

Although Yeats turned to his own country for scenery, the details he selected from it are generic—rock, hill, stream—and are primarily chosen not for the picture of Ireland they convey, but for their symbolic value. "Oisin"'s landscapes may function symbolically, but they serve most immediately as backdrops for action; in the poems of the 1890s, the reverse is true. Landscape may provide the setting for action, but its importance lies in its symbolism. In addition to Blake, occult studies had encouraged Yeats to view the natural world symbolically. The Golden Dawn had taught him that the basic elements of the landscape—earth, water, air, and fire—possessed already established significance.[37] Thus, Yeats could use the four elements and the various forms in which they appear—sea, wind, hills, stars, and more specifically, the hazel tree, the rose—with increased authority and sense of their power.

The poems of the 1890s are not "pictorial" in the way that "Oisin" and "The Island of Statues" are. As Yeats formulated with the Rhymers a desire for simplicity, he stripped his poems of detail. Increasingly, rather than describe symbolic vision as he had so elaborately in "The Wanderings of Oisin," he used symbol to evoke vision. As we saw in chapter 2, this required that he only mention or briefly describe the symbol, thus reducing visual detail. Even when he did re-present vision, as in "The Cap and Bells," he did so frugally.

Decreasing the number of details increased the suggestive powers of those he did select, as fewer elements bore more of the symbolic weight. Thus, Yeats's poems became sparer on the one hand, but richer and more powerful on the other. A passage from Yeats's revision of "The Wanderings of Oisin" for the 1895 *Poems* can illustrate. The opening description of the dewy fragrant woods, which symbolize, as we have seen, the sorrow and joy of mortal life, he compressed into nine lines in which the hunters and hounds "passing the Firbolgs' burial mounds,/Came to the cairn-heaped grassy hill/Where passionate Maive is stony still;/And found on the dove-gray edge of the sea/A pearl-pale, high-born lady" (*VP* 3). The burial mounds, the grayness of the sea's edge, the simple lushness of a grassy hill—the energy of Maeve's passion—carry with greater simplicity and power the same significance as the dripping overabundant forest.

The sparse details of the poems of *The Wind Among the Reeds* evoke landscapes by a variety of techniques, and those landscapes differ in their relation to the poetic world. Many of the poems use natural detail to evoke a scene that comprises a part of the world in which the poem's events happen. Sometimes the poem's action takes place in that landscape, as in the revised section of "Oisin" above, or in "Aedh hears the Cry of the Sedge" which opens: "I wander by the edge/Of this desolate lake/Where wind cries in the sedge" (*VP* 165). Sometimes, especially in poems where the action is mental rather than physical, a detail or series of details suggests a landscape that exists somewhere in the poem's world, but is not "present." In "Aedh tells of the Perfect Beauty,"

> The poets labouring all their days . . .
> Are overthrown by a woman's gaze
> And by the unlabouring brood of the skies

"And therefore," the speaker says,

> my heart will bow, when dew
> Is dropping sleep, until God burn time,
> Before the unlabouring stars and you.
>
> (*VP* 164)

The details evoke a dew-drenched land, a "brood" of stars in a darkening sky, which is not the scene of present action, but which defines a significant time and place somewhere in the poetic world. Such landscapes are often all we know of the physical "look" of that world.

Often Yeats used natural details—both those with already-established symbolic significance and those without—in simile or metaphor, thus charging or further charging them with meaning. In a poem whose physical region has been in some way defined, such details tend to become part of that region and enter it carrying the significance given them by their metaphoric use. "Aedh tells of a Valley full of Lovers" begins:

I dreamed that I stood in a valley, and amid sighs,
For happy lovers passed two by two where I stood;
And I dreamed my lost love came stealthily out of the wood
With her cloud-pale eyelids falling on dream-dimmed eyes
(*VP* 163)

The pale clouds to which the lost love's eyelids are compared function metaphorically, but they also tend to become one more detail in a very sparely described landscape of valley and wood. They enter the landscape, however, full of the suggestiveness imparted to them by their use in the simile, and cannot be separated from it.

When natural details in similes and metaphors occur in a poem whose physical region has not been suggested, they define part of the world of the poem, but the landscape they evoke is entirely symbolic. It cannot exist apart from the meaning given it by the metaphoric use of the detail that suggested it. "A Poet to his Beloved" can illustrate:

I bring you with reverent hands
The books of my numberless dreams,
White woman that passion has worn
As the tide wears the dove-gray sands
(*VP* 157)

The seaside landscape called up by the last line is the most vivid image in the poem, but it is not the scene of the poem's action or projected action as are the landscapes in "Oisin," "Aedh hears the Cry of the Sedge," and "Aedh tells of the Perfect Beauty." Nor can it be attached to a place of action, as are the clouds in "Aedh tells of the Valley full of Lovers," because there is no specified place of action. The landscape "actually" exists somewhere in the world of the poem: the speaker as part of that world must have seen it in order to use it as a simile. But that landscape as we know it can be nothing other than a symbolic representation of how passion wears down a woman. It exists solely for the sake of describing her, and if we imagine it as a place, it must be a symbolic place.

The image of dove-gray sands worn by the tide, even when entirely symbolic, calls up a landscape we at least recognize from our own world. Some of Yeats's landscapes cannot be so identified. These are the world's of dream where the elements of the landscape are familiar to us, but where such relationships as those of size do not pertain. In "The Secret

Rose," the rose's "great leaves enfold/The ancient beards, the helms of ruby and gold/Of the crowned Magi" (*VP* 169). In "Aedh wishes his Beloved were Dead," the speaker addresses the lost love: "Nor would you rise and hasten away,/Though you have the will of the wild birds,/But know your hair was bound and wound/About the stars and moon and sun" (*VP* 176). In each case the image evoked does not correspond to what we know of our world. The rose and its leaves are entirely symbolic, as is the place where such roses enfold beards and helms. So, too, is the world in which a woman's hair is entangled in stars, moon, and sun.

As Yeats decreased the details of his landscapes and increased their symbolic weight, so he reduced the number and brilliance of the colors that had made his poems resemble the pictures he loved and began to exploit their individual symbolic potential. His resolution to write from nature, specifically Irish nature, meant that the old sense of color he had inherited from Turner, Shelley, and the Pre-Raphaelites, who had all gotten it from the Italian landscape, no longer sufficed: "I had a conviction, which indeed I have still," he declared in 1901, "that one's verses should hold, as in a mirror, the colours of one's own climate and scenery in their right proportion; and, when I found my verses too full of the reds and yellows Shelley gathered in Italy, I thought for two days of setting things right . . . by eating little and sleeping upon a board" (*E&I* 5). Motivated by growing nationalism as well as aesthetic values, he solved the problem with more direct action than he had first contemplated. He replaced the gold that had so pervaded "The Island of Statues" and the blues, yellows, reds, and greens of "Oisin" with the cool light of Ireland and the gray of Sligo and the Rosses: "when I had finished *The Wanderings of Oisin,* dissatisfied with its yellow and its dull green, with all that overcharged colour inherited from the romantic movement, I deliberately reshaped my style, deliberately sought out an impression as of cold light and tumbling clouds" (*Au* 74). The landscapes no longer glow with blues, yellows, greens, and reds. Instead there are gray seas and gray twilights, gray cairns and gray shores (*VP* 115, 147, 161, 170), or no color at all.

Yeats did not, however, banish romantic color entirely. Although never present in such abundance after "Oisin," gold remained a favorite, as did red and crimson, outnumbering gray in frequency of use. Green came in not far behind.[38] Yeats had learned that overabundant color, in addition to being untrue to his native scenery, could make one a poet of the picturesque, but he still admired it and believed it could be "full of affection and spiritual meaning" (*L* 98). As this suggests, Yeats was discovering that color might function symbolically and not merely decoratively. Although Blake's colors did not all appeal to Yeats—pink, symbolic of "wholesome," "imaginative" life, never enters his work—he had gained confidence in color's symbolic properties by charting with Ellis Blake's color symbolism.[39] By the time he wrote "The Symbolism of Poetry" in 1900, he was examining the effects and characteristics of the emotional symbols white and purple (*E&I* 161). Whereas color in "Oisin" was at times suggestive, in the poems of the 1890s it is explicitly symbolic. Thus, "Oisin"'s "melting hues" gave way to the red and blue garments of "The Cap and Bells"—symbols of heart and head, passion and intellect—and to the "green drop in the surge" and "chair of gold" in "Fergus and the Druid"—symbols of the glory of mortal life and power.

The decrease in detail in the poems of the 1890s meant that the visual pattern Yeats had adopted from artists could no longer enchant as easily as it had when the landscape was more abundant and pattern, hence, more obvious. Yeats became increasingly skilled, however, in the use of aural pattern whose function in poetry he thought analogous, as we have seen, to that of visual pattern in art. During the 1890s he worked especially hard to refine his rhythm, to create the monotony of the ticking watch made softer and more various (*E&I* 159). After "Oisin," he "loosened" his rhythm, he said (*Au* 74), believing that "serious poetry" must cast out "those energetic rhythms, as of a man running" and cultivate "those wavering, meditative, organic rhythms, which are the embodiment of the imagination" (*E&I* 163) and which have their visual counterparts in such pictures as Rossetti's illustration to "The Maids of Elfen-mere" which Yeats admired.

His loosening of rhythm did not include adoption of vers libre, whose effect (lack of pattern) he associated with the enemies of the Pre-Raphaelites, "Tyndall and Huxley, and Bastien-Lepage's clownish peasant" (*Au* 125). He insisted upon traditional meter but with a "ghostly voice" (*E&I* 524). There were no rules for such rhythm and, discussing the problem with Robert Bridges whose own metrical forays were making poetic news, he lamented his lack of "science on the matter" (*L* 278). Nevertheless, following the French lead and the example of Bridges, he experimented with such devices as the alexandrine—adding in "The Lover tells of the Rose in his Heart" an unstressed syllable to vary the rhythm—and with breaking the monotony of common rhythm by a line of running rhythm (e.g., "The Hosting of the Sidhe").[40] Yeats's method of composition, made famous by Pound's Canto LXXXIII, underscores his belief in the power of rhythm. He chanted his poems, thus practicing the conviction that rhythm could liberate the mind from the pressure of the will and induce a state in which vision would unfold.

The simplification of picture and the increase of its symbolic value extended also to the motifs Yeats transferred during the 1890s from painting to poetry. The poppy, the lily, and especially the rose, so abundant in his poetic regions, came, in part, from Pre-Raphaelite painting, although other sources validated their use. Yeats himself had indicated the debt by drawing attention, in "Symbolism in Painting," to the lilies in Rossetti's *Annunciation* and *Girlhood of Mary Virgin* (*E&I* 147). More importantly and more directly, Yeats borrowed from the Pre-Raphaelites their image of woman. In the poems of the 1890s, however, rather than describe her in elaborate detail as he had in "The Wanderings of Oisin," he chose one or two particular characteristics that evoke a vision of the whole and carry increased symbolic weight. Thus, Niamh's "sunset" lips, "citron" hair and "white vesture" that "flowed/And with the woven crimson glowed/Of many a figured creature strange" are simplifed in "To Ireland in the Coming Times" to a "red-rose-bordered hem" (*VP* 3–4, 137).

The hair of the Pre-Raphaelite women, more than any other detail, fascinated Yeats.[41] It appears again and again in the poems of the 1890s: the "unbound" hair of the Sidhe, the "long dim hair" O'Driscoll dreams of, the "long heavy hair" the curlew sings about, the "dim heavy hair" that makes Michael Robartes moody and long for forgiveness (*VP* 140, 144, 155, 163). Hair was one of the major motifs of the symbolic movement in art in general,[42] and Yeats had noted that in Rossetti's paintings, hair served as a personal symbol: "ears hidden by the hair," he explained, made "one think of a mind busy with inner voices" (*E&I* 147). While he never transferred that particular symbolism to his poems, Yeats did use hair to suggest the dual nature of the Pre-Raphaelite woman. In "The Host of the Air," when the young fairy carries off Bridget, "his neck and his breast and his arms/Were drowned in her long dim hair" (*VP* 145). As elsewhere in Yeats's poetry ("The Heart of the Woman" and "Michael Robartes bids his Beloved be at Peace," for example) that hair represents an allure that is dangerous: it offers both a comforting refuge and a drowning pool.[43]

Similarly, in "The Cap and Bells" Yeats turns the familiar Pre-Raphaelite image of flower-bedecked hair into symbols of desire and fulfillment at the expense of human life. Yeats's women often wear flowers in their hair: the glimmering girl in "The Song of Wandering Aengus," like the woman of Rossetti's *Sea-Spell* (fig. 20) and like Maud Gonne, wears an apple blossom;[44] the beloveds in "Michael Robartes remembers Forgotten Beauty" and "Michael Robartes asks Forgiveness because of his Many Moods" wear roses like the maidens in Rossetti's *Mary Magdalene at the Door of Simon the Pharisee* (fig. 21).[45] But in "The Cap and Bells" the queen does not actually wear flowers: her hair is first "flower-like," then "a folded flower" (*VP* 160, 161). The resolution of the simile into the metaphor follows the poem's general resolution of the world of fragments (heart, soul, cap and bells, queen) whose correspondence can be

Figure 20. Dante Gabriel Rossetti, *A Sea-Spell,* 1877.
Harvard University Art Museums (The Fogg Art Museum),
gift of Grenville L. Winthrop.

described only by simile, into a unified image of the woman in which the previous fragments are identified as one and metaphor describes their relation. The "flutter of flower-like hair" suggests the sensuousness—increased by the image's connection to Pre-Raphaelite women—of the blossom in full bloom (closed flowers do not "flutter"). Its beauty makes the jester's heart "sweet-tongued" in its expression of desire. By contrast,

Figure 21. Dante Gabriel Rossetti, *Mary Magdalene at the Door of Simon the Pharisee,* 1858. Fitzwilliam Museum, Cambridge. Until 1937, this picture was owned by Yeats's friend Charles Ricketts.

"her hair was a folded flower" implies completeness, the result of union—the queen takes to her the jester's cap and bells, and his heart and soul. The agitated motion ("flutter") has been quieted, desire has been fulfilled, but the jester is dead. The folded flower thus not only suggests completeness, but recalls the close-petalled lilies, symbolic of transcendence through death, that Yeats defended in Rossetti's *Annunciation* and *Girlhood of Mary Virgin*.

Figure 22. William Blake, *Thenot and Colinet,* frontispiece to Eclogue I, *The Pastorals of Virgil,* ed. Robert John Thornton, 1821. The illustration shown here is from a complete set of the seven wood engravings printed by Edward Calvert for John Linnell, c. 1825. Rare Book and Special Collections Division, Library of Congress, Washington, D.C.

The decrease in visual detail and the increase in symbolic power that we have seen in Yeats's poems of the 1890s found particular analogues in the work of the landscape painters who had gathered around Blake in his old age. Introduced to Blake by his patron John Linnell, Edward Calvert and Samuel Palmer were inspired by Blake's illustrations for Thornton's edition of Virgil (fig. 22) to portray the simplified symbolic landscapes that Yeats was beginning to want in his poetry. Palmer's etchings, and the early woodcuts and etchings of Calvert that Yeats praised, showed him how lack of color, emphasis on pattern, and reduction in detail could create symbolic art.[46] At times, Yeats's poetic regions bear some visual resemblance to Palmer's and Calvert's art, but even when their pictures differ, poet and painters followed the same symbolic method.

Yeats may have first learned of Palmer and Calvert from Alexander Gilchrist's *Life of William Blake,* which he read around 1881.[47] He cer-

Figure 23. Samuel Palmer, *The Lonely Tower* from *The Shorter Poems of John Milton,* 1889, which Yeats read. Print Collection, The New York Public Library, Astor, Lenox and Tilden Foundations.

tainly encountered their work in the course of his studies for the Ellis-Yeats *Blake* (begun in 1889), which involved visits to the home of John Linnell's children. Yeats's essays of the mid-1890s show that he had read *The Life and Letters of Samuel Palmer* (1892) and *A Memoir of Edward Calvert, Artist, by His Third Son, Samuel,* published in 1893 and illustrated with many prints from the original plates and blocks.[48] By 1901 Yeats had apparently gained a reputation as an expert on Calvert: he planned to write a book on the artist for the Unicorn Press's Artists' Library of Little Engravings series,[49] and when that fell through because of financial difficulties, Pamela Colman Smith, an artist and friend of Yeats, suggested he might "do a book on *Calvert*—with reproductions of the woodcuts" to be printed on her hand press (*LTWBY* 133). Yeats's interest in Palmer and Calvert lasted throughout his life and surfaced in later poems and letters,[50] most importantly in "Under Ben Bulben" where Yeats set them with Blake, Claude, and Richard Wilson (Claude's first English follower) in the same cultural succession to which the Pre-Raphaelites belonged as preservers of the quatrocento's "greater dream":

> When that greater dream had gone
> Calvert and Wilson, Blake and Claude,

Figure 24. Edward Calvert, *The Ploughman,* 1828, from print of original block in *A Memoir of Edward Calvert, Artist, by His Third Son, Samuel,* 1893. Prints and Photographs Division, Library of Congress, Washington, D.C. Yeats owned a copy of this book.

Prepared a rest for the people of God,
Palmer's phrase

(*VP* 639)

In addition to their devotion to Blake, Palmer and Calvert attracted Yeats by their commitment to art's literary connections, their interest in symbolism, and their cultivation of vision as the source of art. Following Blake, they had illustrated Milton and Virgil, and proclaimed that painting and poetry were one.[51] Yeats read Milton's *Shorter Poems* with Palmer's illustrations;[52] one of them, *The Lonely Tower* (fig. 23), became, years later, a major symbol in "The Phases of the Moon." As Calvert's Blakean woodcut, *The Ploughman* (fig. 24), suggests, symbolic vision provided the foundation of much of Palmer's and Calvert's art, especially during their association with Blake.[53] In its first and second states, the print's inscription explains: "Seen in the kingdom of heaven by vision through Jesus Christ our Saviour."[54]

Palmer's and Calvert's reputations in the 1890s encouraged Yeats's interest. Palmer was already highly regarded in art circles when, in 1891, an exhibit of oil paintings and engravings at the British Museum introduced Calvert to the public.[55] Praise for his work and Palmer's followed in the

Figure 25. Edward Calvert, *The Bride,* 1828, from print of original block in *A Memoir of Edward Calvert, Artist, by His Third Son, Samuel,* 1893. Prints and Photographs Division, Library of Congress, Washington, D.C.

periodicals with which Yeats was associated. In 1897, Yeats's friend Charles Ricketts devoted part of "A Note on Original Wood Engraving," an article for *The Pageant,* to Blake's woodcuts for Thornton's Virgil and to the works of Palmer and Calvert, praising especially Calvert's "exquisite prints."[56] Reproductions of Calvert's *The Brook* and *Lady with the Rooks* accompanied the text.

Whereas Yeats viewed Palmer primarily as an advocate in prose of the symbolic method he had learned from Blake, Yeats saw Calvert as a practitioner of that method. Calvert's *The Bride* (fig. 25), which Yeats knew from *A Memoir* and possibly also through Ricketts who owned a copy of it,[57] provides a good comparison in both motif and symbolic method to Yeats's "The Song of Wandering Aengus." The picture reveals that Calvert, like Turner, developed out of the Claudian tradition, as "Under Ben Bulben" suggests. However, Calvert's landscapes, like Yeats's in the 1890s, are explicitly symbolic. In both "The Song of Wandering Aengus" (*VP* 149–150) and *The Bride,* though the region is definite, it is not specific. We know nothing, for example, about the hazel wood except that it existed, and the flowers by the bride's feet are so generalized as to be unidentifiable.[58] The elements of the landscapes clearly exist, not for the pleasures of carefully recorded detail, but for the larger meanings they represent. The inscription to *The Bride* explains its explicitly Christian symbolism: OH GOD! THY BRIDE SEEKETH THEE. A STRAY LAMB IS LED TO THY FOLDS. The bunches of grapes (so ripe that juice drips from one), the bee hives, the flowers along the bride's path signify the fullness of earthly life blessed by divine favor. The stream of life, the well-marked paths leading to the fold, the striding shepherd and bride, naked in their innocence, all resonate with meaning. *The Bride* differs from Morris's visions of Earthly Paradise in that it can never be taken merely as a beautiful work of art. Its symbolism is too insistent. One can never ignore, for example, the pointed meaning of shepherd and flock, as one might overlook, in Morris's profusion of fruits and flowers, the potential symbol of the grapevine in *The Orchard* (fig. 10).

Although less Christian, Yeats's landscape is equally symbolic. The hazel wood, the stream, the "hollow" and "hilly" lands suggest the experience of physical, objective life through which Aengus, poet and lover, pursues the antithetical, subjective life represented by the glimmering girl. The tantalizing appearance of the subjective in the objective is repeated in the elements of the landscape. The hazel tree, as Yeats explained, "was the Irish tree of Life or Knowledge, and in Ireland it was doubtless, as elsewhere, the tree of the heavens" (*VP* 177). While the tree thus exists in and represents the physical world of Life and the Fall into Knowledge through which Aengus wanders, it also suggests the otherworldly realm of the heavens where Aengus's pursuit will end. The poem's heavenly apple tree functions similarly. It bears on one branch the silver and golden apples of sun and moon, symbols of the objective and subjective.[59] The lights of the heavens' fruits combine to dapple the grass, signifying the final union of Aengus and the glimmering girl.

Like the landscapes of Yeats's poems of the 1890s, including "The Song of Wandering Aengus," *The Bride* concentrates symbolic meaning into a few, specifically chosen elements. Unlike Morris, who used in *The Orchard* four different fruit trees, a grapevine, and numerous tufts of flowers to convey the generosity of earth, Calvert used one grapevine, several beehives, and a few flowers. Where Morris used abundant color, Calvert used only black and white. As in Yeats's "Aengus," which reduced the landscape of "Oisin" to uncolored hazel wood, stream, and hollow and hilly lands, fewer elements bear more concentrated meaning.

Calvert's scene, while simpler and more generalized than Morris's, does, nonetheless, contain more detail than Yeats's. Although a symbolist, Calvert still worked within the tradition of representation, and the elements of his symbolic landscape are connected into a recognizable picture. Outline, however, helped Calvert further concentrate symbolic meaning. It could make his forms stand out from their surrounding space, isolating tree, bride, sheep for extra attention. The purpose of outline, Blake had taught both Yeats and Calvert, was not primarily to enhance the look of the picture, but to serve its symbolic purpose. As the "great and golden rule" of symbolic art, the "bounding line" showed, Yeats explained, that the artist had distinguished "the permanent and characteristic" (*E&I* 120) in the forms he drew—had, in other words, apprehended their universal, their symbolic significance. Forms so delineated in art impressed that significance on their viewer, just as Yeats's selection of details did.

In addition to their symbolic method, "The Song of Wandering Aengus" and *The Bride* share symbolic motifs. The stream, the hills and hollows common to both show how easily the symbols of one art can also be those of another. While we cannot attribute Yeats's streams and hills to the influence of Calvert (they are too common in art and in Ireland), the half-light that pervades "The Song of Wandering Aengus" and so many other Yeats poems of the 1890s derives not only from the romantic poets, but from Calvert and Palmer and Blake in the Virgil illustrations. The twilights in Blake's illustrations had so impressed Calvert and Palmer that a full sun rarely shines in their own pictures. Yeats seized on Palmer's praise of the illustrations to Virgil, quoting them often and seconding their identification of the half-light as the most striking quality of the pictures. Palmer, Yeats explained, "has alone praised worthily these illustrations to the first Eclogue: 'There is in all such a misty and dreamy glimmer as penetrates and kindles the inmost soul and gives complete and unreserved delight, unlike the gaudy daylight of this world.'"[60] Palmer's statement probably encouraged Yeats's fondness for the word "glimmer" which had already appeared in "The Lake Isle of Innisfree." During the 1890s the term became a favorite with Yeats to describe that region or state in which "ordinary intelligence" is put away, and the hidden shapes of another world—symbols—emerge in the dim light by which man seeks the truth that will be fully illuminated only at the Last Judgment. In his essay in Shelley, for example, Yeats wrote, "The poet of essences and pure ideas must seek in the half-lights that glimmer from symbol to symbol" (*E&I* 87). Shelley's world—like those of Palmer, Calvert, and Blake in the Virgil illustrations and that of Yeats in the poems of the 1890s—most often glimmers with the half-light of the symbolic morning and evening stars.[61]

In both *The Bride* and "The Song of Wandering Aengus," the half-light of the star signifies that condition in which the earthly apprehends and approaches, but does not reach, the heavenly. The bride returns to the fold of the Lord in a landscape glimmering with the light of a large evening star. Similarly, Aengus catches the fish when "moth-like stars were flickering out" and pursues it, transformed into a girl who has taken on the glimmering light of the stars. Although the clearly marked paths in Calvert's picture may indicate a confidence that the bride's journey will return her to the fold, Calvert has chosen to capture her while she still "seeketh," as the inscription says, leaving the outcome undecided. Yeats's poem makes clear that Aengus's quest will continue as long as the world as we know it exists. Until sun and moon become one, Aengus will wander hollow and hilly lands, as the bride follows her path, under a glimmering half-light.

The half-light of the stars in "The Song of Wandering Aengus" and *The Bride* unifies the scene—the function, Kenneth Clark reminds us, of light in much landscape painting.[62] The starlight, as it glints off the sheep, the trees, the hills, the stream, the bride and shepherd, visually connects the objects in Calvert's landscape. The uniformity of texture the starlight creates, furthermore, conveys Calvert's belief that man and nature are naturally one, a belief reflected also in the companionable glance between the sheep and the bride, in the flowers around her head and in the thatched roof whose curves and hollows blend with those of the hills.

The glimmer of light through "The Song of Wandering Aengus" also creates a unity of scene as the white moths and the silver trout echo the "flickering" of the "moth-like stars." But whereas Calvert's light binds man to nature in an innocent vision of harmony, Yeats's ties nature to the supernatural, and together they conspire to seduce and frustrate man.[63] The "glimmering girl" takes on the flickering light of the stars, allying her to the natural world, as do the apple blossoms in her hair (like the flowers encircling the bride's head) and her assimilation by the "brightening air" of dawn. The girl's glimmering light and the flower in her hair lure Aengus to the chase; her disappearance contrived by nature prevents its successful end.

Yeats found in Calvert's woodcuts and engravings a symbolic region in which one might indeed wander. Calvert's simplification of detail and use of line and symbol declared his art nonrealistic, but his use of perspective, like Turner's, invites us into his scene. Yeats himself recognized that our world and that of Calvert's pictures seem coextensive, as he indicated when, in later life, he wrote Olivia Shakespear about his cottage at Rathfarnham, "This little creeper-covered farm-house might be in a Calvert woodcut" (*L* 799). The poetic worlds of *The Wind Among the Reeds* are at times more accessible than those of Yeats's earlier work. Although the spatial relations in "The Song of Wandering Aengus" may often be unclear ("I went out" is too general to convey a sense of Aengus's place among the physical objects of the poetic world, and where is the floor on which he lays the silver trout?), the poem provides a greater sense of depth than earlier works. The glimmering girl fades through the brightening air, suggesting not only that the light of day obscures her gentler light, but that, as she runs, she disappears into the distance. The "I" of this poem, as in others such as "Aedh hears the Cry of the Sedge," moves through the landscape and implicitly invites us to accompany him. In "The Hosting of the Sidhe," the fairies beckon us directly. The present tense in many of the poems heightens the immediacy of the poem's world: "I hear the Shadowy Horses, their long manes a-shake" (*VP* 154).

But in the end, Yeats's early poetic worlds remain "remote" and "vague," as readers frequently note. The problem is not just that Yeats writes of legendary characters who seem removed from ordinary life; they, after all, people the late poems, which do not seem distant or vague. Nor is it that he doubted—as he had when he pictured the Golden Age—that the world described in the poem was uninhabitable by man. Yeats believed, like Blake, that man lived his daily life in a symbolic world. So why should the symbolic world of the poem not be a congenial place? The problem was more in the nature of literary symbolism as Yeats then practiced it, a problem Calvert did not encounter in his visual symbolism.

In part, we are confronting here the difference between the literary image and the pictorial image. Calvert's symbols, because always present in actual physical form, seem continuous with, or a part of, the physical world of the viewer. But the problem cannot be so easily attributed to differences in media. The images of Yeats's late poems possess a physicality; they seem palpable in a way that even Calvert's literally palpable images do not. The difference between Calvert's symbols and those in Yeats's early poems lies rather in the artists' conceptions of the objects in their created worlds.

In Calvert's landscapes a tree may be a symbol, but it is primarily a tree, derived from those Calvert had observed in nature. In this way, the immediacy of the physical world as directly experienced always entered Calvert's art.[64] For Yeats in the early poetry, however, a tree is primarily a symbol. Despite his vow to take his scenery from Ireland, the hazel wood in "The Song of Wandering Aengus" existed for Yeats not so much as a grove of hazel trees that he saw, say, in Sligo, but as a symbol. In his desire to avoid Wordsworth's error of interpreting "things as they are," Yeats perceived the symbolic value of his landscapes before (or without) seeing them as landscapes. This is the difference between the regions of the 1890s poems and those of the later poems where, for example, the tree seen from the top of the tower is exactly that, and then—or simultaneously—a symbol. In Yeats's finest poems the symbolic landscape never takes precedence over the landscape as experienced. Readers frequently remark the greater immediacy of the later poems, the almost palpable quality of their images, which suggests that the poetic regions are neither vague nor remote.

During the 1880s and 1890s, as Yeats pursued and developed the connections between the visual arts, he experimented with vision, symbol, and the spatial qualities of poems. Despite his claim for "The Wanderings of Oisin" as "an incident or series of incidents," Yeats was never a narrative poet. If poetry does take its place somewhere along a continuum from narrative/temporal to spatial/pictorial, Yeats's tended always toward the pictorial, the placement of images in space. In 1914 he claimed that as the achievement of modern poetry in general: "The whole movement of poetry is toward pictures, sensuous images, away from rhetoric, from the abstract, toward humility" (*UP* 2:414).

By the end of the 1890s, however, Yeats found himself increasingly dissatisfied with the dream world of Pre-Raphaelite art and of his own poetry of vision. The community centered around Pre-Raphaelitism, which had aesthetically and psychologically supported him, had begun to dissolve. In 1896 Morris died, followed two years later by Puvis, Moreau, Beardsley, and Burne-Jones. The Rhymers had disbanded, some sinking into "dissipation and despair" (*Au* 312; *VP* 369). The sense of deterioration encouraged Yeats to question—tentatively at first—both the Pre-Raphaelite art his generation had admired and emulated, and his own poetry so tied to it. Characteristically, Yeats's reservations about his own work surfaced in his discussions of the visual arts, most clearly in comments he made between 1898 and 1901 on the minor artist W. T. Horton.[65] Yeats's evaluation of Horton is an evaluation of himself which prepared the way for the next step of his career.

That Yeats ever admired Horton's monotonous, technically flawed black and white drawings seems strange, but he clearly felt an affinity for this Pre-Raphaelite descendent who worked from vision (fig. 26).[66] Perhaps it was the lack of surface charm in Horton's work that allowed Yeats to identify the problems obscured by the technical virtuosity of the more talented Pre-Raphaelite artists. In Yeats's 1898 introduction to Horton's *A Book of Images*—which Yeats later purged of all references to his friend and reprinted as "Symbolism in Painting" in *Ideas of Good and Evil* (1903)—he sounded, briefly, the criticism that was to become the focus of his dissatisfaction with Horton's art and his own poetry: systematic mystics, among whom he counted Blake and Rossetti, are "not the greatest of artists" because "so august a beauty moves before the mind that they forget the things which move before the eyes" (*E&I* 150). Two years later, in an unpublished letter to Horton, Yeats faulted for this reason thirteen pictures Horton had sent him. The "defect in drawing fig-

Figure 26. William T. Horton, *The Magi*, from *A Book of Images*, 1898. Department of Rare Books and Special Collections, The University of Michigan Library, Ann Arbor. Yeats wrote the introduction to this book.

ures," which he enumerated and described, derived, he thought, from too much reliance on vision and insufficient study of nature. He warned Horton that he was too shaded in "lunar and saturnine shadows" and advised him to "see under a solar influence" by imagining himself "bathed in sunlight" while he worked.[67] In July 1901 Yeats told Horton, in advice less veiled by occult symbols, to "turn from vision for a while."[68] Two weeks later he wrote, "Like most visionary and imaginative artists your difficulty is to force yourself to study not the visionary truth but the form and methods by which it has to be expressed in the world. . . . It is quite certain to me that you should force yourself to study from life and from nature in every form, but this I fear you will not do."[69]

Yeats considered himself among those "visionary and imaginative artists." Although, unlike Horton, he had mastered his craft, he had begun to see that his own poems were as distant from life, as overly dependent on vision, as Horton's art: "all a flight into fairyland," he later said. In 1897 Yeats wrote, "I had finished *The Secret Rose,* and felt how it had separated my imagination from life, sending my Red Hanrahan, who should have trodden the same roads with myself, into some undiscoverable country" (*E&I* 298–299). Like Horton, he had worked in "lunar and saturnine shadows." By 1904, however, he was warning AE against that "dim shadowy region" in poetry: "I have dwelt there too long not to dread all that comes out of it" (*L* 435, 434).

Yeats did not intend to abandon vision, nor did he mean to become a realistic artist, but he recognized that he and Horton both needed to attach their art more closely to life. In 1906 Yeats summed up his analysis of his early poetry in a statement that again illustrates the affinity he perceived between his art and the visual arts:

> I had set out on life with the thought of putting my very self into poetry, and had understood this as a representation of my own visions and an attempt to cut away the non-essential, but as I imagined the visions outside myself my imagination became full of decorative landscape and of still life. (*E&I* 271)

As these comments on Horton's work and on his own suggest, Yeats was groping toward a recognition of aesthetic distance and the roles that space, decorativeness, and the palpability of images played in it. He had imagined his visions outside himself and that distance created, as it did in the worst kinds of art, merely decorative landscape and still life—pictures that seemed to readers distant from life as experienced in this world. The "lunar and saturnine shadows" made both Yeats's and Horton's art too ethereal, too unlike the ordinary life lived by the light of day. Red Hanrahan inhabited not only a space different from Yeats's and the reader's, but one that is "undiscoverable."

Years later, puzzling out in his *Autobiographies* the failure of the tragic generation of the 1890s, Yeats saw distance from life as the major flaw of the Pre-Raphaelite aesthetic, and he held it responsible for the limitations in both the art and the lives of the Pre-Raphaelites and their followers. Of the Rhymers he said, "They all followed Rossetti in his absolute withdrawal into the world of art."[70] In instinctive reaction to the dangers of their separation from life, Yeats made his famous vow to move downward upon it (*L* 469). He did so by taking his work into the theater.

4

From Painted Stage to Sculpted Image

The Theater Years

"When I went to Coole the curtain had fallen upon the first act of my drama," Yeats wrote (*Au* 395). The second act opened in 1897 with the foundation of the Irish Literary Theatre. For more than a decade after its debut in 1899 with *The Countess Cathleen* and Edward Martyn's *The Heather Field,* theater business absorbed Yeats's time and energies. He wrote few poems and devoted himself to learning his new craft. Yeats's career as playwright, producer, and manager, however, is inseparable from his career as poet. As Thomas Parkinson and others have shown, Yeats's experience as a dramatist changed the kind of poetry he would write.[1]

In terms of its relationship to the visual arts, especially, Yeats's later poetry grew out of his practical experience as playwright and producer. Poetry's relation to the visual arts is more obviously realized in the theater where images appear to the physical eye and not the mind's eye alone. So important was the physical image to Yeats that he termed drama in general the "art of making a succession of pictures" (*E&I* 99). He actively participated in the staging of his plays and crusaded for suitable scenery.

The physical presence of the stage pictures and the simple necessity of keeping an audience interested threw into relief one issue with which Yeats had been wrestling in his early poetry: aesthetic distance. Yeats realized that his success as a producer of dramatically effective poetic plays would depend on his ability to manipulate the perceived distance between the audience and the world on stage. His dissatisfaction with the too distant world of his early poems both led to and resulted from his entrance into the theater. In 1903 Yeats wrote hopefully of *On Baile's Strand:* "The first shape of it came to me in a dream, but it changed much in the making, foreshadowing, it may be, a change that may bring a less dream-burdened will into my verses."[2]

Contending with the problem of distance revolutionized Yeats's concept of dramatic images and changed the fundamental alliance between his art and the visual arts. Recognizing the importance of the actor, he first abandoned landscape in favor of portraiture as the appropriate painterly analogy. Ultimately, dissatisfied with the dramatic effect of staged portraits and inspired by the Noh drama, which Ezra Pound introduced him to in 1913, Yeats pulled his subjects out of the picture frame of the proscenium arch, turned them slowly in space to reveal their solid forms, and declared sculpture the new art of the theater. Yeats did not reject Pre-Raphaelite painting, but assimilated its elements into his new concept of stage production.

This radical shift of analogies affected not only the production of plays, but the writing of poetry. To understand the relation between Yeats's later poems and the visual arts as well as his work as a dramatist, it is necessary to follow the development of his concept of theatrical production. Unlike the relationship between the visual arts and poetry of vision, that between the plays and their visual presentation is documented by Yeats's clear, programmatic statements. The new Irish theater movement's demand for a set of artistic goals, and the necessity of educating an audience in the ways of the art, required Yeats to articulate his dramatic theory, giving us a clear view of how he came to formulate it. This chapter, then, will trace Yeats's idea of drama as picture as it evolves into drama as sculpture. Gordon Craig, the great European scenic innovator, animated the first phase; Ezra Pound and the illustrator Edmund Dulac inspired the second.

When Yeats embarked on his career as writer and producer of plays, he turned from the unity of literature and the visual arts offered by poetry of vision to that provided by drama. The theater's opportunities for such unity, in fact, helped animate Yeats's ready enthusiasm for the stage: as early as 1886 he had admired a production of John Todhunter's *Helena of Troas* because its "mood, acting, scenery and verse were all a perfect unity."[3] Although, for Yeats, "the arts" of the theater included music and, later, dance, his early efforts concentrated on producing a stage picture united to words: "our art of the stage is the art of making a succession of pictures."[4] Yeats saw those pictures as paintings, and on several levels he associated writing and producing plays with the works of art he admired. Yeats often saw Pre-Raphaelite paintings as frozen moments of drama, admiring those Rossettis "where there are several figures engaged in some dramatic action" (*E&I* vii). It is not surprising then that when he wrote plays he sometimes worked from such paintings, continuing the practice initiated when J. B. Yeats's drawing inspired his 1884 *Love and Death*. Yeats explained about the last scene of *The Countess Cathleen*'s 1895 revision: "When I was in my twenties I saw a drawing or etching by some French artist of an angel standing against a midnight sky. . . . I imitated it in the old angels at the end of *The Countess Cathleen*" (*VPl* 178). Such associations of picture as stage and play as picture perhaps explain why Yeats's pastels of Coole, drawn around 1900 when he was deep in planning the theater movement's early productions, look so much like set designs (fig. 2).

The new alliances with the visual arts which the theater offered differ in two major ways from those of his early poetry: although Yeats had associated with artists and found in their work analogues and inspiration for his poems of the 1880s and 1890s, he now collaborated directly with them in the production of his visions; whereas the visions called up by the early poems had been visible only to the mind's eye, in the theater they are visible to the physical eye as well.

During the 1890s Yeats had gained some experience in combining words with literal pictures and in working with artists. Responding to the call by the Pre-Raphaelite movement for well-designed and illustrated books, he had tried to secure the right pictures for his volumes of poems and stories.[5] J. B. Yeats, Edwin Ellis, J. T. Nettleship, Aubrey Beardsley, H. Granville Fell, and Althea Gyles all contributed illustrations or cover designs.[6] Many had disappointed Yeats, but Althea Gyles's covers for *The Secret Rose* (1897), *Poems* (1899), and *The Wind Among the Reeds* (1899) pleased him, perhaps because the designs are not separate from the written word but attempt to work with it.[7] They image the books' major occult symbols, declare the author's Irishness by using Celtic lettering, and set the poems and stories in the Pre-Raphaelite tradition by echoing the motifs and patterns of Blake, Rossetti, and Burne-Jones.[8] Yeats's collaboration with artists on the staging of his and others' plays extend these early ventures.

A single problem motivated all of Yeats's experiments in set design: how to stage the world of imagination, to "picture the soul." Yeats's movement downward upon life did not mean abandoning imagination and the visions it produced. Remaining true to his early theories of poetry, Yeats believed that the best drama offered man dreams, and he continued to work from vision. Although his poetry of the 1890s had succeeded in evoking dream worlds, it lacked the dramatic force necessary for stage presentation. His poetic pictures, he knew, were too distant to make an impact on an audience. Yeats thus found himself in the paradoxical position of desiring a stage picture that seemed remote enough to suggest to the audience the world of imagination, but "near" enough to have dramatic effect—otherwordly, but full of the pressure of reality. To manipulate the distance between audience and picture, he needed sets and costumes that would establish the right degree of remoteness so that the world on stage would draw in its viewers, yet would be unlike their ordinary lives. He needed the distance that resulted from imaginative vision and the "closeness" that came from the observation of life he had recommended to Horton.

The theater Yeats entered in 1897, however, was founded in a realistic tradition. Actors, designers, managers, and directors had all been trained to persuade the audience that what passed before their eyes was not a play, but the events of actual lives. This theater's conventions were to deny convention. Illusion succeeded when the audience felt that the stage was an extension of their world, when the audience "believed" they were in a real wood or a real room. Realism's object was to close the gap between audience and stage. Yeats thus found himself with the realism of conventional theater on one hand and the distant dream world of his early poetic regions on the other.

While he clearly recognized that "one must get one's actors, and perhaps one's scenery, from the theatre of commerce," Yeats began to rebel (*E&I* 170). He started by calling for a new decorative scenery subordinate to the actor. He denied the theater's assumption that scenery was "as important as the story." Vigorously objecting to the modern stage's substitution of "the more obvious effects of nature painted by somebody who understands how to show everything to the most hurried glance" for "the descriptions of poetry," he insisted on the supremacy of words (*E&I* 169). "The poet cannot," he argued, "evoke a picture to the mind's eye if a second-rate painter has set his imagination of it before the bodily eye" (*Ex* 178–179). After the 1899 fiasco when the final scene of *The Countess Cathleen* was staged, as James Flannery notes, with "a dazzling Wagnerian panoply of the theatre arts that would have challenged Bayreuth itself,"[9] Yeats set to "writing plays where all would depend upon the player" (*VPl* 1291). Despite the new emphasis on the actor, Yeats never adopted the bare stage of the Elizabethans where all really did depend on the player. He continued to strive for a marriage of his poetry to the visual, but he meant the painter's art to be a more equal partner to his own than had previously been the case in the theater. Scenery should "not overwhelm, as our naturalistic scenery does, the idealistic art of the poet."[10] It should support, not supplant, the pictures poetry created.

Replacing the realistic with the decorative meant first rejecting the distinguishing characteristic of the commercial theater: "Meretricious landscape." The visual arts of the stage, Yeats claimed, should not seek the effects the easel painter could create much better: "the moment an actor stands near to your mountain, or your forest, one will perceive that he is standing against a flat surface. Illusion, therefore, is impossible and should not be attempted" (*Ex* 178). As Pre-Raphaelite paintings and Morris's tapestries had conceded the flatness of canvas or carpet by violating perspective, so now Yeats recommended the theater defy realism and admit its craft: "We should be content to suggest a scene upon a canvas, whose vertical flatness we accept and use, as the decorator of pottery accepts the roundness of a bowl or a jug" (*Ex* 178). The theater should acknowledge its conventions.

Whereas Yeats's poetry of the 1880s and 1890s had evoked a landscape, the theater demanded a different picture. Because the actors were most important, landscape itself must go. Yeats thus turned from Palmer, Calvert, and Blake's illustrations of Virgil to his father's art (figs. 3,4).[11]

The backgrounds for plays, he repeatedly advised, "should be thought out not as one thinks out a landscape, but as if it were the background of a portrait" (*Ex* 109; cf. *Ex*. 88). This view of scenery also allies the picture he wanted to the Pre-Raphaelites, especially Rossetti, who set Elizabeth Siddall, Jane Morris, and others against backgrounds whose decorativeness appealed to Yeats (*Au* 140).

The sense of pattern and color Yeats had learned from the Pre-Raphaelites now became central to his concept of decorative scenery: "You must make the stage a background for your players, but you must get your effects from simple decorative form and decorative colour." [12] Because they would not carry across the footlights, Yeats broadened the intricate details of the Arts and Crafts Movement. The trees for the background of Synge's *The Well of the Saints* derive from the Pre-Raphaelite tradition (as seen, for example, in the pattern of rose branches in Althea Gyles's cover for *The Secret Rose*): "While I write," said Yeats in 1905, "we are rehearsing *The Well of the Saints,* and are painting for it decorative scenery, mountains in one or two flat colours and without detail, ashtrees and red salleys with something of recurring pattern in their woven boughs" (*E&I* 305). He sought an effect like that of a frieze (*Ex* 177) whose repeated shapes combined the sense of pattern and procession he had seen in Morris's tapestries. Yeats also reduced the varied colors of Pre-Raphaelite painting to one or two of his favorites. Dramatic effect required simplicity and boldness. He criticized AE's 1902 costumes and scenery for *Deirdre* as not "simple enough." "One often needs nothing more than a single colour," he advised, "with perhaps a few shadowy forms to suggest wood or mountain" (*Ex* 88).

Against such shadowy backgrounds Yeats would pose the subjects of his portraits in contrasting colors: "we could make our pictures with robes that contrasted with great masses of colour in the back-cloth" (*E&I* 100). To further emphasize the actor, Yeats took care that the line separating the player from the backdrop "should be clear and not broken up into the outline of windows and wainscoting, or lost into the edges of colours" (*Ex* 177). The concept derived from Blake and had been carried on in Pre-Raphaelite painting and design. "The more distinct, sharp and wiry the bounding line," Yeats quoted Blake in 1896, "the more perfect the work of art" (*E&I* 120).

While Yeats's program for set design displays its Pre-Raphaelite ancestry, the adaptation of his forefathers' art distinguishes, in an important way, his pictures from theirs. The boldness of effect and the insistence on Blake's energetic line indicate that the dream world Yeats wanted to present on stage was not his Pre-Raphaelite dream world of the nineties. The "lyric mood," the heightened sensuality based in part on late Pre-

Raphaelite paintings of women, Yeats now rejected, in his movement downward, for the more Blakean masculine energy: "Modern literature, above all poetical literature," he objected, "is monotonous in its structure and effeminate in its continual insistence upon certain moments of strained lyricism." Yeats fought the effeminate and strove to be like the "old writers, the masculine writers of the world, [who] wrote to be spoken or to be sung" (*Ex* 221). He rewrote his plays for "an addition to the masculine element": "To me drama . . . has been the search for more of manful energy, more of cheerful acceptance of whatever arises out of the logic of events, and for clean outline, instead of those outlines of lyric poetry that are blurred with desire and vague regret."[13] That clean outline joined pattern and color to create the decorative scenery necessary for his new sense of the world of imagination.

With decorative scenery installed, Yeats believed he could control aesthetic distance. The more decorative, the less realistic, a set, the more remote the stage picture would seem: "I have noticed that the more obviously decorative is the scene and costuming of any play, the more it is lifted out of time and place, and the nearer to faeryland do we carry it" (*VPl* 454). Whereas he had tried to cast the decorative out of his poetry after "Oisin," he now saw that he could simply vary its degree to have greater flexibility in creating the distance he needed to stage the world of imagination. Further extending his control, Yeats completed the picture with movements—more or less stylized—to complement or contrast with words that were more or less poetic. In the 1904 *Samhain* he summed up his scenic program:

> Having chosen the distance from naturalism which will keep one's composition from competing with the illusion created by the actor, who belongs to a world with depth as well as height and breadth, one must keep this distance without flinching. The distance will vary according to the distance the playwright has chosen, and especially in poetry, which is more remote and idealistic than prose, one will insist on schemes of colour and simplicity of form, for every sign of deliberate order gives remoteness and ideality. But, whatever the distance be, one's treatment will always be more or less decorative. We can only find out the right decoration for the different types of play by experiment, but it will probably range between, on the one hand, woodlands made out of recurring pattern, or painted like old religious pictures upon a gold background, and upon the other the comparative realism of a Japanese print. This decoration will not only give us a scenic art that will be a true art because pe-

culiar to the stage, but it will give the imagination liberty, and without returning to the bareness of the Elizabethan stage. (*Ex* 178)

With this new scenic art Yeats staged *The Shadowy Waters* in 1906. The production exemplifies the practical application of Yeats's theories. Its scenery by Robert Gregory combined pattern and color in a stage picture of Pre-Raphaelite heritage. Designed in two predominant colors—the blues and greens so pervasive in Pre-Raphaelite paintings—the play took place on the deck of a stylized ship: "All the woodwork is of dark green; and the sail is dark green, with a blue pattern upon it, having a little copper colour here and there. The sky and sea are dark blue. All the persons of the play are dressed in various tints of green and blue, the men with helmets and swords of copper, the woman with copper ornaments upon her dress" (*VPl* 317). To make Dectora, the main subject of his portrait, stand out, Yeats dressed her in "a lighter green against the darker tints in sky and boat" (*VPl* 341). Like the women of Yeats's nineties poems, she possessed the Pre-Raphaelite "pale forehead" and "hair the colour of burning" (*VPl* 318). The stage picture satisfied Yeats's desire to show the world of dream: "The effect of this monotony of colour was to my eyes beautiful, and made the players seem like people in a dream" (*VPl* 341). The *Freeman's Journal* praised the play, identifying its theme with its picture in a way that would have pleased Yeats: "The contrast of the sceptical crew and the trustful dreamer, the apparition of the woman yearning for the past, and mystically even for the unending future, constitute a picture painted in colours ethereal, yet intense, pervaded with a cool warmth which cannot stir the blood, but must heat the imagination."[14]

The Shadowy Waters offered one kind of stage picture, but many of Yeats's early plays offered a different kind. While he argued for words as picture makers, advocated unrealistic scenery, and promoted the decorative as a means, Yeats also admitted as scenery "anything that can be represented successfully—a room, for instance" (*Ex* 177). Such an admission assents, however covertly, to the modern theater's expertise in realism, and indicates Yeats's well-documented difficulties in getting the scenery he wanted. Concessions were necessary to his continued life in the theater. Even in *The Shadowy Waters,* rather than rely on an image painted by words to describe the burning strings of Forgael's harp, Yeats turned to the illusion possible to modern stagecraft. At the climax of the play, he committed the sin for which he had damned the realistic theater—he appealed to the eye rather than the ear. Grappling with the difficulty of making Forgael's harp "take fire," Yeats had "to give up the harp for a sort of psaltery . . . where the strings could be slits covered with glass or gelatine on the surface of a shallow and perhaps semi-transparent box" (*VPl* 341). Yeats rationalized his heresy in the name of symbolism: "There is no reason for objecting to a mechanical effect when it represents some material thing, becomes a symbol, a player, as it were" (*VPl* 342). But perhaps the real reason was recognition that his desire to picture dream worlds was limited by the modern theater and its audience schooled to expect realistic representation: "If the harp cannot suggest some power that no actor could represent by sheer acting . . . the enchanting of so many people by it will seem impossible. Perhaps very wonderful music might do that if the audience were musicians, but lacking the music and that audience it is better to appeal to the eye" (*VPl* 342).

Many of Yeats's early plays demonstrate this pragmatic approach by conceding in part to the audience's expectations and relying on the stage's ability to represent a room successfully. In *The Countess Cathleen,* words do not present the picture of Mary grinding a quern or of Teigue setting peat next to a lighted fire. Both mill and hearth form part of a simple but realistic setting. So precise are Yeats's directions for this scene in some versions of the play that he specifies the kind of trees (oak, pine, hazel, quicken) seen through the cottage window (*VPl* 5). This is hardly the "few shadowy forms to suggest wood or mountain" that he had advocated. Even after he had learned to write plays "where all would depend upon the player," his scenic effects rely on the stage's fitness for realism. *The Pot of Broth* (1904) takes place in a "cottage kitchen" (*VPl* 236), *Deirdre* (1907) in a "Guest-house in a wood" (*VPl* 345), *On Baile's Strand* (1904) in a "great hall by the sea close to Dundalgan" (*VPL* 456). While the words of the plays often create a relationship between actors and sets ("I will shut the door"; "this house/Is an old guest-house built for travellers/From the seashore to Conchubar's royal house"; "What's in that big pot? . . . What's in the little pot? . . .What's in that bottle, I wonder?" [*VPl* 456,345,236]), they rarely evoke scenes themselves.

But even when using the stage's realistic abilities, Yeats heeded his own advice. He tried to distance his picture from the audience. Already the mythological subject matter of many of his plays provided an element of unreality. The events that unfolded were not events the audience believed would or could happen in their lives. To further the distance, Yeats insisted on a style of acting for which the Abbey later became famous: "That we may throw emphasis on the words in poetical drama . . . the actors must move, for the most part, slowly and quietly, and not very much" (*Ex* 176). Reducing the player's movement to a minimum allowed the poetry—with its magical ability to conduct the listener into the imagination—to become the center of attention, and made the audience aware that the world on stage was not quite "real." Because one does not stand still and speak in verse in one's kitchen, the stage picture would seem more distant from the audience than that of realistic drama. Even the sets themselves contain evidence of Yeats's desire for remoteness. He introduced to his kitchens and halls details that refer to and evoke Pre-Raphaelite dream worlds. The decorative chairs for *On Baile's Strand,* the embroidered curtain Yeats wanted for the 1903 production of *The King's Threshold,* and the "ancient tapestry" hanging in the medieval-inspired great hall of *The Countess Cathleen* all recall William Morris (*VPl* 456; *L* 409; *VPl* 51). The child in the 1898 production of *The Land of Heart's Desire* has the "red-gold hair" of Pre-Raphaelite women and is dressed in the "pale green" that Yeats had admired at the 1890 Arts and Crafts Exhibition (*UP* 1:185). Although realistic in themselves, the details echo the Pre-Raphaelite dream worlds from which they were borrowed.

Throughout the early years of the Abbey, Yeats experimented with decorative stage pictures, always fighting managers, actors, builders to achieve the effects he needed for proper distance. Edward Gordon Craig, "the greatest stage inventor in Europe" (*UP* 2:393), had provided model and inspiration for the struggle, and Yeats's early efforts culminated in his collaboration with Craig on the 1911 production of *The Hour Glass.* Yeats had first run across Craig in 1901 when he saw Craig's staging of *Dido and Aeneas* and *The Masque of Love:* "Mr. Gordon Craig has discovered how to decorate a play with severe, beautiful, simple, effects of colour," he wrote in the *Saturday Review* (*L* 366). Like Yeats, Craig wanted to carry drama beyond realism, to create a "new world" on the stage, "not to copy the real world imperfectly."[15]

Much has been written on Yeats's debt to Craig, which Yeats himself proclaimed in 1902: "I have now however learnt a great deal from Gordon Craig."[16] Yeats owned Craig's book of stage designs, *Towards a New Theatre,* and subscribed to *The Mask* in which his own "The Tragic Theatre" and "*The Hour Glass:* A Preface to the New Version" appeared (*YL* 65, 169–171). But Yeats was by no means a slavish follower. He quarreled particularly with what he found to be a lack of unity in Craig's stage pictures. For Craig, unlike Yeats, the purely visual effects counted for more than the powers of poetry. Yeats found Craig's 1903 scenery for *The Viking* "amazing but [it] rather distracts one's thoughts from the words" (*L* 398). In 1904 he criticized the "externality" of Craig's fantastic lighting effects. And by 1905 Yeats felt confident that his own designs improved on the master's: he thought Florence Farr would prefer the scenery for *The Shadowy Waters* to Craig's work because "It is more noble and simple (*L* 456). True to his own ideas on poetic drama, he insisted on sets whose simplicity and nobility would contribute to the "evocation," but would guarantee that the scenery did not call attention to itself.

Despite the disagreements, in 1910 Craig's invention of movable screens for staging plays revived Yeats's waning enthusiasm for the theater.[17] The tall, hinged screens that rolled on castors would, Yeats proclaimed to Lady Gregory, "be a fine new start for us and put a new force in much that we do" (*L* 545–546). He believed the invention would revolutionize the staging of not only his plays, but realistic drama as well: "we shall have a means of staging everything that is not naturalistic, and . . . out of his invention may grow a completely new method even for our naturalistic plays" (*L* 546). On 12 January 1911 the Abbey Theatre, using the screens, produced *The Hour Glass* and Lady Gregory's *The Deliverer.* "At last," Yeats declared, "one composes like a painter."[18]

The stage pictures painted by Craig's screens for *The Hour Glass* and for a later production of *The Countess Cathleen* show how far Yeats had come from preferring the background of Rossetti's paintings. The "recurring patterns" of "woven boughs" were replaced by the pattern of vertical lines made by the angles of the screens. All detail, even that of "shadowy forms," was gone. Color, though important, was achieved not by paint but by colored lights trained on the off-white screens. Yeats praised the effects for *The Hour Glass* that "depend but little on colour, and greatly upon delicate changes of tone" (*VPl* 644). Most important was the change in general atmosphere. Despite windows and doors frequently opening onto outdoor scenes, Pre-Raphaelite paintings create an intimate space, a sense of enclosure, as do the portraits of J. B. Yeats. Gordon Craig's screens, on the other hand, were monumental; they created vast, seemingly endless spaces. Their large scale attracted Yeats. He exulted that "by means so simple that one laughs" he would be able "to lay the events of my plays amid a grandeur like that of Babylon" (*UP* 2:392). Yeats's own sketch for *The Countess Cathleen* shows an actor dwarfed by the huge screens (fig. 27). Their "great cyclopean proportions" (*UP* 2:393) rendered the stage pictures unhuman. The grandeur of Babylon was completely foreign to the ordinary world of the Irish theatergoer. Craig's screens, even more than the "decorative scenery" Yeats had been advocating, created the aesthetic distance necessary for presenting the world of imagination.

Despite Yeats's enthusiasm for the possibilities of Craig's screens, they were rarely used fter 1912. Technical difficulties, problems with collaboration, a disappointing audience, and changing theories of dramatic presentation cooled Yeats's interest in Craig's invention and discouraged his efforts to write plays for the modern stage.

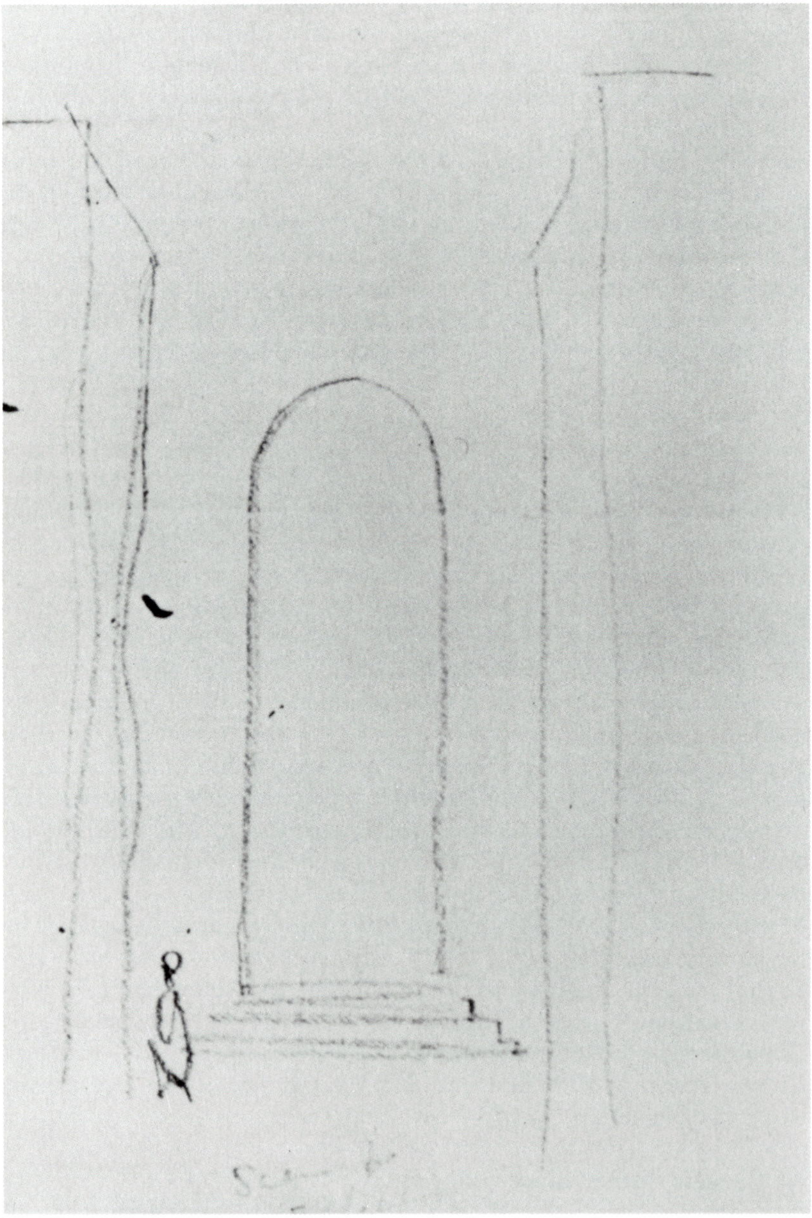

Figure 27. William Butler Yeats, sketch for 1911 production of *The Countess Cathleen* with Gordon Craig's screens. Courtesy of Michael B. Yeats and Anne Yeats.

Although they rolled on castors, Craig's screens proved more difficult to move for quick scene changes than both Craig and Yeats had hoped. Their unfortunate habit of toppling over tried the patience of stage hands, actors, and audience. Further, as James Flannery has noted, they required a skilled, imaginative director to achieve their full range of effects.[19] With the departure of Nugent Monck in 1912, the Abbey lost that director.

Craig, furthermore, turned out to be a more difficult collaborator than Yeats had foreseen. Jealous of his invention, Craig refused the Abbey Theatre Company permission to tour with his screens unless he was present to manage them.[20] He insisted on closely supervising their use at the Abbey, but his directions were vague and of little practical value. To the impoverished Abbey he suggested silk, oak, and bronze as possible materials for the screens, and doggedly claimed that although the screens rolled, the Abbey's sloped stage posed no problem. Craig's letters to Yeats show the designer's testy responses to Yeats's proposed changes. When Yeats directed his carpenter to add doors to the screens because Craig had omitted entrances and exits from his design, Craig responded, "please Mister Yeats your carpenter mustn't. *He mustn't add or take away anything whatsoever*; but if any fault is found in said screens *I will always be glad to do what I can to rectify it*" (*LTWBY* 242). Yet, as other letters indicate, Craig took months to reply to calls for help (e.g., *LTWBY* 234, 236). While Craig's scenery and costumes for *The Hour Glass* excited him, Yeats clearly wanted more autonomy in controlling his stage pictures.

Yeats was also increasingly discouraged by the Abbey audience. At the outset of the national theater project, he had envisioned the audience as an extension of the Pre-Raphaelite community he had allied himself with in the 1890s. "Why should we thrust our works . . . before those quite excellent people who think that Rossetti's women are 'guys,' that Rodin's women are 'ugly,' and that Ibsen is 'immoral'?" he polemically asked in 1899 (*E&I* 166). Convinced that an Aran Islander would understand Gustave Moreau (*Au* 321–322), he welcomed the peasant to the Pre-Raphaelite elite: "We must make a theatre for ourselves and our friends, and for a few simple people who understand from sheer simplicity what we understand from scholarship and thought. We have planned the Irish Literary Theatre with this hospitable emotion," he claimed (*E&I* 166). But it became clear that such an audience did not exist. By 1912 Yeats found himself trapped between the need for a theater and its intolerable demands: "I have begun to shrink from sending my muses where they are but half-welcomed," he later explained. "Yet I need a theatre; I believe myself to be a dramatist" (*VPl* 415).

There was, however, another reason for Yeats's failing enthusiasm. Early on he had begun to question the very concept of staging as picture.

In 1904 Yeats explained in *Samhain:* "There are two kinds of poetry, and they are commingled in all the greatest works. When the tide of life sinks low there are pictures, as in the *Ode on a Grecian Urn* and Virgil at the plucking of the Golden Bough. The pictures make us sorrowful. We share the poet's separation from what he describes "(*Ex* 163). He saw that picture making itself implied a necessary separation between viewer and viewed, and he understood that, in his early poetry, picture making in the tradition of Keats and Virgil had helped make his poetic worlds distant. The discovery extended to his dramatic program founded on the same principles. In the theater, as in poetry, picture making separated audience and work too much. Even given the dramatist's ability to control the decorative for more or less distance, the world on stage seemed too far away, too divorced from the world of the audience. Increased realism could decrease distance, but for a Yeats attached to nonmimetic art, that offered no solution.

Yeats was, however, beginning to see a new possibility in the visual arts for dramatic model. Although he had argued in 1901 for a fan-shaped theater whose sight lines would improve the theater's picture-making ability (*E&I* 99–100), he admired those productions in which the sculptural asserted itself against the pictorial. In 1902 he praised DeMax and Bernhardt in *Phèdre:* "For long periods the performers would merely stand and pose . . . the whole scene had the nobility of Greek sculpture" (*Ex* 87). Two years later he lamented the modern theater's proscenium stage and longed to violate the two-dimensionality of the picture it created. He wanted to move the actors out of the picture frame of the proscenium arch and onto an apron: "The necessities of a builder have torn from us, all unwilling as we were, the apron . . . We would have preferred to be able to return occasionally to the old stage of statue-making, of gesture" (*Ex* 173). In an effort to move the picture closer to the audience, Yeats slowly over the course of a decade rejected painting and adopted sculpture as his dramatic model.

Yeats's experiments with Craig's screens marked the culmination of his theatrical picture making, but one of them—Nugent Monck's 1911 production of *The Countess Cathleen*—also showed Yeats how sculpture could work as dramatic model.[21] Although he saw the screens as backgrounds for two-dimensional pictures (the linearity of his sketch for *The Countess Cathleen* and his claim that they allowed him to compose like a painter demonstrate that), they are more sculptural than pictorial. Their square, boxlike shapes insisted that the stage had depth as well as height and width. Monck's *Countess Cathleen* carried that insistence further. In addition to using the screens, Monck extended the Abbey stage to create the apron Yeats had wanted. With the actors playing in front of the pros-

Figure 28. Jacob Epstein, *Sun God*, c. 1910.
Permission of Richard Buckle, C.B.E.

Figure 29. Henri Gaudier-Brzeska, *Boy with a Rabbit (Boy with a Coney)*, 1914. Permission of Mary De Rachewiltz.

cenium arch and entering through the audience, the notion of a stage picture could no longer be maintained. The production demanded that the playgoers recognize the three-dimensionality of the players.

The possibilities Yeats saw in drama as sculpture were encouraged in general by a growing interest in that form of art, and in particular by Ezra Pound. During the winter of 1913–1914, Pound introduced Yeats to the works of the young sculptors Jacob Epstein and Henri Gaudier-Brzeska and to the Noh drama. We do not know what Yeats thought of Pound's enthusiasm for Vorticist sculpture, but its conjunction with Pound's enthusiasm for Japanese Noh was surely suggestive. Yeats subsequently found in the Noh a form that solved his problems with theater and audience, and encouraged sculpture as stage model.

Yeats met Pound in London in 1908, and although he thought the younger poet had "more sound principles than taste," by 1913 he was looking to Pound's often harsh criticism to help him "get back to the definite and the concrete away from modern abstractions,"[22] the same problem whose solution he had earlier sought in "picture." During the winter of 1913–1914, Pound accompanied Yeats to Stone Cottage, Sussex, as his secretary. Pound had anticipated boredom—"Yeats will amuse me part of the time and bore me to death with psychical research the rest"—but soon had to admit "we are both, I think, very contented."[23] Pound's contentment came in part from finding Yeats "much finer *intime* than seen spasmodically in the midst of a whirl," and in part, surely, from discovering Yeats unexpectedly receptive to his various enthusiasms.[24] Two in particular occupied Pound that winter: his discovery of Jacob Epstein and Henri Gaudier-Brzeska (figs. 28, 29)—the two sculptors who, with Pound, Wyndham Lewis, and the painters Frederick Etchells and Edward Wadsworth were soon to form the Vorticist movement whose panarts emphasis must have intrigued Yeats; and Ernest Fenollosa's translations of Japanese Noh drama which Pound was reworking for publication.

Epstein and Gaudier-Brzeska participated in the reemergence of sculpture as a major art form. Despite the activity of sculptors such as Jules Dalou and Constantin Meunier, painting had held center stage in the nineteenth century. There were few Pre-Raphaelite or Impressionist sculptors. But with Rodin and his ambition to restore sculpture to the heights of Michelangelo, it regained its position among the arts (fig. 30). As early as 1899 Yeats knew about Rodin and had linked him to both the Pre-Raphaelites and the theater, deploring, as we have seen, those theater audiences who thought Rodin's women "ugly" and called Rossetti's women "guys."[25] Twenty-six years later Rodin's *Eternal Idol* joined Burne-Jones's women as examples of *A Vision*'s phase 14 (*AV-A* 68), and Rodin himself became the chief example of the modern phase 21

Figure 30. Auguste Rodin, *Mask of Man with the Broken Nose,* 1863–1875. Philadelphia Museum of Art, Rodin Museum. Gift of Jules E. Mastbaum.

(c. 1800–1875) which would also include Blake and the Pre-Raphaelites (*AV-A* 211).

Pound's response to Rodin was only lukewarm, for precisely those reasons that Yeats admired him, but Pound recognized in Rodin a presence in the world of sculpture worth discussing. In 1914 he sent Harriet

Monroe news of the Rodin exhibit at South Kensington and offered to send her photos.[26] But he preferred the work of Epstein and, especially, Gaudier-Brzeska, whose sculpture often experimented with the ideas of Michelangelo and Rodin.[27] The Rodin exhibit, Pound wrote Monroe, "does look like muck after one has got one's eye in on Epstein's Babylonian austerity. And Brzeska's work, for all that he is only 22, is much more interesting."[28]

Pound had met both artists in 1913 and quickly declared their excellence. "Epstein is a great sculptor," he wrote his mother in November just before leaving for Sussex with Yeats.[29] Several weeks later he purchased two statuettes by Gaudier, bought with the prize money Yeats had returned to *Poetry* with the recommendation that it be given to Pound.[30] From Stone Cottage he wrote William Carlos Williams that Gaudier-Brezska was "*the* coming sculptor. . . . I like him very much."[31] When Gaudier died in the trenches in 1915, Pound was named his executor.

There is no published evidence of Yeats's immediate response to Pound's interest in Epstein and Gaudier, but Pound certainly introduced them to Yeats. We know that in January 1914, Pound and Yeats were among a group that presented a Gaudier sculpture to Wilfred Scawen Blunt for his seventy-fourth birthday, and that in 1915 it was Yeats who told Pound that John Quinn purchased "an Epstein."[32] In 1931 Yeats read H. S. Ede's *The Savage Messiah,* an account of the life and work of Gaudier (*L* 782), and he owned Horace Brodsky's 1933 *Henri Gaudier-Brzeska, 1891–1915* (*YL* 44). In 1913–1914, remembering the "grandeur like that of Babylon" that Craig's screens imparted to his play productions (*UP* 2:392), Yeats may have been responding in part to the "Babylonian austerity" Pound detected in Epstein.

In any case the combined talk of sculpture and Japanese Noh drama surely encouraged Yeats's developing concept of theater as sculpture. A letter Pound wrote in 1916 when rehearsals for Yeats's first Noh-inspired play, *At the Hawk's Well,* were under way illustrates how closely Yeats's life and work were intertwined with Pound and his interest in sculpture:

> My occupations this week consist in finally (let us hope) dealing with Brzeska's estate; 2, getting a vorticist show packed up and started for New York; 3, making a selection from old father Yeats' letters, some of which are very fine (I suppose this will lap over into next week), small vol. to appear soon; 4, bother a good deal about the production of Yeats' new play.[33]

Yeats's response to the Japanese Noh, unlike that to Epstein and Gaudier, is well documented. He immediately recognized in the Noh a dramatic form that liberated him from the constraints of the conventional theater and stage, solved his problem of unreceptive audiences, and invited the use of sculptural effects. Yeats found the Noh drama so satisfying that most of the plays he wrote after 1914 employ its techniques.

The Noh allowed Yeats, first, to move his plays from the Abbey stage into the drawing room. "My blunder has been," he proclaimed, "that I did not discover in my youth that my theatre must be the ancient theatre that can be made by unrolling a carpet or marking out a place with a stick, or setting a screen against the wall. Certainly those who care for my kind of poetry must be numerous enough, if I can bring them together to pay half a dozen players who can bring all their properties in a cab and perform in their leisure moments" (*VPl* 415). Because the properties were few and inexpensive, production did not require a large, paying audience. His muse, whom he had been hesitant to send before the Abbey audience, would be welcomed by a small group with a taste for poetry.

Staging plays in the drawing room meant Yeats could do away with the exaggerated acting and set design needed for dramatic impact in the theater. "Violence of passion" would seem "indecorous in our sitting-room," and it gave way to dance as conveyor of emotion (*E&I* 221). A chandelier rather than a spotlight could provide illumination. Most important, scenery could be abolished: "It has been a great gain," Yeats claimed after his first success with Noh-inspired drama, "to get rid of scenery, to substitute for a crude landscape painted upon canvas three performers who, sitting before the wall or a patterned screen, describe landscape or event . . . Painted scenery, after all, is unnecessary to my friends and to myself, for our imagination kept living by the arts can imagine a mountain covered with thorn-trees in a drawing-room without any great trouble, and we have many quarrels with even good scene-painting" (*VPl* 415–416). In the theater, Yeats claimed, too much action had prevented verbal description of place; in the drawing room, where constant action was unnecessary to maintain the audience's attention, words could finally assume their supremacy (*E&I* 233). They, not the set, would evoke the scene. The musicians of *At the Hawk's Well* (1914), which established the techniques of the new drama and can serve as example, "call to the eye of the mind/A well long choked up and dry/And boughs long stripped by the wind" (*VPl* 399). Instead of dimming lights, the first musician says "Night falls;/The mountain-side grows dark" (*VPl* 400). Yeats's earlier realistic interiors are replaced in *The Only Jealousy of Emer* (1919) by the words "I call before the eyes a roof/With cross-beams darkened by smoke;/A fisher's net hangs from a beam,/A long oar lies against the wall" (*VPl* 531, 533).

With poetry assuming the duties that landscapes and even the backgrounds for portraits had performed in the theater, picture making could not rule the visual presentation of the play. The lack of scenery and the intimacy of the drawing room focused attention on the players as the creators of visual effects. Musicians were "substituted," as Yeats said, for scenery. Not separated from the action by the picture frame of the proscenium arch, the audience viewed the actors in the round. Yeats had understood, in arguing against illusion in scene painting, that unlike the two-dimensional backdrop, the actor "belongs to a world with depth as well as height and breadth" (*Ex* 178). He now wanted to exploit the three-dimensionality of the actors. Sculpture, the modeling of three-dimensional form, was the art of Yeats's new theater.

Yeats's early concept of staging as picture had recognized distance as an aesthetic issue. With sculpture as stage model, Yeats confronted, although not consciously, two more factors that had troubled his early verse: space and the palpability of his images. Two-dimensional space had ruled his experiments in theater as picture, as it had many of his early poems. When Yeats moved his actors off the stage and out of the picture frame, he suddenly saw that three-dimensional space facilitated access to the dramatic world, and he began learning how to manipulate its effects on his audience. With the actors and props so close to the audience, Yeats's dramatic images, unlike those of his early poems, achieved a physical immediacy. They were literally palpable; the audience could reach out and touch them.

Nugent Monck's production of *The Countess Cathleen* had taught Yeats that placing actors like sculpture among his audience could be dramatically effective. "It is well to be close enough to an artist to feel for him a personal liking, close enough perhaps to feel that our liking is returned" (*E&I* 224). Yeats discovered that, paradoxically, reducing physical distance did not abolish aesthetic distance. In fact, the closeness of the actors created a strangeness that conducted the audience into the world of imagination. "Where no studied lighting, no stage-picture made an artificial world," the actor "receded but to inhabit as it were the deeps of the mind. One realised anew, at every separating strangeness, that the measure of all arts' greatness can be but in their intimacy" (*E&I* 224). Yeats's Noh-inspired drama gathers its effect from the tension between intimacy created by physical proximity, and "separating strangeness" created by the use of dramatic conventions explicitly acknowledged as such.[34] By insisting on the three-dimensionality of the actors, Yeats carried to an extreme the recognition of medium that he had earlier argued for in decorative scenery: "We should be content to suggest a scene upon a canvas, whose vertical flatness we accept and use, as the decorator of pottery accepts the roundness of a bowl or jug," he had said (*Ex* 178). As sculpture produces excitement because it occupies the same space in the same three-dimensional way as its viewer yet is clearly artifice, so does

Yeats's Noh drama: the actors' closeness and roundness make them part of the audience's world, yet they remain part of the play.[35]

That juxtaposition of the world of artifice and the daily world of the audience produces a tension that not only holds the audience's attention but dramatically underscores the main theme of Yeats's Noh plays: the opposition of the mortal and the immortal. The struggles of the Old Man with the Guardian in *At the Hawk's Well,* of Cuchulain's human fallibility with his dream of perfection, are echoed in the audience's experience of the play. The tension they feel between the recognition of the actors as humans like themselves and the strangeness of the artifice, between the ordinary and the extraordinary, is the tension the play dramatizes.

The visual conventions Yeats adopted to achieve "separating strangeness" themselves continually asserted the sculptural quality of the production. Masks, ritualistic movement, and dance furthered the distance created by a poetry made more explicitly formal through increased repetition and the addition of music. Yeats had learned about masks from Gordon Craig and had been enthusiastic about using them for his 1911 production of *The Hour Glass*—a time when he was moving firmly toward his new concept of the sculptural (*L* 554). The Noh drama three years later gave Yeats both a tradition and a compelling dramatic reason for employing them.[36] Since the physical distance between audience and player was not sufficient in the drawing room to blur the edges of individual personality, Yeats used masks to assure that his "heroic or grotesque types" would keep "an appropriate distance from life" and so "seem images of those profound emotions that exist only in solitude and in silence" (*VPl* 416). The masks themselves should be works of art, "the fine invention of a sculptor" (*E&I* 226). "We are accustomed to faces of bronze and of marble," he argued, "and what could be more suitable than that Cuchulain, let us say, a half-supernatural legendary person, should show to us a face . . . moulded by some distinguished artist?" (*VPl* 416). He praised Cuchulain's mask for the first production of *At the Hawk's Well:* "Ainley, who is the hero, wears a mask like an archaic Greek statue" (*L* 610). When the performance was over, the masks could be "hung upon the walls where they will be fine ornaments" (*E&I* 222). Yeats thought it would be a "stirring adventure" to collaborate with an artist in creating them (*VPl* 416).

For his Noh drama Yeats advocated, as he had before, a minimum of movement, and that should be slow and rhythmical (e.g., *VPl* 780). But the movement of Yeats's Noh follows a more precisely prescribed order than that of his earlier drama, and is thus made more ritualistic. As the mask idealizes the face and makes it more strange, ritualistic movement idealizes stage action and further distances it. The ceremonious folding and unfolding of a cloth signifies the beginning and end of many of the plays. The musicians, like attendants in religious rite, take the same places on "stage," play after play. In *The Dreaming of the Bones,* the three characters walk ritualistically once around a circle to represent their climb to the mountain summit (*VPl* 773).

Yeats extended this formalized movement at moments of dramatic intensity. *At the Hawk's Well, The Only Jealousy of Emer, The Dreaming of the Bones, Calvary, A Full Moon in March, The Cat and the Moon,* and *The Death of Cuchulain* all climax in dance. "Instead of the disordered passion of nature, there is a dance" (*E&I* 230). The use of the masks had already exerted a pressure toward dance by forcing the actors to make their bodies, not their faces, expressive (*VPl* 416). Furthermore, Yeats realized in 1911 that the acting style he had formerly advocated resulted in "too statuesque a pose" (*VPl* 1299). When he began to use sculpture as an explicit model, he saw that because the stationary audience cannot walk around the sculpture to discover for itself the unfolding of the form, he would have to move the sculpture. The highly ordered pattern of dance maintained the artifice, but allowed the movement necessary to reveal form. The pattern that had once decorated flat backgrounds, now extended into space. The rhythms of painting gave way to the rhythms of sculpture. In adopting dance, Yeats married the spatial quality of the visual arts to the temporal quality of literature: the visual forms of his plays unfold in both space and time.

The sculptural quality became the center of Yeats's later dramas to such an extent that he declared, "Perhaps in the end one would write plays for certain masks" (*VPl* 1305). In 1929 he even sacrificed the poetic for the sculptural. Inspired by Hildo Krop's masks for a production of *The Only Jealousy of Emer,* Yeats rewrote the play to better show off the sculptor's work (fig. 31).[37] Considering himself "lucky" to "collaborate with a great sculptor" (*VPl* 567), he simplified the dialogue to highlight the masks, to give full range to the talent of the dancer Ninette de Valois, and to set off George Antheil's music.[38] "*Fighting the Waves* is in itself nothing, a mere occasion for sculptor and dancer, for the exciting dramatic music of George Antheil" (*VPl* 567). Despite the deprecation, Yeats found the results exciting and declared "the birth of a new art" (*L* 765; cf. *L* 768).

Yeats's staging of the Noh and his suggestion that a screen serve as its background derive from his earlier experiments with Craig's invention. But more than the plays he staged with Craig's screens, Yeats's drawing-room drama relies on the pattern he had admired in Pre-Raphaelitism.[39] While the decreased importance of color and the reliance on the sculptural mark a step away from the Pre-Raphaelites, Yeats's writing of the

Figure 31. Hildo Krop, mask for Cuchulain in *The Only Jealousy of Emer,* artist's replica of 1922 mask. Collection of Stedelijk Museum, Amsterdam.

first part of his autobiography had renewed his interest in them. Begun the same year that Pound introduced him to the Noh, Yeats's "Reveries over Childhood and Youth," which mused on "the first effect upon me of Bedford Park and all it meant in decoration" (*L* 589), inspired a return to the Pre-Raphaelites' decorative and detailed pattern for his screens and costumes. He revised, for example, the stage picture of *The Countess Cathleen* to achieve "the effect of missal painting" (*VPl* 5). Moreover, it encouraged him to replace the stark, monumental grandeur of Craig's screens with an intimacy like that of Rossetti's interiors. The intimacy was created partly by the smallness of the drawing room and partly by the detailed pattern on screens and costumes.

Aesthetic and practical as well as sentimental reasons recommended such a return to Pre-Raphaelitism. The detail that had not carried across the theater footlights before could now be clearly seen in the drawing room. Yeats no longer needed to broaden and simplify pattern to achieve effect as he had with his earlier decorative backdrops. Furthermore, now that he was exploiting pattern of movement (dance) and pattern of sound (song), supporting pattern in screens and costumes would help unify his productions.

It is not surprising, then, that when Yeats chose a designer for his Noh plays, he picked the illustrator Edmund Dulac, an aesthetic descendent of the Pre-Raphaelites. The two met in 1912 or 1913.[40] "We had in common," Dulac recalled, "many intellectual and aesthetic interests."[41] In addition to participating in occult ventures together and collaborating on the production of Yeats's early Noh dramas, Dulac designed a ring and a bedspread for Yeats, illustrated three of his books and a broadside, and created the unicorn logo that appeared on three of Yeats's Cuala Press books.[42] Yeats owned *The Green Lacquer Pavilion* illustrated by Dulac and written by Dulac's longtime companion Helen Beauclerk (*YL* 16). Despite occasional quarrels, Yeats and Dulac's friendship was close and lasted until Yeats's death.[43] After World War II, when Yeats's body was moved to Sligo from Roquebrune, France, where he had been buried, Dulac designed the tombstone to mark the original grave.[44]

Contemporary reviews inevitably noted Dulac's connections to Pre-Raphaelitism.[45] Beardsley, Burne-Jones, Puvis, and Moreau were frequently cited as influences. For Dulac as for Yeats, color and pattern comprised the most important features of Pre-Raphaelitism, and they became the distinguishing characteristics of his own work. The interest in the repeated shapes of Dawn's unfurling cloth in the first illustration for *Omar Khayyám* and the use of precise detail both recall Burne-Jones and Gustave Moreau (fig. IX). The clear color clearly derives from the Pre-Raphaelites. The blues of this and many other pictures became a hallmark of Dulac's work and must have been a special attraction for Yeats.[46]

As an illustrator, Dulac worked in the tradition established by Pre-Raphaelite concern for fine book design. His interest in symbol and his preoccupation with evoking dream worlds both further recommended him to Yeats.[47] In 1913, when Yeats was deep in recollections of his Pre-Raphaelite past, Dulac, prompted by an interest in Eastern art, was painting pictures in flat colors with heavily patterned surfaces, qualities Yeats admired in the Pre-Raphaelites.

As Craig had been the main inspiration for Yeats's scenic programs in the first half of his dramatic career, so Dulac was in the second half. "My Noh plays," Yeats said, "have to be worked out with Dulac" (*L* 643). Dulac, however, turned out to be a more amenable collaborator than Craig. Perhaps because as an illustrator he often needed to subordinate his work to someone else's conception, Dulac, unlike Craig, was willing to let Yeats have free rein with the plays' presentation. Because Dulac was a more conventional artist and not an innovator whose genius needed room to work, clashes of artistic purpose were rare.

Their collaboration in 1916 on *At the Hawk's Well* fired Yeats's enthusiasm for the possibilities of the Noh. In addition to writing the music, Dulac designed the masks and costumes for the Old Man and Cuchulain and the costume for the Guardian (figs. 32,33,34). Yeats opened his introduction to Pound's Fenollosa translations of the Noh plays: "I am writing with my imagination stirred by a visit to the studio of Mr. Dulac, the distinguished illustrator of the Arabian Nights. I saw there the mask and head-dress to be worn in a play of mine by the player who will speak the part of Cuchulain, and who, wearing this noble, half-Greek, half-Asiatic face, will appear perhaps like an image seen in reverie by some Orphic worshipper" (*E&I* 221). The bulging forehead and cheeks of the Old Man's mask, the flat planes of nose and eyebrows of both masks, and the large elaborate headdress and curved horn of Cuchulain's mask all emphasize the sculptural. The costumes for all three players, but especially that for the hawk, gather their effect from repetition of shapes. The patterns exert the hypnotic power Yeats had admired in Pre-Raphaelite art (*E&I* 159), which helps lead the audience into the play's imaginative world.

The combination of the dancer Michio Ito's slow, rhythmical movements as the hawk with Dulac's masks and costumes delighted Yeats. It confirmed the power and possibilities of the model he had chosen. The impact of sculptural form created by the proximity of the actors and extended by dance and mask, and the evocative effect of pattern in costume, poetry, music, and dance, created a striking strangeness. When he saw the first production of *At the Hawk's Well* in 1916 in Lady Cunard's drawing room, he triumphantly declared, "The form is a discovery and the dancing and masks wonderful. . . . It was all very strange" (*L* 611).

Figure 32. Edmund Dulac, mask for Old Man in *At the Hawk's Well*, 1916. Photograph by Alvin Langdon Coburn, George Eastman House, Rochester, New York. Courtesy of The Universal Order.

Figure 33. Edmund Dulac, mask for Cuchulain in *At the Hawk's Well*, 1916. Photograph by Alvin Langdon Coburn, George Eastman House, Rochester, New York. Courtesy of The Universal Order.

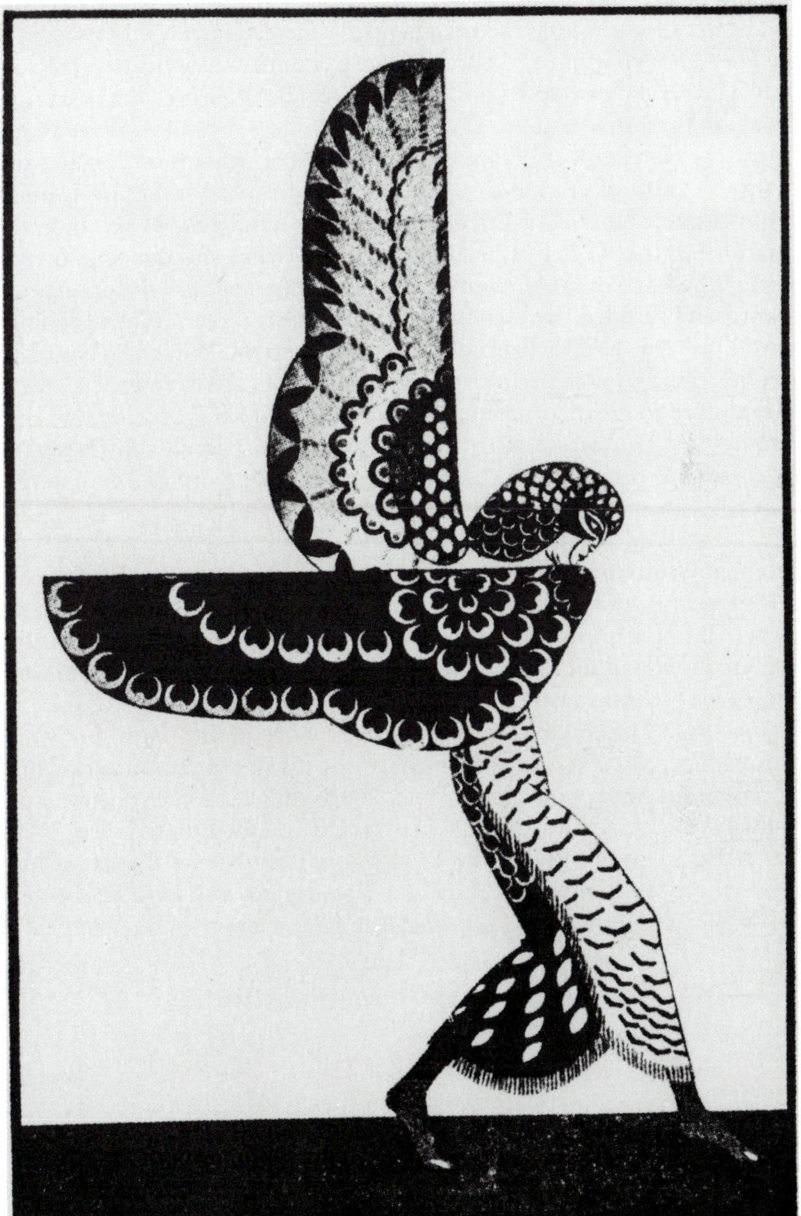

Figure 34. Edmund Dulac, drawing for costume of the Hawk in *At the Hawk's Well*, 1916. Courtesy of M. G. Anderson.

Years later, his life altered by the experiences leading up to *A Vision* and his creative impulses focused on poetry instead of plays, Yeats saw *At the Hawk's Well* again and felt the same excitement as at its first production. The revival prompted him to dedicate *The Winding Stair* (1933) to Dulac. In the public letter to Dulac which prefaces that book Yeats wrote: "I saw my *Hawk's Well* played by students of our Schools of Dancing and Acting a couple of years ago. . . . Watching Cuchulain in his lovely mask and costume, that old masked man who seems hundreds of years old, that Guardian of the Well, with your great golden wings and dancing to your music, I had one of those moments of excitement that are the dramatist's reward and decided there and then to dedicate to you my next book of verse" (*VP* 831). The dedication was appropriate. What the Noh had taught Yeats about centering drama on the actor, about using the effects of sculpture to create dramatic tension, and about heightening that tension by the obvious use of convention and ritual had all contributed to the method and effect of the later poems, including those of *The Winding Stair.*

Yeats's notion of theater as sculpture grew largely out of dramatic necessity, but he developed and extended it to his poetry as he expanded his knowledge of art. His interest in sculpture in general and his receptivity to Pound's talk about Epstein and Gaudier-Brzeska and Noh drama were part of his growing awareness of art outside the narrow realm of the Pre-Raphaelites. Yeats organized his new knowledge in the "Dove or Swan" section of *A Vision* (1925), which charts the history of the Western world by observing changes of artistic style. Much of Yeats's later poetry, especially in its connections to the visual arts, is founded on the view of art and artists "Dove or Swan" displays. Before examining the relationships between the visual arts and Yeats's later poetry, we will look, in the next chapter, at his expanding knowledge and the order it assumed in *A Vision.*

Figure I. Dante Gabriel Rossetti, *The Annunciation* (*Ecce Ancilla Domini!*), 1849–1850. Tate Gallery, London.

Figure II (*left*). William Butler Yeats, *Head of a Young Man,* 1887. The National Gallery of Ireland, Dublin.

Figure III (*below*). Frank Potter, *Little Dormouse*. n.d. Tate Gallery, London.

Figure IV. Dante Gabriel Rossetti, *Dante's Dream at the Time of the Death of Beatrice,* 1871. Walker Art Gallery, Liverpool.

Figure V. J. M. W. Turner, *The Golden Bough,* exhib. 1834. Tate Gallery, London.

Figure VI. William Morris, *Strawberry Thief,* printed fabric, 1883.
By permission of Birmingham Museums and Art Gallery.

Figure VII. Dante Gabriel Rossetti, *Monna Vanna* (*Belcolore*), 1866. Tate Gallery, London.

Figure VIII. Bed valence and curtains for William Morris's Kelmscott Manor, c. 1893, designed by May Morris, worked by Lily Yeats and others. Courtesy of the Society of Antiquaries of London, Kelmscott Manor, London. Photo by Anthony F. Kersting.

Figure IX. Edmund Dulac, *The First Quatrain* from *The Rubáiyát of Omar Khayyám*, 1909, watercolor. Private Collection.

Figure X. Two Martyrs. Detail from the mosaics of St. Apollinare Nuovo, sixth century, Ravenna. Scala/Art Resource, New York.

5

Our More Profound Pre-Raphaelitism

A Vision and the Visual Arts

The years from around 1911 to 1925 were for Yeats a period of growth and change. After giving up some of his management responsibilities at the Abbey, he concentrated once more on writing poetry, for which he gathered stimulation from a new generation of poets in London. His pursuit of Maud Gonne ended with her final refusal and his marriage in 1917 to Georgie Hyde-Lees. In 1919 his daughter was born, in 1921 his son. Involvement in the occult, reanimated by experiments conducted with Elizabeth Radcliffe between 1910 and 1914, intensified as he and his wife gathered through automatic handwriting and "sleeps" the material that was to become the first version of *A Vision*, published in 1925.

Those years also brought a change in the relationship between Yeats's poetry and the visual arts. Beginning with *Responsibilities* (1914), the visual arts became more frequently a source for poetic images. Particular artists and works of art began to appear explicitly in the poems, sometimes as examples in a debate about Art, sometimes as symbols whose significance derives from their positions in *A Vision*'s lunar system. Sculpture replaced painting as the guiding analogy. The Pre-Raphaelites and those Yeats's early circle had associated with them faded from his writing.

The impulses for some of these changes emerged from his experiments in stage production and his evolving concept of a poetry tied to life. But behind them all lay his expanding knowledge of art history and the ordering of his new knowledge in *A Vision*. Yeats's career shows his remarkable openness in matters that affected his poetry and his unfailing desire to extend his own limits. Nowhere is this truer than in his interests in the visual arts as reflected in the new variety and range of artists his writing mentions. Even in the midst of his most ardent defenses of Pre-Raphaelite principles, Yeats had approvingly noted that while Blake vehemently promoted certain artists in public, "in private, Palmer has told us, he could find 'sources of delight throughout the whole range of art,' and was ever ready to praise excellence in any school" (*E&I* 123–124). The same ability to appreciate became increasingly characteristic of Yeats as he happened upon and sought out excellence, acquiring a knowledge of art he had not had before. Yeats's early, concentrated vision of an art world dominated by the Pre-Raphaelites opened into a panoramic view of art history ranging from early cave paintings to Brancusi's sculptures. Unlike Blake, Yeats did not keep his appreciation private. By the time he finished *A Vision* in 1925, he was talking publicly and confidently about Phidias and Callimachus, Byzantine mosaics and Greek pots, Michelangelo, Titian, Poussin, and others. As this list shows, his interest in sculpture as well as painting prospered and grew.

Yeats's extended knowledge of the visual arts placed the Pre-Raphaelites in a new perspective. When seen against the works of the past, their achievement appeared minor, and developments in twentieth-century art confirmed that judgment. A few artists followed the path set by Rossetti, Morris, and Burne-Jones, but Post-Impressionism and Cubism made it clear that Pre-Raphaelitism was not to be the wave of the future as the young Yeats had hoped.

Although he rarely mentioned them in his writings, however, Yeats did not abandon the Pre-Raphaelites. His appreciation of their art, which had been so public, continued in private. Moreover, in his 1913 essay "Art and Ideas," Yeats repudiated the aesthetic view of Pre-Raphaelitism he and his generation had held and broadened his concept of the unity they had represented for him. The essence of the "more profound Pre-Raphaelitism" (*E&I* 355) that resulted was not just unity of the arts with each other, but with the culture at large. Around this broad ideal of unity is built *A Vision*'s system, which organized Yeats's knowledge of all aspects of life, including art.

Yeats's later poetry in its connections to the visual arts depends on his expanded knowledge and on the organizing framework *A Vision* gave it. Before discussing the poetry, it will be useful to set out the terrain of Yeats's continuing education in the visual arts: the sources of his new knowledge, *A Vision*'s debt to his reevaluation of the Pre-Raphaelites in "Art and Ideas," and the continuities and discontinuities between his early Pre-Raphaelitism and the arts that especially interested him, those at phase 15.

Some of Yeats's new knowledge of the visual arts may be credited to the communicators who, beginning in 1917, taught him through his wife's automatic handwriting and speech the philosophy set out in *A Vision*. Most, however, resulted from the more mundane experiences offered by art exhibitions, travel, books, and the talk of friends. Yeats's knowledge of art began expanding as early as 1904 when, seeing Manet's *Eva Gonzales* in an exhibition of Hugh Lane's collection, he started to understand, as a sign of the modern concern for the individual and particular, the French art that he had once scorned in the name of Pre-Raphaelitism (*E&I* 241–242; *UP* 2:331). In 1908, in an attempt, he said, to find out if he was "a romantic of some kind, or only an ignorant man, puzzled in the middle of a revolution that has changed all about him," he recorded a newfound appreciation for the Impressionists' ability to see nature "afresh," a major concession for one who had damned them for their slavish realism.[1] The next year, Thomas Bodkin overheard him praising Cézanne, Gaugin, van Gogh, and Matisse at a Post-Impressionist show.[2] By 1913 a photograph of a Gaugin painting hung over his breakfast table (*E&I* 354–355).

Tours to Europe, where Yeats saw firsthand works he had previously known only through conversation or reproductions, extended his education. In northern Italy with Robert and Lady Gregory in 1907, he marveled at the wonders of Renaissance and Byzantine art. With his wife he traveled to Sicily in 1924 to see the Byzantine mosaics at Palermo, and in February 1925 he spent a week in Rome visiting the Borghese Palace and the Vatican galleries, and taking rolls of photographs of the Sistine ceiling.[3]

He also began to buy books on art, many with the Nobel Prize money he won in 1923. His library contains over 130 books, journals, and catalogs on art. Those he acquired later in life demonstrate his diverse interests (*YL* 267, 294, 95, 71): Josef Strzygowski's *Origin of Christian Church Art* (1923), Arthur Waley's *An Introduction to the Study of Chinese Painting* (1923), Elie Faure's *History of Art* (1921–1924), and O. M. Dalton's *Byzantine Art and Archaeology* (1911). George Harper and Walter Hood's notes to their critical edition of the 1925 *A Vision* provide excellent documentation of the influence of such works on the views expounded in Yeats's system.

Ezra Pound's talk of Vorticism, as we have seen, and the erudition and example of the connoisseur and artist Charles Ricketts—whose Friday evenings Yeats began to attend frequently in 1915 (*L* 595)—helped broaden Yeats's sense of the world of art. Yeats had known Ricketts and his companion, the painter Charles Shannon, since the early 1890s when the two entertained the leading aesthetes of the day at their home, the Vale, where Whistler once lived. Yeats and Ricketts collaborated on productions of *The King's Threshold* (1914) and a revival of *On Baile's Strand* (1915).[4] Now at those Friday evenings, Yeats gathered from the wide-ranging talk of his hosts and their guests knowledge and appreciation of such artists as Titian, Giorgione, Watteau, Michelangelo, Raphael, and da Vinci.[5] In Ricketts and Shannon's extensive art collection he saw Greek vases,[6] a Roman copy of a lost torso by Praxiteles,[7] a twenty-third century B.C. wood and plaster figure,[8] and numerous works by European and oriental masters.[9] Yeats called Ricketts and Shannon "my friends and in certain matters my chief instructors" (*Au* 169); in *A Vision* he acknowledged a particular debt to Ricketts, "my education in so many things" (*AV-A* 208).

Yeats's reading and his conversations with Ricketts and Shannon, as well as Pound, further developed Yeats's interest in sculpture. Ricketts and Shannon collected sculpture and talked much about Rodin who had influenced Ricketts's own work. They promoted living sculptors they admired, including Ivan Meštrović—whom Yeats met at their house in the

1890s and later invited to submit designs for Ireland's new coinage[10]—and their special protégé Ernest Cole, whose Michelangelesque work excited Yeats.[11] Yeats also began to acquire books on sculpture. His interests ranged from Arthur Gardner's *French Sculpture of the Thirteenth Century* (*YL* 102; 1915), to Laurence Binyon's *Examples of Indian Sculpture at the British Museum* (1923), to M. Curcin's *Ivan Mestrovic* (*YL* 71; 1919), to Leigh Ashton's *An Introduction to the Study of Chinese Sculpture* (*YL* 8; 1924).

While Yeats explored new interests in the arts, the Pre-Raphaelites and those he associated with them remained important. "Rossetti came often into his talk," L. A. G. Strong remembered of Yeats during these years.[12] Other friends confirmed his continued Pre-Raphaelitism in the gifts they chose for him: a copy of the Kelmscott Chaucer illustrated by Burne-Jones for his fortieth birthday; a drawing of Lucretia Borgia by Rossetti, given him by H. C. Grierson and others in 1935; a stained-glass window by Burne-Jones, a gift from Charles Ricketts.[13] These pleased Yeats, and he praised them. Furthermore, Yeats worked actively on several fronts to perpetuate the spirit of Morris. He supported his sisters' efforts to carry the Arts and Crafts Movement to Ireland: he searched out designs worthy of Lilly's embroidery talents (e.g., *L* 604), praised the cradle Lolly painted for Yeats's daughter Anne (*L* 674), and constantly lent money and editorial advice to the Cuala Press. His own plans for Thoor Ballylee, the Norman tower he bought in 1916, followed Pre-Raphaelite principles. By hiring local craftsmen and designers to work together restoring the tower, Yeats tried to re-create the medieval spirit of common enterprise. His continued admiration for the decorative and for Pre-Raphaelite color prompted the painting of the ceiling in the bedroom "blue and black and gold."[14] Inspired perhaps by the table around which he and others had gathered at Morris's Kelmscott House (*Au* 140), Yeats commissioned a large trestle table for Ballylee. When the tower was finished, he expressed his satisfaction by invoking the age that had inspired the Pre-Raphaelites: "It is a great pleasure to live in a place where George makes at every moment a fourteenth century picture."[15]

Yeats's new interests in art, however, were not as limited by a particular aesthetic program as were his enthusiasms of the 1880s and 1890s. He maintained a commitment to the Pre-Raphaelites by admiring, as we will see, much that they had admired. But he could not find in Gothic architecture "the creation of a new communal freedom" that they found (*AV-A* 198), and he became quite interested—perhaps under the influence of Eugenie Strong's measured and broad-minded *Apotheosis and After Life*[16]—in Roman sculpture with all of its functional and mimetic aims. Yeats never admired without a reason, however quirky and personal, but in the years leading up to *A Vision* he explored the arts with less of the self-justification that had marked his early responses.

A Vision is Yeats's most important late prose statement on the visual arts. "Dove or Swan"—the only part of the book that so satisfied Yeats that he did not extensively revise it for the 1937 edition—organizes Yeats's knowledge of the history of art and, in its method, extends his early use of the analogies between art and literature. In both specific content and overall conception, *A Vision* derives, as scholars have shown, not only from the mysterious communicators, but from numerous other sources, including Yeats's own earlier work. The book is, Thomas Whitaker notes, "a typically romantic achievement."[17] Its underlying premises, however, can be found not only in Yeats's view of the romantic poets, but in his 1913 reconsideration of their descendents, the Pre-Raphaelite painters.

Yeats's broadened awareness of art, combined with his desire to remake himself, prompted a general adjustment of his sense of the Pre-Raphaelites and his relation to them. The Pre-Raphaelites appear rarely in *A Vision,* in part because his new knowledge put their historical importance in perspective, and in part because he had already explored and set in order his early relation to them in "Reveries over Childhood and Youth" (1914) and "The Trembling of the Veil" (1922). But more important, in his 1913 essay "Art and Ideas," Yeats reexamined his early assumptions about the Pre-Raphaelite aesthetic as the pursuit of art-for-art's-sake, and broadened his concept of it in such a way that it became the implicit basis for evaluating the artists who now interested him. By claiming "integration" as the major principle of what he called "our more profound Pre-Raphaelitism," Yeats abstracted from a historical movement an ahistorical aesthetic standard.

In "Art and Ideas"—a loose, autobiographical essay, full of perplexing turns that often make it, as Thomas Parkinson has pointed out, confused[18]—Yeats tries to grapple with a limitation of his early thought and practice. In rejecting Victorian "moral enthusiasm" (*E&I* 350), Yeats and his generation had, under the banner of Pre-Raphaelitism, spurned all ideas and championed art arising from "the impression made by the world upon their delicate senses" (*E&I* 347). Yeats uses "ideas" here broadly, to cover any influence on art that is not purely sensory: literature, "elements from the general thought" (*E&I* 347), religion, politics, science, and even past works of art. Yeats's conclusions about the aestheticism he had professed and the contradictions it gave rise to are not profound and may appear obvious to readers of his early work. Pre-

Raphaelite art, he decided, was not free of ideas—it was founded on them; indeed, no art could be free of ideas, and, he concluded, he had never been able in practice or thought to support wholeheartedly the rejection of ideas. Such discoveries allowed Yeats to understand his own practice and to connect—he might say "integrate"—his early, unstated longings, such as his love for the religious and literary in art, to his current aims for powerful art attached to life.

By casting out ideas, Yeats now thought, he and his friends had robbed art of one of its greatest sources of power. They had cut it free of its nonsensual moorings and set it adrift. Most important, since art founded on exquisite sensation required a special audience, they had cut art off from all but a small group of people and all but the most refined sense of life. Aestheticism had, in other words, helped bring about the very fragmentation that Yeats, with his desires for unity of thought and a popular theater, had been struggling against. It violated one of the ideals that Pater had held up: the integration of all aspects of life and thought that had existed before the Renaissance brought dissolution. Yeats ends his essay with a resonant call to recover this lost integration:

> Shall we be rid of the pride of intellect, of sedentary meditation, of emotion that leaves us when the book is closed or the picture seen no more; and live amid the thoughts that can go with us by steamboat and railway as once upon horseback, or camel-back, rediscovering, by our reintegration of the mind, our more profound Pre-Raphaelitism, the old abounding, nonchalant reverie? (*E&I* 355)

Yeats's desire here to reconnect the artist and the work of art with life as it is lived reflects his own attempt to move downward upon life. But whereas he had previously thought that movement was a revolt against the failures of Pre-Raphaelitism, he now saw it as a fulfillment of the Pre-Raphaelites' most profound ideal.

The elaborate fictional account of *A Vision*'s origin in the 1925 introduction asks us to consider the connection between Yeats's system and "Art and Ideas." Michael Robartes, whose reconstruction and annotation of Giraldus' "Speculorum Angelorum et Hominorum" *A Vision* supposedly presents, bears often-noted similarities to Yeats himself. Thirty years before the events narrated in the introduction, Robartes had been "an uncompromising Pre-Raphaelite" (*AV-A* xv), as Yeats was thirty years before *A Vision* was first written. The project that culminated in *A Vision* began, the introduction explains, when Owen Aherne came upon his old friend Michael Robartes in the National Gallery, where "he stood before the story of Griselda pictured in a number of episodes, the sort of thing he had admired thirty years ago" (*AV-A* xv). Yeats echoes here the beginning of "Art and Ideas": "Two days ago I was at the Tate Gallery to see the early Millais's, and before his *Ophelia,* as before the *Mary Magdalene* and *Mary of Galilee* of Rossetti that hung near, I recovered an old emotion. I saw these pictures as I had seen pictures in my childhood" (*E&I* 346). *A Vision* answers on several levels the call for a more profound Pre-Raphaelitism that Yeats's experience in the Tate prompted.

By enabling a union of poetry with ideas, and hence with life, *A Vision* helped Yeats effect integration. His new conviction that art, instead of spurning ideas, must be founded on them, encouraged the development of a philosophy on which to base his work. *A Vision*'s system fulfilled the need. It offered, furthermore, a guide to interpreting individual human lives as well as historical movements. A reader, encountering *A Vision*'s philosophy in a poem, would find, as "Art and Ideas" advocated, significance that he could take away with him into his own individual daily life of "steamship and railway."

Reintegration is also *A Vision*'s fundamental principle. All civilizations, according to the system, approach, then fall away from, phase 15, where "Thought and Will," "effort and attainment are indistinguishable" (*AV-A* 69–70). This is the "phase of complete beauty," of complete integration (*AV-A* 69). The idea may have come directly from the communicators, but it was an explicit part of Yeats's new Pre-Raphaelitism and an inherent part of his early view of the movement. When he had admired those Rossetti women in whom "the ecstasy of the lover and of the saint are alike" (*E&I* 53), he anticipated by twenty-three years his characterization of phase 15 where all opposites are reconciled, where "contemplation and desire, united into one, inhabit a world where every beloved image has bodily form, and every bodily form is loved" (*AV-A* 70). As Yeats understood, none of the Pre-Raphaelites, not even Rossetti, succeeded in such complete integration; but he saw the effort as central to their work, and it became in *A Vision* the impulse by which all civilizations could be measured.[19]

Yeats's exhortation in "Art and Ideas" against "emotion that leaves us when the book is closed or the picture seen no more" suggests that his notion of reintegration included the alliance of visual art and literature (*E&I* 355). Perhaps in response to arguments, voiced by Pound and others, against the modern tendency to confuse the arts, Yeats asserted in his essay his belief in a necessary union: "Nor had we better warrant to separate one art from another, for there has been no age before our own wherein the arts have been other than a single authority, a Holy Church of Romance" (*E&I* 353). This assertion underlies Yeats's ambitious reading of history through art in the "Dove or Swan" section of *A Vision.*

A Vision, in general, insists on the continuing alliance of Yeats's poetry and thought, with vision and the visual arts. The vision of the book's title encompasses and extends Yeats's use of that term in describing his early verse as poetry of vision. Like much of that early poetry, the book's philosophy derived from occult experiences. The vision Yeats's communicators conveyed through scripts and sleeps, however, was metaphorical, not literal—a conception of the world, not a picture of it. But Yeats's understanding and expression of that conception depended on visual models: a pair of inverted triangles, the interpenetrating gyres of civilization's opposing tendencies, and a circle representing the twenty-eight phases of the moon. Yeats was so concerned that the latter, most important visualization be right that he commissioned Edmund Dulac to design the woodcut of it printed in both published texts.

The historical manifestation of *A Vision*'s philosophy in "Dove or Swan" relies heavily on civilizations' visions of themselves in art. Yeats charted history in part by charting the development of the visual arts, setting out and organizing the knowledge he had been gathering. Furthermore, the representation of eyes in depictions of the human body became one of the central motifs in "Dove or Swan." Yeats extended his father's belief that a good portrait revealed the personality of the sitter, and applied the concept to a whole age. A civilization's handling of the eyes in its depictions of the face revealed not only the age's technical innovations or the prevailing style of art, but the general character of its people:

> The Greeks painted the eyes of marble statues and made out of enamel or glass or precious stones those of their bronze statues, but the Roman was the first to drill a round hole to represent the pupil, and because, as I think, of a preoccupation with the glance characteristic of a civilization in its final phase. . . . They could now express in stone a perfect composure, the administrative mind, alert attention where all had been rhythm, an exaltation of the body, uncommitted energy. (*AV-A* 187–188)

The assumptions of Yeats's historical method in "Dove or Swan," however, reveal a deeper connection between the arts than the mere presence of the visual arts or Yeats's interest in eyes suggest. "Dove or Swan" is a broad attempt to draw historical interart analogies, particularly between the literature and visual art on which it depends for example and evidence. It proceeds on the major premise that art and literature reveal, in Mario Praz's phrase, "the hand of the age"[20] and, conversely, that that hand can be detected in both art and literature, creating a bond between them. The connections between the arts that Yeats had drawn early in his career focused on the exchange of subject (painters painting what poets wrote, etc.), the borrowing of visual motifs (the rose, the lily), and the comparability of technique (aural rhythm functioning like visual pattern). Now he claimed a more radical connection. In addition to finding unity in a lateral exchange between a poem and a picture, or more generally between literature and the visual arts, he now discovered it in the common characteristics that gave rise to the arts. To this view of the interart analogy

he added this:

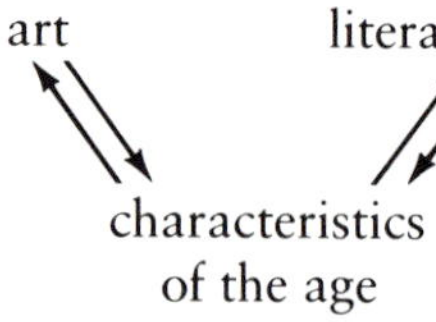

Yeats detected in the ornament of Romanesque architecture, for example, "the same impulse that created Merlin and his jugglery" (*AV-A* 198). Applying this premise more broadly, he made such statements as, "The period from 1300 to 1380 . . . finds its character in painting from Giotto to FraAngelico, in the chronicles of Froissart and in the elaborate canopy upon the stained glass of the windows" (*AV-A* 200). Recent scholarship might discredit this method of connecting the arts, but Yeats used it unaware of or uninterested in the theoretical difficulties it poses.

Yeats's system also extended and systematized his practice of seeing himself and his own art in relation to visual artists and their work. *A Vision*'s ultimate usefulness lay not in the philosophical offerings themselves, but in what they could tell Yeats about his own art. He studied the phases to find places for Blake, Shakespeare, Titian, Michelangelo, and the rest, but more important, he studied them to find a place for himself. Although Yeats dropped all explicit references to himself in the book's published texts, the communicators placed him at phase 17, among Shelley, Landor, Dante, Homer, Botticelli, Burne-Jones, and Rossetti.[21] The grouping invited Yeats to compare himself to the visual artists as well as to the writers. Indeed, Yeats most longed to be part of the world of medieval Byzantium, which he saw entirely in terms of its visual arts. He was not disturbed that poets, as he noted, played little role in the unity of art and life that marked the Byzantine world (*AV-A* 191). His long-standing sense of his own art's alliance to the visual arts made him imagine himself quite at home among mosaic workers and goldsmiths.

What *A Vision* gave Yeats's work most directly was metaphors (*AV-B* 8). It provided the gyres, wheels, and phases of the moon that appear in the late poems. But more important, *A Vision*'s system endowed the past, including its art and artists, with significance that enabled Yeats to use it metaphorically. As we will see in the next chapter, the art and artists of "Dove or Swan" frequently enter the poems carrying the significance *A Vision* gave them.

Of all the arts, Yeats's history in "Dove or Swan" relies most heavily on sculpture for example. Sculpture's predominance reflects Yeats's interest in that form and was bred by the book's methodology. Sculpture lasted longer than its frailer sister arts and thus comprised most of the available evidence for Yeats's observations on ancient cultures. In his discussion of each successive age, the repeating gyres of history returned Yeats to his comments on the ancients and to the art he had used there as example. He was thus encouraged to take sculpture as a standard for comparing and contrasting the phases' manifestations in various ages. Yeats found precedent for such a method in at least one of his major sources, Flinders Petrie's *The Revolutions of Civilization*. Petrie observed in his introduction that sculpture "is available over so long a period, in so many countries . . . that it may be well to begin with that as a standard subject for comparison."[22]

In *A Vision*, the painting and poetry as well as sculpture that interested Yeats most were to be found, of course, at the phases around 15 where integration was complete, where his more profound Pre-Raphaelitism was realized. The arts that appear at phase 15, and Yeats's view of them, were legacies from the Pre-Raphaelites and those associated with them. Although Yeats had been more absorbed in Pre-Raphaelitism itself at the time, Greek, Renaissance, and Byzantine art had been much discussed in his youth, and those discussions formed part of Yeats's education. When his interest in past arts began expanding, Yeats returned to the views he had earlier heard, supplementing them with new reading in the history of art, which itself had developed from work done in the late nineteenth century and often bore its attitudes.

Romantic fascination for the Greek art of Phidias—especially as displayed by the Elgin marbles in the British Museum (figs. 35, 36, 37)—was handed on to Yeats's circle by the Pre-Raphaelites,[23] and, most important, by Pater. Yeats's own interlocking gyres—the pull of Westward-moving against Eastward-moving influences in Greek art—derived in part, as Whitaker notes, from the concept of centrifugal and centripetal forces that Pater developed in *Greek Studies*.[24] So, too, do their specific manifestations in the Ionic and Doric styles—graceful Asiatic art full of "freedom and happiness" opposed to "severe simplification," in Pater's phrases; the "light limbed dandy" versus the "athlete," in Yeats's.[25] For

Figure 35. Horsemen, west frieze of the Parthenon, c. 440 B.C. Courtesy of the Trustees of the British Museum, London.

both Pater and Yeats, the Doric and Ionic unite in Phidias. Yeats found a similar account of Phidias in George Redford's *A Manual of Ancient Sculpture: Egyptian—Assyrian—Greek—Roman* (1886) which he owned (*YL* 223). In Redford and in Furtwangler's *Masterpieces of Greek Sculpture* (1895), which Yeats read sometime between 1920 and 1925,[26] he also learned about Callimachus, sculptor of phase 16, whose work revived the Ionic art of the phases before 15. *A Vision* displays in general Yeats's sympathy for those who, like the Pre-Raphaelites, attempt to bring new life to art by reviving past styles. Like Redford, who connected the archaistic movement—of which Callimachus was a part—with that of the "preraphaelite painters of our day,"[27] Yeats associated Callimachus and those the sculptor imitated in phases 13 and 14 with the heroes of his own youth. Although Phidian art represented the civilization's perfection and would later claim Yeats's greatest interest, it is in phases 13 and 14, Yeats explained, that he found "the visible art that interests us most to-day, for Phidian art, like the art of Raphael, has for the moment exhausted our attention" (*AV-A* 181). Yeats's description of the arts of phases 13 and 14

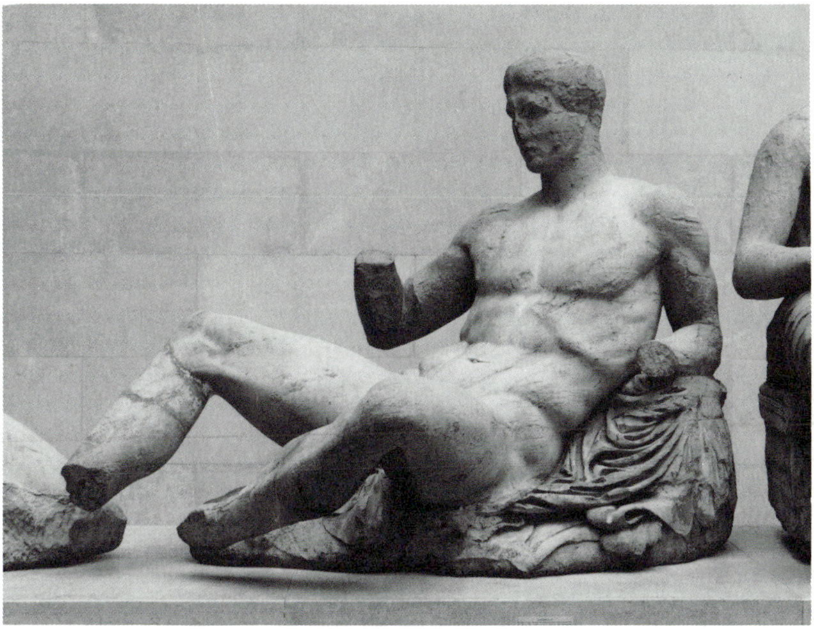

Figure 36. Dionysus, east pediment of the Parthenon, c. 438–432 B.C. Courtesy of the Trustees of the British Museum, London.

reveals this implicit connection to the Pre-Raphaelites and their followers, especially to Beardsley, Burne-Jones, and Dulac: "clarity, meaning, elegance, all things separated from one another in luminous space."[28] Callimachus' revival of this Ionic elegance in the only examples of his work known to us, a marble chair and a bronze lamp shaped like a palm, surely recalled to Yeats the Arts and Crafts Movement's attempts to reunite art to use.[29]

The modern era comes to perfection, not surprisingly, during the Renaissance whose artists took their ideals from the arts of the ancient phase 15. The Renaissance had, of course, been the great preoccupation of the late nineteenth century. Botticelli, Crivelli, Mantegna, and da Vinci occupy the historical phase 15 (*AV-A* 203). Botticelli had been a favorite of the Pre-Raphaelites and of Blake, and had captured the interest of Yeats's fellow Rhymer, Herbert Horne, who, as Yeats commented, wrote "the one standard work" on the artist (*Au* 169). Yeats knew Leonardo from Pater, whose famous description of *La Giaconda* Yeats divided into lines and printed as the first modern poem in *The Oxford Book of Modern Verse* (1936). He had also read Leonardo's *Notebooks,*[30] which he

Figure 37. Three Goddesses, east pediment of the Parthenon, c. 438–432 B.C.
Courtesy of the Trustees of the British Museum, London.

quoted as early as 1897 in *The Secret Rose.* The phases before 15 belong to Masaccio—whom Yeats likened to Beardsley, but whose art he thought showed a "naturalism that begins to weary us a little," a naturalism that had bothered Pater, too[31]—and to Donatello, whose "hardness and astringency" mark him as the modern equivalent of the ancient Doric artists (*AV-A* 201). Phase 15 is followed by Raphael, Michelangelo, and Titian, whose forms, like those of Rossetti, "awaken sexual desire" (*AV-A* 204). Although Raphael had been faulted as the originator of the form that was codified by his followers into academic convention, many of his paintings had been admired and praised—especially for their rhythm, that visual quality so attractive to Yeats—by the Pre-Raphaelites, even in their earliest, most revolutionary days.[32] Michelangelo, a poet as well as painter and sculptor, had influenced Blake and many other artists Yeats admired as a youth, including Gustave Moreau[33] and Burne-Jones[34] who kept small copies of the Medici tomb statues on his mantlepiece (figs. 38, 39).

Yeats's Pre-Raphaelite vision of the past is clearest, however, in his discussions of Byzantine art, the art of phase 15 that had not exhausted

Figure 38. Michelangelo, tomb of Giuliano de'Medici, with figures of *Night* (left) and *Day* (right), 1526–1534, New Sacristy, S. Lorenzo, Florence. Alinari/Art Resource, New York.

Figure 39. Michelangelo, tomb of Lorenzo de'Medici, with figures of *Dusk* (left) and *Dawn* (right), 1524–1534, New Sacristy, S. Lorenzo, Florence. Alinari/Art Resource, New York.

his attention and that of all art he most admired in *A Vision*. His association of Byzantine art with the aims and qualities of Pre-Raphaelitism derives mainly from the interest in Byzantium his acquaintances of the 1890s had displayed.[35] Gordon and Fletcher in *Images of a Poet* offer a survey of that interest, noting in particular: Arthur Symons's descriptions of Ravenna in *Cities of Italy* (1907) and of Constantinople in *Cities* (1903), which Yeats's library contains (*YL* 274); the similarity between Oscar Wilde's concept of Byzantine art in *The Decay of Lying*, which he read to Yeats one Christmas Eve, and Yeats's own; and the specific interest Burne-Jones took in the "heavenly churches" of Ravenna.[36] Yeats's description of Byzantium in *A Vision*, as well as his concept of it, owe something, furthermore, to Ruskin's description of the Byzantine St. Mark's in *The Stones of Venice* which Yeats owned.[37]

As Thomas McAlindon has shown, however, Yeats's "chief of men," William Morris, exerted perhaps the most powerful influence. Drawn by its achievements in the decorative arts, Morris spoke often of Byzantium and was especially attracted by the Persian-influenced use of continuous line that Yeats singled out for special attention in *A Vision*.[38] "Morris seems to have seen in Pre-Raphaelitism," McAlindon observes, "a resurrection of the Byzantine spirit."[39] Yeats's only early reference to Byzantium, in "Rosa Alchemica," shows his early perception that admiration for Byzantine-inspired art was consistent with Pre-Raphaelitism: the narrator-hero, a Pre-Raphaelite admirer, comments, "I opened the door, and found myself in a marvellous passage, along whose sides were many divinities wrought in a mosaic, not less beautiful than the mosaic in the Baptistery at Ravenna, but of a less severe beauty."[40]

Yeats's vision of Byzantium during the reign of Justinian embraced the features of Pre-Raphaelite art that Yeats had especially admired in his youth. There, according to Yeats, the integration of art and society that underlies a "more profound Pre-Raphaelitism" flourished: "I think that in early Byzantium, and maybe never before or since in recorded history, religious, aesthetic and practical life were one" (*AV-A* 191). Where the Arts and Crafts Movement failed, Byzantium succeeded in uniting art to the daily life of the people because the community, so important to the Pre-Raphaelite Brotherhood, included not only artists and their few admirers, but society at large: "architect and artificers . . . spoke to the multitude and the few alike" (*AV-A* 191).

The art created within this community also resembled the Pre-Raphaelites in its emphasis on decoration. Yeats found the "appropriate symbol" of such decoration in a motif that recalls Morris: "a vine whose tendrils climb everywhere and display among their leaves all those strange images of bird and beast" (*AV-A* 192). The color and pattern that had attracted him in Pre-Raphaelitism he also saw as hallmarks of Byzantine art. Such mosaics as those at St. Apollinare Nuovo in Ravenna (fig. X), which he had seen in 1907 and knew from the books he was reading, gave him ample reason for seeing "pattern" as one of Byzantium's achievements and for admiring "their little glimmering cubes of blue and green and gold," colors among his favorites in Pre-Raphaelite art (*AV-A* 191, 192).

The nonmimetic art was, for Yeats, the typical art of vision of which Pre-Raphaelite art and his own poetry were later manifestations. Yeats devotes considerable space in *A Vision* to emphasizing the visionary qualities of Byzantine art. Speaking of the ascetic, Yeats says, "all about him is an incredible splendour like that which we see pass under our closed eyelids as we lie between sleep and waking, no representation of a living world, but the dream of a somnambulist" (*AV-A* 191). "Could any visionary of those days," he asks rhetorically, "passing through the Church named with so un-theological a grace 'The Holy Widsom,' can even a visionary of to-day wandering among the mosaics of Rome [later revised to "Ravenne"] and Sicily [as Yeats had in 1907, 1924, and 1925] fail to recognise some one image seen under his closed eyelids?" (*AV-A* 192).

Yeats's "more profound Pre-Raphaelitism," whose simple principle, integration, underlay *A Vision,* was more an acknowledgement of something he had always felt than a complete revamping of his sense of the movement. He came to recognize consciously his love for the religious and literary in art and his desire to attach his own work to Irish legend as signs of the knowledge he had always possessed but could not realize while he and his generation fought Victorian moralism: art must depend on ideas to possess its full power. Aestheticism had been, as he said, "a good switch while the roads were beset with geese" (*E&I* 349).

A wider knowledge and appreciation of art helped Yeats see the switch for what it was, and seeing, in turn, encouraged his exploration of the visual arts. Both indicate the increasing control Yeats was gaining over his world and his own thought. Yeats claimed that *A Vision,* by presenting a coherent view of personal and historical life, gave him the control—it helped him "to hold in a single thought reality and justice" (*AV-B* 25)—but the book is more likely a symptom of it. The mastery extended to his poetry. Most critics agree that after 1917 Yeats wrote out of a clear understanding of his aesthetic aims and with a firm grasp of his craft. The control is evident in the later poems' use of the visual arts. Rather than hovering on the fringes of a poem, held to it by Yeats's suggestive analogies but not part of it, the visual arts now enter the poetry explicitly and consistently. With a sure hand Yeats turned his knowledge of art and artists endowed with the significance of their lunar phases to poetic purpose.

6

Picture and Book Remain

The Visual Arts in the Later Poetry

Only an aching heart
Conceives a changeless work of art
(*VP* 421)

Yeats's later poems are rich in allusions to the visual arts. They constantly proclaim his varied interests in sculpture and painting, modern and ancient, and their images call up works of art that may have been the poems' sources. Some of the most famous poetic evocations of art occur in Yeats's later poems: "Lapis Lazuli," "Sailing to Byzantium," "Byzantium."

As all of this suggests, the visual arts are much more evident in Yeats's later poetry than they were in the early verse. More and more, Yeats began to gather images from the visual arts, often turning them, as he did other elements of his world, into symbols. Drafts show us that frequently Yeats had the visual arts in mind, even when no mention of an image's origin remains in the final version.[1]

The later poems contain many more explicit references to visual arts in general and to specific artists and works of art than do the early poems. The exploration of aesthetic issues that had earlier been carried out in the essays, now often occurred in the poems. Now, as then, the visual arts provided evidence and example for discussion, continuing Yeats's practice of examining his own art by analogy to the visual arts. Furthermore, *A Vision* had, by ordering the visual arts according to lunar phases, opened up a whole realm of symbols to Yeats. Works of art, instead of being sources for symbols that could be transferred into poems without reference to their original context, now became, along with the artists who produced them, symbols themselves.

The most important aesthetic issue the poems discuss is the function of art as monument, an idea that arose from *A Vision*'s survey of civilization's surviving monuments and that affected Yeats's sense of his own art. The monuments the poems most frequently invoke are those around phase 15: Byzantine mosaics, the works of Michelangelo and of Phidias. Yeats's final preference for the more naturalistic art of Greece and the Renaissance suggests a shift in his own aesthetic aims away from the static, brilliant decorative art of the Pre-Raphaelites to a more mimetic and plastic art of the body.

As the criticism of the later poems—from *Responsibilities* (1914) on—shows, Yeats increasingly mined the visual arts for poetic images.[2] Many of his greatest poems revolve around such images: "Sailing to Byzantium," "Byzantium,"[3] "Leda and the Swan,"[4] and "News for the Delphic Oracle,"[5] to name a few. The fact of the visual sources is, in itself, important for it tells us something about the things of this world to which Yeats was alive. David R. Clark's account of "Her Triumph" demonstrates just how easily a variety of painters and paintings came into Yeats's mind during the process of composition and, again, how closely they are connected to poetic sources.[6] In the manuscripts to that poem, Carpaccio, "Titians Perseus," and the vaguer "some great painters winged Perseus" appear explicitly. The poem's dragon image also suggests the possible inspiration of other works Yeats knew: Paris Bordone's *St. George and the Dragon,* Perino del Vaga's *Andromeda and Perseus,* Cosmè Tura's *St. George and the Dragon,* and J. T. Nettleship's "Blake drawings," among them.[7] Clark concludes that the principal sources, those that best match the details of the poem, are Blake's engraving for *Milton* of two lovers on a rocky shore with an eagle screaming above them and, more important, Burne-Jones's picture on the Perseus story, *The Doom Fulfilled,* and Burne-Jones's literary source, Morris's "The Doom of King Acrisus" in *The Earthly Paradise.*

As the variety of possible "real sources" for this poem and others suggests, Yeats rarely took his images whole from the visual arts. Even when the source is certain and clear in the poem—as in "On those that Hated 'The Playboy of the Western World', 1907," based on Charles Ricketts's painting of Don Juan in Hell (*L* 525; fig. 40)—Yeats, instead of entering into the painter's phantasmagoria as he had tried to do in such early experiments as "On Mr. Nettleship's Picture at the Royal Hibernian Academy," adopts and adapts it for his own. Don Juan's leg thus becomes the focal point, the "sinewy thigh," apt metaphor for *Playboy*'s bawdy vigor, the envy of the painting's eunuchs and the play's critics.

Yeats's new ability to rule instead of be ruled by the visual art he admired allowed him to return to poems on pictures with greater success than he had had in the 1880s. "On a Picture of a Black Centaur by Edmund Dulac" (written 1920) can serve as example of how Yeats in the later poems most characteristically used an image explicitly drawn from the visual arts: to explore an aesthetic issue of interest to him. The poem differs most markedly from "In Church" or "On Mr. Nettleship's Picture at the Royal Hibernian Academy" in straying from the work named in the title. It is, in fact, unclear what picture by Dulac inspired the poem: Dulac's biographer and others assume that the centaur is one pictured in the design for a bedcover that Lilly Yeats was to embroider—"male & female, with trees"[8]—but it could as easily derive from the centaur motif in Dulac's cover and illustrations for Hawthorne's *Tanglewood Tales* (fig. 41). Dulac was at work on this project when Yeats approached him in 1917 about doing the portrait of Giraldus for *A Vision.*[9] In February 1918 Dulac sent Yeats a sketch for Giraldus and some preliminary sketches for

Figure 40. Charles Ricketts, *Don Juan in Hell,* from *The Studio,* 43 (1908).

Tanglewood Tales.[10] While writing the poem, Yeats also saw a watercolor by Cecil Salkeld which "made the thing clear" and whose details, according to Salkeld's description of the painting, match those of the poem more closely than Dulac's.[11]

The poem first appeared in *Seven Poems and a Fragment* (1922) as "Suggested by a Picture of a Black Centaur." When reprinting it in *The Tower* (1929), Yeats added Dulac's name, never mentioning Salkeld

Figure 41. Edmund Dulac, *The Good Chiron Taught His Pupils How to Play upon the Harp,* from Hawthorne's *Tanglewood Tales,* 1918 (London: Hodder and Stoughton, 1919). Rare Book and Special Collections Division, Library of Congress, Washington, D.C. Courtesy of M. G. Anderson.

and honoring his friend. But the title does more than publicly declare friendship: it sends readers not just to pictures, but to Dulac's pictures, and in so doing provides a visual aid to the poem's major interpretive problem—the identity of the centaur. Even without specifying a particular picture, the title's reference to Dulac calls up images whose stylization counters the animal force of the centaur in the poem's first lines: "Your hooves have stamped at the black margin of the wood,/Even where hor-

Figure 42. Edmund Dulac, *The Centaurs and the Lapith Women*, 1937. Private Collection. Courtesy of M. G. Anderson.

rible green parrots call and swing" (*VP* 442). Dulac's pictures thus help establish the Yeatsian contention that drives the poem: mind, which selects and orders experience into such nonmimetic art as Dulac's—as opposed to body, which lives violently and unthinkingly.

But the poem does not deal in such simple bifurcation, as Dulac's art again indicates.[12] His centaur, in itself, represents "the wisdom of a man and the strength of a horse, a fusion of the worlds of culture and of nature."[13] Dulac depicted the centaur's animal physicality in such pictures as *The Centaurs and the Lapith Women* (fig. 42). Yeats's title, in calling up Dulac's centaur, calls up its meaning in Dulac's art and suggests at the very start that the centaur of the poem similarly signifies such unity and cannot be read simply as a representative of brute force.

Clearly, however, Yeats takes Dulac's notion of the centaur and makes it his own, seeing the creature as a symbolic actor in a personal drama of the creative process. Others have proposed that the centaur represents Irish art, the poet's muse, or his daimon.[14] As union of mind and body, however, the centaur is more Yeats's Image of Unity of Being. It encompasses those opposites the poet strives to unite. This Image of Unity of Being functions here not so much as a guiding ideal, but as a harsh judge of the poet's creative efforts. Most important, it is created by the poet himself, not sent by any external power. The symbolic centaur's creation reflects the opposites it unifies: it is a being imagined by the artist—as its mythological existence and Dulac's highly stylized renderings remind us—which has assumed an independent, violent, physical life of its own. The centaur, like Hanrahan whom Yeats calls up in "The Tower," now exists apart from his creator. Yeats explained in "The Trembling of the Veil," published the same year as the poem, that the images of the mind "might move of themselves and with some powerful, even turbulent life, like those painted horses that trampled the rice-fields of Japan" (*Au* 194). The poem's speaker, like Yeats here, recognizes that the seemingly harmless "horse-play" of mere imagined beings can, in fact, be "a murderous thing." He is filled with both awe at the centaur's power and sadness for the destruction that accompanies its judgment: "My works are all stamped down into the sultry mud" (*VP* 442).

The powerful physicality of this centaur, like Dulac's, is balanced by its supernatural wisdom. In Oxford, where Yeats spent time between 1918 and 1922, he had seen at the Ashmolean Museum "certain pots with strange half supernatural horses dark on a light ground" (*AV-A* 182)—the same kind of Greek vases on which Dulac based his *Tanglewood Tales* illustrations[15]—and associated them in *A Vision* with the self-realization of phases 13 and 14, whose art "interests us most today" (*AV-A* 181). Dulac's art clearly belongs to those phases characterized by "clarity, meaning, elegance, all things separated from one another in luminous space" (*AV-A* 182), and his frequent depictions of the centaur-sage Chiron (e.g., fig. 40) emphasize the creature's wisdom.

Yeats's centaur, in destroying the works, serves the artist. He inhabits the margin of the wood where, as with other margins in Yeats's poems, true creativity occurs. "Even" though they threaten, the centaur keeps vigilant watch over the temptingly brilliant, but "horrible" green birds of the art that "parrots" by formula.[16] When the artist, "driven half insane/ Because of some green wing," produces art too full of the otherworldly and of the intellect that grinds "old Mummy wheat" "grain by grain"—as Yeats had in reaction to prevailing tastes for the realistic—the centaur tramples it into the mud. His act condemns the art and teaches a lesson: such works must attach themselves to earth.

The poem's speaker has learned the lesson. He, too, now comes to the margin of the wood, abashed by the centaur's verdict on his past works, but hopefully bringing his new art, "full-flavored wine." The phrase suggests the earthiness of "What wholesome sun has ripened," but the wine comes, at the same time, out of the mysterious deeps of the sleeping mind. It has not been made by "the mill of the mind" (*VP* 575), but "found/Where seven Ephesian topers slept and never knew/When Alexander's empire passed, they slept so sound" (*VP* 442). The speaker says he is now "fit," as he had not been before, to "keep/Unwearied eyes upon those horrible green birds," for his work has attained Unity of Being. He has come, out of love for this creature who has caused him such pain and served him so well, to take over the watch that the centaur might sleep.

Yet the very assertiveness of the poet's claim "And there is none so fit [as I] to keep a watch" suggests how tenuous is the artist's fitness to rule by himself the margin of the wood. Like the seven Christian martyrs whose two-hundred-year sleep in a cave near Ephesus foreshadows the centaur's "long Saturnian sleep," the centaur may awake to find on the throne a king of failing faith, unable to maintain unity, to successfully fuse the heavenly and the earthly.

In the careful order of *The Tower,* "On a Picture of a Black Centaur by Edmund Dulac" falls appropriately between "Leda and the Swan" and "Among School Children." Its vision of unity tentatively and painfully achieved is the intermediate step from the separability of mind and body implicit in Yeats's genuine question, "Did she put on his knowledge with his power/Before the indifferent beak could let her drop?" to the triumphant discovery of necessary unity proclaimed in the rhetorical "O body swayed to music, O brightening glance,/How can we know the dancer from the dance?" (*VP* 441, 446).

In addition to deriving their images more often from the visual arts, Yeats's later poems also refer more frequently to the visual arts in general and to specific artists and works of art. Longhi, Giorgione, Palmer, Veronese, Michelangelo's "Sistine roof," his *Night* and *Day,* "Phidias' famous ivories," Mantegna, Callimachus, and Delacroix all appear explicitly in the poems, as does talk of statues, mosaics, pictures, the sculptor's and the painter's craft. The reasons for this proliferation of art and artists are two. First, the exploration of aesthetic issues Yeats had earlier carried out in the essays he now often carried out in the poems. The poems through *In the Seven Woods* (1903) embody aesthetic principles set out elsewhere; beginning with *The Green Helmet and Other Poems* (1910) those principles increasingly became the subject of poetry as well. In the later poems, as in the earlier essays, the visual arts serve as evidence and example for discussion and provide Yeats with a way of talking, by analogy, about his own art.

Second, *A Vision* taught Yeats, or systematized his growing awareness, that artists and works of art, instead of being simply sources of symbols, could themselves be symbols. Whereas before he had transferred visual elements, such as the rose, into his poetry, Yeats now began appropriating whole works of art, indeed, whole eras of art, for symbolic use. Most obvious, the arts and artists around phase 15—those of Phidian Greece, Byzantium, and Renaissance Italy—enter the poetry as symbols of Unity of Being and of the characteristics it embodies.

The aesthetic concerns Yeats probed in the poems were at times those that had occupied the earlier essays. In "The Realists" (1912), for example, "Paintings of the dolphin-drawn/Sea-nymphs in their pearly wagons" join "books of men that wive/In a dragon-guarded land" in a poetic continuation of the Morrisian argument for the value of "the arts" in a realistic age (*VP* 309). But the major aesthetic issue the poems discuss is one precipitated by age and the lessons of *A Vision:* the notion of art as "monument." The word appears explicitly in the familiar phrases of "Sailing to Byzantium," "Meditations in Time of Civil War," "Nineteen Hundred and Nineteen," and "Meru." Yeats's use of the term perhaps derived from his reading in history where "monument" commonly designated a past work of art,[17] but it clearly carried for him particular connotations. It implied, above all, permanence. Age and its infirmities increased Yeats's already well-formed sense of his own mortality and quickened a natural desire to outlive himself. The restoration of Thoor Ballylee—aimed, as we have seen, to make it an art object in the Arts and Crafts Movement tradition—most baldly reveals the impulse: the tower, Yeats wrote John Quinn in 1919, requires "another year's work under our own eyes before it is a fitting monument and symbol" (*L* 659). Yeats's instructors, worldly and other-worldly, had taught him that man's immortality rests in his art. "All that survives of a nation is its art," Charles Ricketts had observed.[18] "Dove or Swan," in its reading of the past through monuments, shows that Yeats assumed such assertions as the foundation of his thought. Art's permanence as opposd to man's impermanence is, of course, the best-known theme of Yeats's later poems: "Byzantium"'s "monuments" offer "the artifice of eternity" to an "aged man" (*VP* 407–408). Conversely, Yeats thought that only the man who felt life's decay could ever create such monuments: "only an aching heart/Conceives a changeless work of art" (*VP* 421).

"Monument," however, also suggests the physical presence of the art object. Yeats had always believed that art embodies essence, but in his revolt against mimesis he had earlier emphasized imaginative, nonmaterial qualities. Now, in keeping with his movement downward upon life, he became more aware of art as a physical object. If art is permanent, then it is permanent only insofar as any physical thing can be. As the gyres whirl,

A Vision taught, all must be destroyed. The knowledge that art's ability to immortalize man is, at best, provisional contends in the later poems with the knowledge that art is man's best hope for permanence. The dual awareness surfaces, for example, in the bitter frustration of "Nineteen Hundred and Nineteen":

> Come let us mock at the great
> That had such burdens on the mind
> And toiled so hard and late
> To leave some monument behind,
> Nor thought of the levelling wind.
> (*VP* 432)

As the poems makes clear, the ultimate value for Yeats must finally lie not in the work of art, but in the dignity and courage of creating despite the leveling wind. Paradoxically, however, the struggle can be heroic only if the artist strives to create "monuments of unaging intellect": "Did not Leonardo da Vinci warn the imaginative man against preoccupation with arts that cannot survive his death?" (*Au* 216).

While Yeats valued the arts that survive the artist's death because they grant him some measure of personal immortality, he also viewed art's permanence in its larger cultural and historical aspects. "Monument" connotes a public, perhaps more than a private, sense of art. "Dove or Swan" names particular artists and thus attests to art's ability to immortalize the individual, but it primarily sees art as monument to its civilization. Yeats thus read in the changing eyes of the statues the evolution of the cultural mind from ancient Greece through the Roman Empire (*AV-A* 187–188). In the poems, "learned Italian things/And the proud stones of Greece" (*VP* 415) spoke to Yeats not only of Michelangelo or Phidias, but of Renaissance Italy and Athenian Greece as cultures.

Yeats's own continued service to Irish art, especially the visual arts, illustrates his commitment to art as national monument. The idea both validated and encouraged his efforts to reanimate Irish culture. As Yeats's standing as a national figure grew, he became more involved in Irish politics and used his position to further the cause of worthy national monuments. As a member of the Irish Senate from 1922 to 1928, he pressed the government to appoint an Advisory Committee of Artists and secured promises from William Orpen, Charles Shannon, and John Lavery to serve on it.[19] "I am also trying," he wrote John Quinn in 1924, "to get the designs of Irish lace improved" (*L* 704). A few years later he chaired the committee that solicited designs and offered advice on the new coinage to be issued by the Free State. Perhaps influenced by Dulac's interest in medals and coins as art objects,[20] and by Pound's reverence for them as enduring representatives of civilizations,[21] Yeats and his committee called upon some of the finest sculptors of the day, Carl Milles and Ivan Meštrović among them, to submit designs for these small monuments.[22] Even Yeats's participation in the fight to secure Hugh Lane's art collection for Ireland was indebted to his desire for Irish monuments.[23] Yeats believed Lane's modern, mostly French, paintings might help rescue his country and its artists from the provinciality that produced second-rate art. By studying the monuments Lane had gathered, as the speaker of "Sailing to Byzantium" advises more generally, Ireland might create worthy ones of her own. Yeats further exercised this conviction as a governor of Ireland's National Gallery from 1924 until his death.[24]

In exploring the idea of art as monument, both personal and cultural, the poems often take the visual arts as example, but Yeats, as always, is speaking, too, of his own art.[25] Sometimes "the arts" are named explicitly and linked in common purpose, as when paintings and books together oppose "The Realists" (*VP* 309), or when the speaker of "Under Ben Bulben" instructs: "Poet and sculptor, do the work,/Nor let the modish painter shirk/What his great forefathers did" (*VP* 638). Often poetry or song and the visual arts are implicitly associated. In "Sailing to Byzantium" Yeats ties them through simile—"O sages standing in God's holy fire/As in the gold mosaic of a wall,/Come from the holy fire, perne in a gyre,/And be the singing-masters of my soul" (*VP* 408)—and through the image of the singing golden bird. At times Yeats proceeds by analogy: Dante "set his chisel to the hardest stone" (*VP* 369). At times, as in "Long-legged Fly," he speaks only of visual art, but the poems and prose have prepared us to see Michelangelo painting "the Pope's chapel" in silent concentration as the representative of all great artists, as Helen is of great beauties and Caesar of great leaders (*VP* 617–618).

Yeats thus extended the idea of art as monument to poetry, and as he explored the notion in poems he simultaneously set about creating his own monuments to himself and to his national culture. The poems became more explicitly autobiographical, and in many Yeats himself, transformed but recognizable, appears and speaks. In prose Yeats declared his poetic intention, using again a metaphor from the visual arts: contrasting his early poetry of vision to his present endeavors, he wrote J. B. Yeats in 1913, "Of recent years . . . I have tried for more self portraiture" (*L* 583). As with his turning from landscape to portraiture for dramatic model, Yeats's metaphor here expresses a desire for immediacy, as we will see in the next chapter. But it also aligns his work with the traditional impulse behind portraiture: to perpetuate the image of the sitter. Yeats had, of course, grown up amidst talk of the portrait's function, and he repeatedly admired the portraits at Coole and the Municipal Gallery for their ability to convey the presence of their subjects.

Yeats's poetic self-portraiture was not only founded on analogy to the visual arts, but often created by reference to them. He frequently depicted himself through the things of his world, and among those things were the works of painters, sculptors, and architects. The most obvious, Thoor Ballylee—itself a self-consciously created monument to its owner—provided the poems from "Ego Dominus Tuus" (1917) on with both a setting for the portrait and an indicator of the sitter's character.[26] The tower is ancient, solitary, dignified. The "mysterious wisdom won by toil" that it and its light at times represent is itself developed in "The Phases of the Moon" by analogy to the visual arts: "The lonely light that Samuel Palmer engraved" in *The Lonely Tower,* an illustration to "Il Penseroso" (fig. 23).[27] Like Thoor Ballylee, the paintings and sculptures of the Municipal Gallery, Coole's "Old marble heads, old pictures" (*VP* 491), Lissadell, "that old Georgian mansion" (*VP* 475), and other works of visual art contribute to the self-portraiture.

Yeats sought, however, more than personal immortality. His later poems, even those most obviously monuments to himself, are also monuments to his national culture. He became a public poet and was pleased when Archibald MacLeish commended his "public language."[28] Earlier Yeats had believed that art must be founded in local soil. The recent political instability of Ireland, reinforced by that of the world, lent to that belief a desire to preserve his nation in art. World War I, the Easter Rebellion, the Irish Civil War, and *A Vision*'s prophecy of a coming annunciation impressed on him the tenuousness of modern civilization in general and Ireland in particular. "I had no idea that any public event could so deeply move me," he wrote Lady Gregory of the 1916 uprising, "and I am very despondent about the future" (*L* 613). Yeats responded to his country's turmoil, as he did to the uncertainty of life in old age, with a compensating desire for the permanence and stability of monuments.

By locating his poems, including those that seem most self-portraiture, in particular Irish places, Yeats immortalized Ireland. But increasingly he created monuments to his age and country more explicitly by exploring one frequent function of monuments: to memorialize people and events. Yeats was concerned by 1913 with this function of monuments; he first used the term "monument" in "To a Shade," where it designates the statue of Charles Stewart Parnell (*VP* 292–293). Many of Yeats's later poems are memorials—to "Easter 1916," "September 1913," Parnell, Alfred Pollexfen, Roger Casement, Lionel Johnson, Con Markiewicz, Eva Gore-Booth, Maud Gonne, Robert Gregory, and others. Yeats implicitly allied his own memorials to those created by visual artists. His poems and prose refer to tombs, sepulchres, and other works of art that memorialize: Oliver Sheppard's statue of Cuchulain (*VPl* 1063; *VP* 611; fig. 43); "The Three Monuments" to Lord Nelson, Parnell, and

Figure 43. Oliver Sheppard, *Cuchulain*. General Post Office, Dublin.

Daniel O'Connell (*VP* 460); Michelangelo's figures on the Medici tombs (*VP* 386; figs. 38, 39). More important, many of his own memorials begin with meditation on or reference to visual memorials, as in "A Bronze Head" or "The Municipal Gallery Revisited," or his tributes to Henley and Morris in the *Autobiographies*.[29] At times, his monuments to others develop by comparison to past monuments: Lionel Johnson with "the delicate strong features of a certain filleted head of a Greek athlete in the British Museum, an archaistic Graeco-Roman copy of a masterpiece of the fourth century" (*Au* 222); or Maud Gonne, whose "face, like the face of some Greek statue, showed little thought" and whose "whole body seemed a master-work of long labouring thought, as though a Scopas had measured and calculated, consorted with Egyptian sages, and mathematicians out of Babylon, that he might outface even Artemisia's sepulchral image with a living norm" (*Au* 364–365).

Yeats's exploration of art as monument and his attempts to create monuments himself were elevated, by art's symbolic function, above the mere desire for self or national glorification. Works of art exist in Yeats's later poems as physical objects, but they also serve as symbols. Their meaning derives most often from their place on *A Vision*'s Great Wheel. Art, thus, not only immortalizes the artist and the civilization, but symbolizes particular characteristics. It survives the death of its maker and its age both because it is more permanent and because it possesses larger significance. Michelangelo's Sistine ceiling is just that, but it also symbolizes "Profane perfection" (*VP* 639). Yeats, as opposed perhaps to many whose art he took as symbols, was always conscious of trying to make a work of art that would itself by a symbol. As early as 1896 he had, in a rhetorical question, gently pointed to one of Blake's limitations: "and yet . . . he forgot how he who wraps the vision in lights and shadows, in irridescent or glowing colour . . . until form be half lost in pattern, may compel the canvas or paper to become itself a symbol of some not indefinite because unsearchable essence."[30] Yeats wanted his own works to be symbols, as his desire that Thoor Ballylee be "a fitting monument and symbol" suggests. Yeats's use of art as symbols in the poems thus contributed, as his concept of art as monument did, to his constant exploration, through analogies to the visual arts, of his own art's form and function. He sought in his poetic references to the visual arts adequate symbols for art which would include his own poetry.

"Lapis Lazuli" (written 1936; published 1938) is Yeats's most famous poetic exploration of the arts' function as monument.[31] Here he asserts baldly what he knows to be true: "All things fall." Yet the poem, instead of bitterly lamenting that inevitability as "Nineteen Hundred and Nineteen" had, finds compensation in the process of artistic creation: "All

Figure 44. Lapis Lazuli Mountain, Ch'ien Lung period (1739–1795).
Courtesy of Michael B. Yeats and Anne Yeats.

things fall and are built again,/And those that build them again are gay."[32] The lapis lazuli's Chinamen become, of course, symbols of those who rebuild (fig. 44). As in other poems, the artists, like Yeats himself, are old and full of sorrow as they "stare" "On all the tragic scene." Gone is Yeats's confidence that those with aching hearts create changeless works of art. The Chinamen respond to the scene with "mournful melodies," with music, the most impermanent of the arts. All that endures is their gaiety, which proclaims the immortality of the human spirit and imagination.[33]

Yet the poem is full of Yeats's desire to believe in art's permanence despite his knowledge. Although he spoke with spirits and argued for the claims of the nonmaterial world, Yeats often had more faith in what man could see and touch. The syntactic strategy of the poem's passage on Callimachus subtly undercuts the lines' overt meaning:

> No handiwork of Callimachus,
> Who handled marble as if it were bronze,
> Made draperies that seemed to rise
> When sea-wind swept the corner, stands
> (*VP* 566)

By delaying the verb and placing it in the position of greatest emphasis, Yeats creates a sense of the presence of Callimachus' handiwork in a sentence whose point is its absence.

More obviously, by taking the poem's title and the images of its last two stanzas from a two-hundred-year-old piece of carved lapis lazuli, Yeats celebrates art's longevity, if not its immortality. Like other works of art in Yeats's late poems, this gift from Harry Clifton, to whom the poem is dedicated, becomes itself a symbol—here of those monuments that survive their maker. Moreover, Yeats makes clear that the artist's gaiety is not reserved for those whose art is music. The references to Callimachus and Shakespeare insist, as always, that what applies to one art applies to the others as well. The piece of lapis lazuli itself embodies the union of the arts the poem claims: the front presents an image; the back contains a Chinese poem in four seven-syllable lines.[34]

The lapis lazuli further performs a function Yeats found characteristic of monuments: as a work of art on which he meditated, it, like the mosaics of "Sailing to Byzantium," served as his "singing school."[35] Like "On a Picture of a Black Centaur by Edmund Dulac," the last two stanzas of "Lapis Lazuli" are based on a work of art. But, whereas in the earlier poem the reader must bring with him a knowledge of Dulac's art, here Yeats describes the picture for us:

Two Chinamen, behind them a third,
Are carved in lapis lazuli,
Over them flies a long-legged bird,
A symbol of longevity;
The third, doubtless a serving man,
Carries a musical instrument.
(*VP* 566)

The poem's use of its visual inspiration is seemingly more straightforward than in the "Black Centaur." One look at the lapis lazuli, however, reveals that here, as before, Yeats makes free use of his source. The long-legged bird actually appears on the back of the piece, not on the front with the Chinamen, and the "plum or cherry branch," which "doubtless" "Sweetens the little half-way house/Those Chinamen climb towards," is, in fact, a pine tree.

Such changes served Yeats's poetic purposes. Moving the bird allowed for compression by relieving Yeats of an awkward "On the front . . . On the back." More importantly, by declaring the bird a symbol of longevity and placing it over the Chinamen, Yeats makes clear that these are wise old men, while avoiding that cliché. The position of the bird also suggests that these artists, unlike those whom the women of the first stanza malign, are protected and dignified by an almost heavenly power. The plum or cherry branch—along with Yeats's reading of "Every discoloration of the stone,/Every accidental crack or dent" as "a watercourse or an avalanche,/Or lofty slope where it still snows"—reinforces the notion that the Chinamen's climb is a symbolic ascent, threatened by natural dangers, but rewarded, finally, by spring's flowers and the fruits they promise. The final six lines of the poem take leave altogether of the scene actually depicted, as Yeats's explicit "and I/Delight to imagine them seated there" tells us.[36] This creation of an original vision, like the transformation of Dulac's picture, confirms Yeats's belief that studying monuments of unaging intellect inspires the imaginative activity, which, in turn, produces new monuments.[37]

Yeats's use of the lapis lazuli as object of meditation and source of inspiration differs, however, in one important way from his use of Dulac's centaur. In "Lapis Lazuli," Yeats sets his meditation in a larger social and political context, thus declaring this monument's place in the public as well as the private domain. "On a Picture of a Black Centaur" opens immediately into a world inspired by the picture's (or pictures') images. As readers, we are unaware of Dulac's picture as itself existing in a larger context. Yeats narrows our vision because the subject of his poem is narrow: the artist's relation with his own works. "Lapis Lazuli," however, does not mention the work that provides his primary inspiration until well into the poem. When it enters, we see it in the midst of, and as an answer to, a world in decay whose hysterical women voice the age-old argument against artists who do nothing for the public good. The delayed introduction thus allows both the lapis lazuli itself and the scene it depicts to argue that art is not escapist, nor the artist merely self-gratifying. In keeping with "monument's" implied public nature, the piece of lapis lazuli and Yeats's poem based on it proclaim the value of artistic activity as the very maker and preserver of civilization.

Yeats never indicated what phase his lapis lazuli might occupy, but the visual monuments or symbols the later poems most often name are those around phase 15, with which Yeats, of course, wanted to identify his own work. Yeats most notably associated the word "monument" in his poems with the art of Byzantium, and that city with its stylized, brilliantly colored mosaics became for Yeats the symbol of the world of art, as the extensive scholarship on the Byzantium poems has amply shown. Byzantium not only carried the importance of all phase 15s in *A Vision,* but, as we have seen, embodied the principles and characteristics Yeats's Pre-Raphaelite education had taught him to love. It was so central to his later thought that for a while he considered calling *The Winding Stair* (1933) *Byzantium,* and sent the title poem to T. Sturge Moore "hoping that it may suggest symbolism for the cover" Moore was designing (*LTSM* 164). It seemed that Byzantine art might provide a fitting visual symbol for Yeats's poetry.

But the volume remained *The Winding Stair,* and by 1938 Byzantium had disappeared from Yeats's view of the past: "Civilisation rose to the high tide mark in Greece, fell, rose again in the Renaissance but not to the same level" (*OTB* 29). As Harold Bloom has observed, "The later Yeats tended to find only two full moons in the history of civilization."[38] In the poems, Yeats turned more frequently to Renaissance and ancient Greek art than he did to Byzantium, finding particularly in Michelangelo and Phidias more adequate symbols for his own sense of the creative act and for his own work.

In 1928, a year after publishing "Sailing to Byzantium," Yeats set out his doubts about Byzantine art in an essay against a censorship bill then before the Irish Senate. His comments there reveal not only what troubled him about Byzantium, but what attracted him to Greece and the Renaissance. The essay pits Plato, who "placed in the brain" the "rational soul," and the "Platonizing theology of Byzantium" against "St. Thomas's opinion, to which we adhere . . . that the soul is wholly present in the whole body and in all its parts" (*UP* 2:478). He developed his argument by reference to the visual arts:

> Amidst the abstract splendour of its [Byzantium's] basilicas stood saints with thought-tortured faces and bodies that were but a framework to sustain the patterns and colours of their clothes. The mosaics of the Apse displayed a Christ with face of pitiless intellect, or a pinched, flat-breasted virgin holding a child like a wooden doll. Nobody can stray into that little Byzantium chapel at Palermo, which suggested the chapel of the Grail to Wagner, without for an instant renouncing the body and all its works. (*UP* 2:478)

To this he opposed "an art of the body" and those who practiced it, naming Giotto, Andrea del Sarto, Raphael, Orcagna, and Titian. "Are we prepared," he then asked his readers, "to exclude such art from Ireland and to sail in a ship of fools, fools that dressed bodies Michael Angelo left naked, Town Councillors of Montreal who hid the Discobulus in the cellar?"[39]

As this passage suggests, Yeats's disenchantment with Byzantium centered on its disregard for physical life.[40] Yeats responded to the physical deterioration of old age with the realization and celebration of the body's magnificence. The later poems gather their power and strength from a sense of life lived in the body, a life not imaged in Byzantium's stiff, stylized figures. The arrangement of *The Tower*, published the same year as the censorship essay, carried into the poetic realm and turned to poetic use the argument Yeats had articulated so clearly for political purpose. "Sailing to Byzantium" opens the volume. Burdened by old age, the speaker looks for relief to Byzantine art where mind and spirit reign so supreme the body's ills no longer matter; he pleads with the sages, "Consume my heart away . . . and gather me/Into the artifice of eternity" (*VP* 408). But in the next poem, "The Tower," the "aged man," in words echoing Yeats's censorship essay, resents and resists the Byzantine refuge to which failing physical life consigns him: "It seems that I must bid the Muse go pack,/Choose Plato and Plotinus for a friend/Until imagination, ear and eye,/Can be content with argument and deal/In abstract things" (*VP* 409). Yeats thus not only uses Byzantium to establish one of the volume's main themes—the permanence of art—but uses his quarrel with it to set up the book's major dramatic conflict—old age raging against its own condition.

The "art of the body," particularly that of Michelangelo, resolved in many ways the difficulties Byzantium presented. The Sistine ceiling and

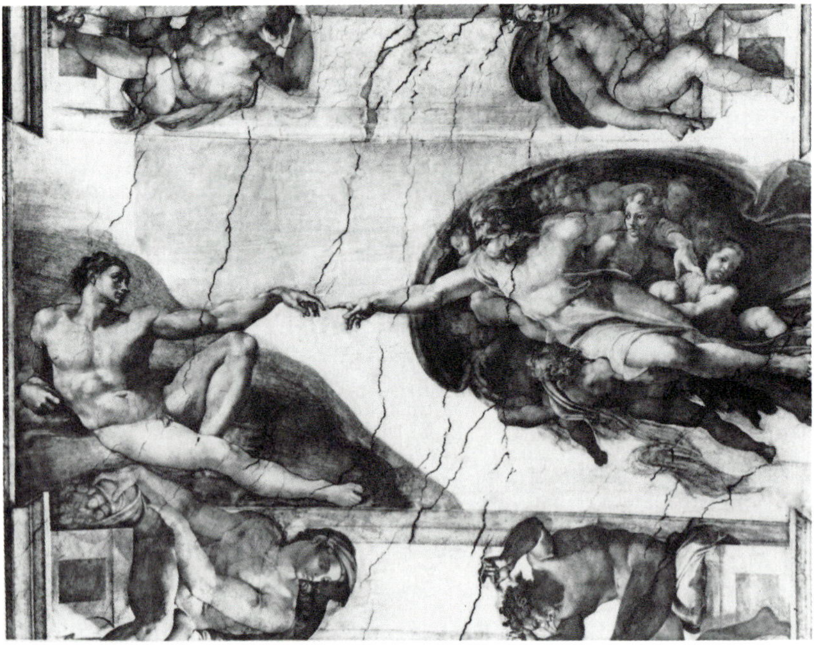

Figure 45. Michelangelo, *The Creation of Adam,* detail of the Sistine ceiling, 1508–1512, Vatican, Rome. Alinari/Art Resource, New York.

the figures on the tombs of Giuliano and Lorenzo de'Medici (figs. 45, 38, 39) appear in the poems as representatives of art that insists on sensuous physical life.[41] Yeats first used Michelangelo in "Michael Robartes and the Dancer" (1920), where "He" argues, as Yeats would later about Byzantine art, that thought from the mind alone and not the whole body is dangerous. Standing before a Renaissance altarpiece of St. George and the Dragon, "He" calls on Veronese and Michelangelo for support:[42]

Paul Veronese
And all his sacred company
Imagined bodies all their days
By the lagoon you love so much,
For proud, soft, ceremonious proof

That all must come to sight and touch;
While Michael Angelo's Sistine roof,
His "Morning" and his "Night" disclose
How sinew that has been pulled tight,

Or it may be loosened in repose,
Can rule by supernatural right
Yet be but sinew.

(*VP* 386)

Yeats here again speaks through these painters of his own art. In an extension of the desire for "more of manful energy" (*VP* 849), which had led him away from the 1890s into his theatrical experiments, Yeats, in turning to the Renaissance, looked to an art the Pre-Raphaelites had sometimes admired for its elegance and sensuousness, but saw there what he could not find in them: vigor and energy. Furthermore, although Rossetti in particular had painted portraits, Pre-Raphaelite art in general is curiously divorced from the human. There often seems to be more delight in the luxurious flowers and vines than in the subjects they adorn. Michelangelo, like Yeats in the later poems, attended almost exclusively to human life. In a 1924 manifesto that Yeats wrote for a group of young poets and artists, he declared allegiance to this vigorous and powerful art of the body:

> We are Catholics, but of the school of Pope Julius the Second and of the Medician Popes, who ordered Michelangelo and Raphael to paint upon the walls of the Vatican, and upon the ceiling of the Sistine Chapel, the doctrine of the Platonic Academy of Florence, the reconciliation of Galilee and Parnassus. We proclaim Michelangelo the most orthodox of men, because he set upon the tomb of the Medici "Dawn" and "Night," vast forms shadowing the strength of antideluvian Patriarchs and the lust of the goat, the whole handiwork of God, even the abounding horn. (*UP* 2:438)

Fifteen years later, in "Under Ben Bulben," Yeats turned again to Michelangelo for the last time to reassert the value of art founded in physical life and to place him in the tradition to which Yeats belonged:

Michael Angelo left a proof
On the Sistine Chapel roof,
Where but half-awakened Adam
Can disturb globe-trotting Madam
Till her bowels are in heat,

Proof that there's a purpose set
Before the secret working mind:
Profane perfection of mankind.

(*VP* 638–639)

For Yeats, part of the appeal of Michelangelo's forms, as both "Michael Robartes and the Dancer" and "Under Ben Bulben" show, was that they seemed so lifelike. Unlike the mosaic saints of Byzantium whose bodies "were but a framework to sustain the patterns and colours of their clothes" (*UP* 2:478), Michelangelo's Adam seems so alive that he "Can disturb globe-trotting Madam/Till her bowels are in heat." Michelangelo did not ignore the spirituality that made Byzantine art so attractive to Yeats, but his figures "disclose/How sinew . . . Can rule by supernatural right/Yet be but sinew." Byzantine art, in contrast, seemed "abstract."

Yeats's interest in the mimetic qualities of art seems a shift of alliances for a man who had spent his early life arguing for the nonmimetic. In the context of artistic climates, however, the change appears less radical. When Yeats first championed the nonmimetic, he had fought a world dominated by a passion for imitation. By 1920, however, Cubism was well established and Yeats had felt its effect in England, most notably in the work of his friend Wyndham Lewis.[43] Faced with such nonrealistic art, Yeats began to seek more and more the imitative, as his desire for poetic self-portraiture, with all its connotations of "likeness," shows. He was encouraged to explore the idea of imitation in art by J. B. Yeats, who had written to his son in 1916 about "all art as imitation." Yeats had responded, "imitation seems to me to create a language in which we say things which are not imitation" (*L* 607). Imitation could give the artist the tools to go beyond mere mimesis. Imitation in poetry, Yeats decided several days later, was "drama and the pictorial element" (*L* 608), the "dramatization and picture" with which he had tried early on to counter "abstraction."

What allowed Michelangelo's forms to "rule by supernatural right/Yet be but sinew" was rhythm. Although Yeats had always spoken of rhythm and pattern in the visual arts as one principle and continued to use the terms interchangeably, he came to distinguish the pattern of whole form he found in Michelangelo's figures from the pattern of surface decoration he saw in Byzantine art and elsewhere. One implied an attachment to life, the other a removal from it. One implied the "concrete," the other the "abstract." Yeats, recognizing from the beginning his own dangerous tendency toward abstraction, sided with all that would aid his "movement downward upon life." Both Impressionism and Cubism were, Yeats observed, "abstract" because they lacked rhythm: "Rhythm implies a living body, a breast to rise and fall, or limbs that dance, while the abstract is incompatible with life" (*L* 608). Despite their varying aims in regard to imitation, Impressionism and Cubism shared with Byzantine art an attention to surface pattern that was divorced, according to Yeats, from a sense of life. The bodies of those Byzantine saints remained mere frameworks, no matter how beautiful the pattern and colors covering them. Greek and Renaissance art, on the other hand, depended on the rhythms, not of surface decoration, but of the forms themselves. This rhythm saved art from being purely imitative: "The element of pattern in every art is, I think, the part that is not imitative," Yeats wrote J. B. Yeats in 1916, repeating a tenet he had held since he first admired Pre-Raphaelite pattern (*L* 607). Rhythm, however, also encouraged art to retain an imitative function: the rhythm of Michelangelo's forms "implies a living body," indeed cannot be separated from the depiction of it.

The imitative qualities of Greek and Renaissance art also appealed to Yeats because they partially resolved a dilemma inherent in desiring immortality through art. Byzantium was such a fit symbol for "monuments of unaging intellect" precisely because its art appeared so changeless. Its static figures and draperies—such as those of the saints and prophets on the walls of St. Apollinare Nuovo (fig. X), the source, perhaps, of Yeats's sages in "Sailing to Byzantium"—never seemed to move, or ever to have moved. They thus epitomized the "artifice of eternity." But the Byzantium poems themselves raise Keatsian doubts about such eternal changelessness. The golden bird, whose form the speaker of "Sailing to Byzantium" so desires for his own, is "set" upon a golden bough to perform mechanically for a "drowsy Emperor" (*VP* 408). While Yeats sang the "glory of changeless metal" in "Byzantium," his heart lay, perhaps despite himself, with the "mire and blood" of mortal life, as the poem's last stanza suggests (*VP* 498).

Yeats knew, of course, that all art fixes life and thus destroys much of its wonder and pleasure, yet Renaissance and Greek art gave an impression of physical life absent in Byzantine works. In Greek sculpture, Pythagorean numbers "moved or seemed to move/In marble or in bronze" and "Michaelangelo's forms threaten us."[44] Significantly, the visual analogue Yeats offered T. Sturge Moore for "Byzantium"'s dolphin, representative of "blood and mire," came from the Italian Renaissance. In opposition to the purged images of the abstract, bodiless art of the holy city, Yeats saw the unpurged as "Raphael's statue of the Dolphin carrying one of the Holy Innocents to Heaven."[45]

In addition to providing a symbol of the art of the body, Michelangelo and his work embodied for Yeats the creative mind in ways that Byzantium's art and craftsmen could not.[46] Yeats began increasingly to associate the wild imaginative excitement that attended his old age with physical, often sexual, power. He frequently found images for that power in art. As early as 1911, the "sinewy thigh" of Ricketts's Don Juan served as symbol not only of the censored sexuality of Synge's work, but of the supple vitality of his imagination. Michelangelo's "half-awakened Adam," his *Morning* and *Night,* whose sinew echoes Don Juan's, thus became for Yeats symbols of imaginative activity.

Yeats attributed to Michelangelo himself the imaginative intensity the works symbolized. Michelangelo thus entered the poems as symbol, specifically of the creative vigor Yeats had or wished to have. Yeats placed him in phase 16 with William Blake:

> At one moment they are full of hate . . . and their hate is always close to madness; and at the next they produce the comedy of Aretino and of Rabelais or the mythology of Blake, and discover symbolism to express the overflowing and bursting of the mind. There is always an element of frenzy, and almost always a delight in certain glowing or shining images of concentrated force; in the smith's forge; in the heart; in the human form in its most vigorous development; in the solar disc; in some symbolical representation of the sexual organs; for the being must brag of its triumph over its own coherence.[47]

Yeats invoked this madness and frenzy in "An Acre of Grass" (1938), a poem that shows Yeats's own delight in "images of concentrated force." The speaker, his "strength of body" gone, vows to "remake" himself as "a mind Michael Angelo knew":

> Grant me an old man's frenzy,
> Myself must I remake
> Till I am Timon and Lear
> Or that William Blake
> Who beat upon the wall
> Till Truth obeyed his call;
>
> A mind Michael Angelo knew
> That can pierce the clouds,
> Or inspired by frenzy
> Shake the dead in their shrouds;
> Forgotten else by mankind,
> An old man's eagle mind.
>
> (*VP* 576)

Yeats sets Michelangelo as presiding mind over those other old men, Timon and Lear, and Yeats's own early hero, Blake, whose energy he had always admired. "Strength of body" will not return for any of them; yet they have what Yeats wants—imaginations so strong and active they seem physical. Their minds "beat," "pierce," and "shake," as their bodies no longer can.[48]

Michelangelo, furthermore, represented the artist's solitude. Yeats had always known that art was lonely business, yet he had longed for the communal creativity, first, of Rossetti, Morris, and Burne-Jones painting the Oxford Union, then of Byzantium's craftsmen. Experience, however, taught him that in "our individualistic age" solitude is the necessary condition of the artist (*Au* 547). This recognition underlies his emphasis in *A Vision* on the "discovery of solitude" that preceded the flowering of Greek and Renaissance art (*AV-A* 181, 201). J. B. Yeats had suggested the concept before the communicators did: in 1914 he wrote his son, "*art is solitary man*" and suggested "M. Angelo" as example. His letter provides a context for Yeats's exploration of the idea twenty-five years later in "Long-legged Fly:

> Now intensity is not art, yet it is the parent of art and its groundwork. Yet here also the artist must work as a solitary, otherwise the intensity is spoiled by the intrusion of what is alien. It does not come on one with the same strangeness—a strangeness yet with something familiar—one's secret heart answers to it as to a language learned in one's infancy and then forgotten. This is the quality of naïveté so noticeable in the drawings of some of the ancient PreRaphaelite Masters—you find it in M. Angelo, seldom in Raphael, who indeed is not intense.[49]

Yeats's poem echoes J. B. Yeats in its idea of intensity working in solitude, in the notion of shutting out the alien and disruptive, and in the implied naïveté of Helen, of the girls who find in Michelangelo's art their "first Adam," and of that art itself:

> That girls at puberty may find
> The first Adam in their thought,
> Shut the door of the Pope's chapel,
> Keep those children out.
> There on that scaffolding reclines
> Michael Angelo.
> With no more sound than the mice make
> His hand moves to and fro.
> *Like a long-legged fly upon the stream*
> *His mind moves upon silence.*
> (*VP* 617–618)

Here, again, Yeats identifies himself with Michelangelo. The silent mouse connects this stanza to "An Acre of Grass," where the speaker calls the frenzy of "A mind Michael Angelo knew" into the silence of "an old house/Where nothing stirs but a mouse" (*VP* 576, 575). That silence, which had signified lack of activity, thus becomes the enabling condition of the most productive and frenzed activity, that of the mind. Yeats himself, we know, required such silence and solitude for work.[50]

For Yeats, the art of ancient Greece, like that of the Renaissance, was an art of the body: "rhythm, an exaltation of the body, uncommitted energy. . . . Those riders upon the Parthenon had all the world's power in their moving bodies" (*AV-A* 188). But whereas Yeats found in Michelangelo the frenzy of the imagination, he saw in Greek sculpture, especially the Parthenon statues attributed to Phidias (figs. 35, 36, 37), the "Doric discipline" that brought it under control and gave its forms universality.[51] That discipline was not primarily a matter of fine craftsmanship (although there was that, too), but of the underlying mathematical conceptions of ideal proportion based on Pythagorean theory. While Yeats the old man loved the physical energy of a Michelangelo, its historical manifestations—the unbridled violence of World War I and the Irish Civil War—frightened him and showed him that such frenzy required the control of rational order. What inspired his flirtation with fascism also inspired his more attractive belief in the efficacy of "mathematic form."[52]

Following Blake's dictum "Grecian is Mathematic Form: Gothic is Living Form, Mathematic Form is Eternal in the Reasoning Memory: Living Form is Eternal Existence," Yeats had always rejected mathematic form and its implication of mechanically worked-out pattern.[53] But unlike Blake, Yeats viewed Greek, not Gothic, art as exemplary of living form and in 1906 used it to argue against mathematic form. Contemplating two pictures, one by Canaletto, one by Frans Francken, he observed:

> Neither painting could move us at all, if our thought did not rush out to the edges of our flesh, and it is so with all good art, whether the Victory of Samothrace which reminds the soles of our feet of swiftness, or the *Odyssey* that would send us out under the salt wind, or the young horsemen on the Parthenon, that seem happier than our boyhood ever was, and in our boyhood's way. Art bids us touch and taste and hear and see the world, and shrinks from what Blake calls mathematic form, from every abstract thing, from all that is of the brain only, from all that is not a fountain jetting from the entire hopes, memories, and sensations of the body. (*E&I* 292–293)

By the early 1920s, however, Yeats was reading John Burnet's *Early Greek Philosophy* and marking the passages on Pythagoras and numbers.[54] And by 1938 he could claim in "Under Ben Bulben":[55]

> Measurement began our might:
> Forms a stark Egyptian thought,
> Forms that gentler Phidias wrought.
> Michael Angelo left a proof
> On the Sistine Chapel roof
>
> (*VP* 638)

Yeats had come to see that "measurement"—a term that encompassed geometry, the foundation of mathematic form—gave power not only to the more abstract forms of Egyptian art, but to the art of the body he so admired.[56] In his later writings he evoked the pictorial resolution of the human body and mathematics—a man inscribed in a square and a circle (fig. 46)—when, following Dante, he symbolized Unity of Being as "a perfectly proportioned human body" (*Au* 190). He noted that the proportions derived "from the measurement of ancient statues" (*AV-A* 202).

As "Under Ben Bulben"'s "our" suggests, Yeats included himself among the artists who found might in measurement. In two principal ways, the idea of art founded on mathematics forged new ties between Yeats's poetry and the visual arts. Yeats, like Phidias, worked out of a geometrical concept of the world. As Pythagorean numbers offered a coherent explanation of the universe and related its parts to its whole, so *A Vision*'s system of circles and gyres ordered and related history and the individual life. The relation of *A Vision* to Yeats's poetry, however, differs from that between Pythagoras' numbers and Greek art. Greek artists, by following the rules of ideal proportions, could create works of art whose beauty would reflect the harmony of a universe ordered by the same mathematical system. Yeats's system offered him "metaphors for poetry" (*AV-B* 8), but no prescriptions for artistic form. The concept of "measurement," however, linked the formal foundations of Yeats's art to those of the other arts: indeed, measurement united the arts under one canon. There are measures of music, dance, and poetry as well as measurement in painting and sculpture.[57] Yeats used the term "measure" in relation to all the arts, often to suggest their connection.[58]

Yeats's famous conclusion to the introduction for the 1937 edition of *A Vision* proposes a specific analogy between geometrically founded visual art and *A Vision* and the poetry built on it: "now that the system stands out clearly in my imagination I regard them [my circuits of sun and moon] as stylistic arrangements of experience comparable to the cubes in the drawings of Wyndham Lewis and to the ovoids in the sculpture of

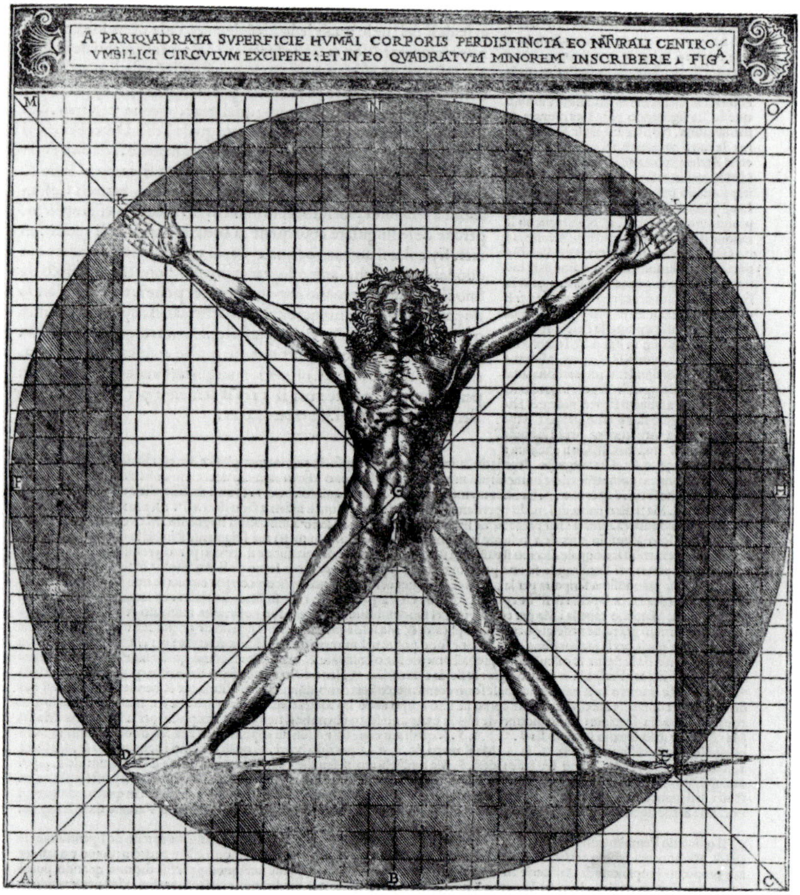

Figure 46. Man inscribed in a circle and a square, from Cesare Cesariano's edition of Vitruvius's *De Architectura,* 1521. Lessing J. Rosenwald Collection, Library of Congress, Washington, D.C.

Brancusi" (*AV-B* 25). Wary of abstraction, but alive to the possibilities of mathematic form, Yeats had been both repelled and interested in the geometrically based art Ezra Pound championed. As critics have noted, the Vorticists' metaphor for creative activity and major visual motif, the vortex, bears some relation to Yeats's gyre.[59] Yeats would, perhaps, have sympathized with Pound's desire to humanize mathematics, but he would not have condoned Pound's attempts to formulate an equation analogous to the poetic image.[60] He never overcame his conviction that Wyndham Lewis confused the "abstract" and the "rhythmical" and thus created art divorced from the "living body" (*L* 608; fig. 47). Yeats's comparison of *A*

Figure 47. Wyndham Lewis, *Composition,* 1913. Tate Gallery, London. Estate of Mrs. G. A. Wyndham Lewis.

Vision's system to the geometrical underpinnings of Lewis's and Brancusi's works is an attempt to place his own work in the modern movement, which so often considered him the old guard. In the end, however, Yeats turned to the more compatible art of Phidias, whom Pound thought had "corrupted sculpture," Yeats reported (*VP* 856), presumably by obscuring geometric form with naturalistic flesh. Yeats's impulse to link his art to the mathematically based visual arts found better expression in his late programmatic poem "The Statues," which takes Phidian sculpture as artistic ideal.

"The Statues" (1939; *VP* 610–611), originally titled "Pythagorean Numbers,"[61] makes clear that Yeats found in Phidian sculpture the fitting symbol of the art he wanted for himself and for Ireland.[62] "Pythagoras planned it," the poem opens. "It" is Yeats's art of the body—lifelike, but purged of individuality ("character") and elevated to the ideal by measurement. "His numbers, though they moved or seemed to move/In marble or in bronze, lacked character."

In the 1937 edition of *A Vision* (23), Yeats had compared his system to "the Pythagorean numbers" and now built both a public and a private artistic program on the analogies between Phidian Greece and modern Ireland. The last stanza of the poem, where the speaker turns to the present tense, sees an Ireland under the dark moon of civilization's first phase and offers ancient Greece as parallel to the new era Ireland will usher in. Yeats had advised the Irish in prose to prepare for its future: "Teach nothing but Greek, Gaelic, mathematics and perhaps one modern language" (*OTB* 28). Greek language, like mathematics, would give children "coordination or intensity" (*OTB* 28), the ability to order and mold. The Greek sculptors in stanza two, "That with a mallet or a chisel modelled these/Calculations that look but casual flesh," argue for the political power of the artist and provide historical validation for Yeats's lifelong efforts to achieve Irish freedom by reviving Irish culture. As the Greek sculptors, ordering by measuring, "put off" the "many-headed foam at Salamis," so must Irish artists put down "this filthy modern tide" of war and revolution that Ireland is "thrown upon."

They cannot do so by responding to the "mire and blood" of human life with such sentimental art as the statue of Cuchulain erected in the General Post Office to memorialize the 1916 rebellion (fig. 43). "Cuchulain is in the last stanza," Yeats explained to Edith Shackleton Heald, "becaus Pearse and some of his followers had a cult of him. The Government has put a statue of Cuchulain in the rebuilt post office to commemorate this" (*L* 911):

> When Pearse summoned Cuchulain to his side,
> What stalked through the Post Office? What intellect,
> What calculation, number, measurement, replied?

Cuchulain, whom Yeats associated with the Greek heroic tradition,[63] required, Yeats thought, a better monument than Oliver Sheppard's seeming pastiche of Michelangelo's slaves (fig. 48). A "bad statue," Yeats called it.[64] His poetic questions, then, are not purely rhetorical; they chide the Irish

Figure 48. Michelangelo, *Dying Slave*, 1513–1516. Louvre, Paris. Alinari/Art Resource, New York.

on to glory. Intellect, calculation, number, measurement, like those of the Greeks, must temper the fervor and mimesis Ireland seemed to love: "There are moments," Yeats said in an often-quoted passage, "when I am certain that art must once again accept those Greek proportions which carry into plastic art the Pythagorean numbers, those faces which are divine because all there is empty and measured" (*OTB* 37). "We Irish," Yeats persuades by asserting, take Greek sculpture founded on Pythagoras' numbers as model and "Climb to our proper dark, that we may trace/The lineaments of a plummet-measured face."

"We," of course, included Yeats himself. Toward the end of his life he looked consciously to Greek literature and art for models. He had written and produced his own version of *Oedipus at Colonnus* by that Phidian man, Sophocles (*AV-A* 182), and had seen "that the wood of the Furies in the opening scene [of that play] was any Irish haunted wood" (*OTB* 28). "The Statues" expresses by allusion Yeats's dissatisfaction with Pre-Raphaelite art as model for poetry and sets in its place Phidian sculpture. Stanza three's description of Buddha derived from several sources, including Yeats's reading of A. Foucher's "The Greek Origin of the Image of Buddha" in *The Beginnings of Buddhist Art,*[65] but the particular rendering resembles, as many critics have noted, Yeats's portrait of Morris in the *Autobiographies* (141–142). The poem's image represents civilization's "subsidence into the void" of primary life.[66] Buddha, like Morris, is "a fat/Dreamer of the Middle Ages," but absorption in dream for both produced "emptiness" and art that could only image dream and not life: "Mirror on mirror mirrored is all the show."[67] Like Byzantine art, such art is static.[68] Yeats's late poetry replaces the passive dream reflections of Buddha, Byzantium, and the Pre-Raphaelites with an art of the body that actively affects its audience. Like Michelangelo, Yeats wanted to "disturb globe-trotting Madam"; like Phidias, he wanted not to mirror dream, but to "give" dreams, to inspire boys and girls to press "Live lips upon a plummet-measured face." By using the geometry of *A Vision,* as Phidias had used Pythagoras' numbers, Yeats would put down the modern tide of formless violence with an art at once active and ideal.

A Vision's communicators brought Yeats "metaphors for poetry" in several ways. The people and events the system used as examples acquired from their places on the wheel symbolic significance that Yeats could poetically exploit. He could use them as metaphors in poetry. But they also brought, especially in "Dove or Swan," examples of art that could serve as metaphors, analogies, for Yeats's own art. All arts of phase 15 appealed to Yeats, who sought for his work their Unity of Being. But he was particularly attracted to the art of sculpture, which played an important role in the historical phases and came to particular flowering in ancient Greece and the Renaissance, those phase 15s that most interested Yeats. The title of "The Statues" calls attention both to the monumental function of art that Yeats explored in his poems and wanted them to fulfill, and to the sculptural form such monuments most often took. Yeats's own late poems frequently adopt the characteristics and effects of the sculpture he admired.

7

Yeats's Sculptural Poetry

Although I saw it all in the mind's eye
There can be nothing solider till I die
("The Double Vision of Michael Robartes," *VP* 383)

The integration characterizing *A Vision*'s "more profound Pre-Raphaelitism" influenced and grew out of Yeats's own increasing sense of integration with the world around him. As he moved downward upon life, the world acquired a physical presence it had not possessed before. Objects that had seemed evanescent, now took on solid form; those vague and distant, he now walked among. Instead of seeing the world as hostile and foreign, Yeats began to feel himself a part of it.[1]

The nature of the visions from which he continued to derive poetic inspiration and images also changed. They often appeared, like Michael Robartes's double vision, "solid" (c.f., *E&I* 397). Yeats became interested in more palpable forms of vision than he had experienced before and began experimenting with materializations, calling up spirits to the physical eye.[2]

As his sense of the world changed and affected his poems, the analogies to the visual arts that Yeats used so frequently to describe his art began to shift. The gap between poet and subject that had been reflected in the painting-poem analogy now diminished. The poetry became explicitly autobiographical: Yeats, transformed but recognizable, entered his own poems, and as in life, stood among the people and objects of their world. Frequently, those people—Lady Gregory, Robert Gregory, and others—became the center of attention; displacing the landscapes of Sligo and the Rosses that had so predominated in the early poems. Yeats's descriptions of his psychical experiments indicate the nature of the change: "there may float before our eyes a mask as strange and powerful as the lineaments of Servian's *Frowning Man* or of Rodin's *Man with the Broken Nose*" (fig. 30).[3] Painting would never disappear as metaphor, but more and more Yeats compared his poetry to sculpture. It conveyed better than painting the solid, humanly oriented sense of the mental and physical worlds he now held.

Yeats's experiments in the theater, as we have seen, taught him that taking sculpture as model for dramatic presentation allowed him to manipulate aesthetic distance for dramatic effect in a way that painting as model could not. That lesson Yeats adapted to poetry by using poetic space and form to create tension as the sculptor and dramatist use literal space and form. The sculptural analogy, furthermore, accorded with Yeats's desire to create monuments. History showed him that stone and bronze outlived paint, and he naturally conceived of his own monuments as analogous to those that survived the centuries. The twin impulses for dramatic effect and durability thus joined a new sense of the world in encouraging Yeats to adopt the sculptural analogy for poetry.

The "later poetry," from *Responsibilities* (1914) through *Last Poems* (1939), encompasses a wide range and contains its own divisions,[4] but sculpture as the predominant visual analogy persists throughout. From the poems of *Responsibilities* emerged the techniques for sculptural effects that Yeats later developed and mastered when his experiments with stage productions, his sense of life, and the experience of *A Vision* encouraged in numerous ways the sculptural analogy. *The Tower* is the height of Yeats's achievement in sculptural poetry, but all of the later volumes contain examples.

The variety of Yeats's later verse is too great to expect the sculptural analogy to account for all its effects. It does, however, describe many of the most characteristic, as its frequent appearance in discussions of Yeats's later work suggests. Daniel Albright, for example, speaks of the "chiselled magniloquence" of "News for the Delphic Oracle" (1939); Frank Kermode proposes that the pastoral offered Yeats in "Shepherd and Goatherd" (1919) "a possibility of achieving an interesting stoic coldness, as of carved flames"; Edward Engelberg, who identifies Yeats as a spatial poet, discovers in the poems "images of Space, concrete images of sculpture"; and Richard Ellmann thinks that Yeats's "last years" in general "suggest the violence of some Hellenistic statute with Yeats 'ravening, raging, and uprooting that he may come/Into the desolation of reality.'"[5] As these comments suggest, however, the analogy is often used casually and with no specific sense of what sculpture is or what effects it creates. Without an understanding of how sculpture differs from painting, it is difficult to say precisely why Yeats's later poems seem sculptural rather than pictorial. Examining Yeats's own use of the sculptural analogy as well as the nature of sculpture itself will, then, establish a context for discussing how Yeats's poetry can be called sculptural.

Yeats's own conscious or half-conscious efforts to create sculptural poetry account, in part, for the poetic effects that prompt critics to the sculptural analogy. As his use of Michelangelo in the later poems and his preoccupation with monuments suggest, Yeats came to think of his craft as violently active, of his material as hard and sometimes resistent, and of his product as solid and permanent. He no longer saw poems as Pre-Raphaelite tapestries or himself as a weaver. Nor did he conceive of his women as Rossetti portraits or of his scenes as Palmer or Calvert landscapes. At times Yeats used an architectural analogy for his later work, as when he wrote his biographer Joseph Hone in 1916: "Your difficulties have come from my house being still unfinished, there are so many rooms and corridors that I am still building upon foundations laid long ago."[6] In Stockholm to accept the Nobel Prize in January 1924, Yeats had been impressed by the city's buildings.[7] A month later, probably encouraged as well by Pound, who believed that in a renaissance "architecture comes first, being the finest branch of advertisement," Yeats publicly wished for "a fine school of building here in Dublin."[8] In the end, however, and despite Thoor Ballylee's fitness as monument and symbol, architecture lacked the explicitly human focus and suppler forms of Yeats's world. Those he found in Greek and Renaissance sculpture.

Sculpture joined painting and poetry as "the arts" Yeats mentioned in the later poems and prose (*E&I* 396), the chisel appeared with the pen as the representative tools of the trade (*Myth* 339; c.f. *VP* 623), and "mould" became a favorite verb for creative activity (e.g., *E&I* 354). Yeats described the process of calling up images, the poet's job, as analogous to the sculptor's work. In the second of the four states of mediation he found "the dreamer creating his dream, the sculptor toiling to set free the imprisoned image;"[9] by the third, there is "nothing left but the statue and dream."[10] Sculpture also provided frequent examples of *A Vision*'s lunar phases by which Yeats measured and placed his own artistic creativity. Occasionally, he thought explicitly of himself and the poets he admired as sculptors, working most often in stone. Dante, who shared Yeats's phrase, "set his chisel to the hardest stone,"[11] and Yeats described his own writing in similar terms: "Tragic drama must be carved out of speech as a statue is out of stone."[12] In *Per Amica Silentia Lunae* (1918) Yeats indicated the change that had come over his verse when he called Morris's muse "indolent," his own "marmorean" (*Myth* 328, 325).

Both romantic and modern concepts of art offered Yeats precedent for the idea of poetry as sculpture. A. W. Schlegel in the early nineteenth century had distinguished the ancient world from his own by establishing a correspondence between literature and the visual arts: "the spirit of ancient poetry is *plastic,* and that of the moderns *picturesque.*"[13] Yeats, who may have known Schlegel's distinction from Coleridge,[14] had explicitly rejected the late nineteenth century's decadent descendent of the "picturesque" (*L* 98) and espoused the "plastic," which Yeats, too, identified with the ancients, especially those at phase 15. Indeed, Yeats considered plasticity a prerequisite for Unity of Being in life and art in any age. Discussing Gen. Eoin O'Duffy, leader of Ireland's Fascist National Guards, Yeats wrote in 1933:

> He seemed to me a plastic man but I could not judge whether he would prove plastic to the opinions of others, obvious political current, or to his own will ('Unity of being'). The man plastic to

> his own will is always powerful. The opposite kind of man is like a mechanical toy, lift him from the floor and he can but buzz. (*L* 814)

Yeats, opposed always to the mechanical, conceived of the self not as evanescent, but as solid and malleable, and of the man who can mold himself as possessing Unity of Being. Similarly, he thought of the artist's material as plastic and knew the artist must mold it to his will to achieve a unified work of art. In *The Oxford Book of Modern Verse* Yeats consequently set W. J. Turner above Pound for his "control of plastic material," his "power of emotional construction," which gave his work the unity Pound's lacked (*OBMV* xxviii).

Unlike Schlegel and the romantics, however, Yeats did not think of plastic form, of sculpture, as still.[15] He had encountered the stillness of classical statues in Pater as well as in Coleridge and Keats.[16] His own early poems—"The Wanderings of Oisin," "The Island of Statues," and the prefatory lyric to *Vivien and Time,* written when he was most under romantic influence—had played with the implications of sculpture as calm, cold, and seemingly wise.[17] But by 1909 Yeats had discovered in Greek sculpture, as Whitaker has observed, "not repose and moderate passion but 'that energy which seems measureless.'"[18] The active nature of Phidias' and Michelangelo's sculptural forms emerged as a theme in the later poems, as we have seen.

Yeats heard the sculptural analogy most vigorously expressed in his own day by Ezra Pound. Despite his campaign against the arts that defined themselves in terms of one another, and his denial that Vorticism had anything to do with him as a writer,[19] Pound constantly spoke of his art as analogous to the visual arts, especially sculpture.[20] He claimed that his poem "The Return," which Yeats admired,[21] "is an objective reality and has a complicated sort of significance, like Mr. Epstein's 'Sun God,' or Mr. Brzeska's 'Boy with a Coney'" (figs. 28, 29). The analogy extended to form as well as "significance": Pound described his *imagiste* poems, which include "The Return," as the "sort of poetry where painting or sculpture seems as if it were 'just coming over into speech.'" Pound, like Yeats, saw the chisel as analogous to the pen: in 1916 he advised the poet Iris Barry to follow the "sculptor's directions: 'Take a chisel and cut away all the stone you don't want.'"[22]

Pound acquired some of his fondness for the sculptural analogy from Théophile Gautier, the inspiration of the Aesthetic Movement, who in *Victor Hugo* (1835) had "announced that the difference between a block of stone and a statue lay in its form, that the poet, too, was a sculptor, for he carved ideas and images out of words."[23] Gautier's idea of art had influenced the English poets of the 1890s, and their poems may have affected Yeats's as well as Pound's claim for the sculptural effects of poetry.[24] Pound explicitly admired the hardness of Lionel Johnson's work, and Yeats remembered the same poet "creating, to use a favorite adjective of his, 'marmorean' verse," an adjective Yeats later adopted for his own muse.[25] Yeats also surely knew Rossetti's claim,

> A sonnet is a moment's monument . . .
> Carve it in ivory or in ebony . . .
> A sonnet is a coin[26]

But both Pound and Yeats conceived of the stone they cut as larger than that of Gautier, Rossetti, or their followers. Pound might admire the craftsmanship of the lapidary verse inspired by Gautier's *Emaux et Camées* (Enamels and Cameos), but he rejected its limited ambition. "Mauberley 1920" suggests that medallions will not do as poems, and Pound went to work on the enormous stone, *The Cantos*.[27] There is no evidence to suggest that Yeats was tempted to work in the lapidary mode. He engaged wholeheartedly in soliciting designs for the new Irish coins in 1928, but from the beginning he conceived of his work as grander. In the *Autobiographies* he described his desire to emulate the 140-foot tomb of Mausolus, whose statues he saw at the British Museum,[28] those "monumental effigies" Pound invoked in "Homage to Sextus Propertius" (fig. 49).[29]

Pound as sculptural poet, however, wanted the angular forms of Gaudier-Brezska or Epstein to emerge under his hand, while Yeats wanted the Parthenon horsemen or Michelangelo's Medici tomb sculptures (figs. 35, 38, 39). Pound praised the geometrical art of the ancient Egyptians who inspired the Vorticists; Yeats deemed them, as "Under Ben Bulben" says, "stark." While he half admired the unbridled energy of Epstein's *Stone Drill*,[30] Yeats preferred the "gentler Phidias," whose statues possess the curves of living, not abstract, form, and who referred all back to the human body made perfect by mathematical proportion, not to mathematics alone.

Despite the differences, Yeats's use of sculptural analogies to describe his own work was supported by those he admired both past and present. He sometimes grouped the pictorial and the sculptural together and admired pictures whose figures presented the illusion of sculptural form, but painting and sculpture were for Yeats distinct, if related, arts. His use of the sculptural analogy for poetry, as for stage presentation, thus reflected a desire to achieve effects the pictorial analogy did not suggest. Yeats sensed, although he did not always clearly express, the important differences between painting and sculpture, and many of his later poems reflect that difference.

Figure 49. Mausolus from the Mausoleum Halicarnasus, 359–351 B.C. Courtesy of the Trustees of the British Museum, London.

The sculptural analogy as used in general is often, Austin Warren and René Wellek observe, "merely a vague metaphor."[31] The vagueness derives from the lack of a clear definition of sculpture itself and from the consequent difficulty of systematically exploring how poetry might achieve sculptural effects.[32] Traditionally, sculpture has been considered "a subsidiary art that merely translates the innovations of painting into three dimensions."[33] Yeats's own statements, however, show that his sense of sculpture was not so simplistic. We know that he considered its material hard and durable, as opposed to paint, and that it offered the movement he missed in the Pre-Raphaelite paintings and Byzantine mosaics he also admired. There is more, too, than Yeats's overt statements indicate. As earlier with the pictorial analogy, his use of the sculptural analogy involves a more complex sense of the art than he was aware. That sense, nevertheless, shows itself in the poems and prompts our impulse to call them sculptural.

Aesthetic discussions, which have begun to distinguish sculpture as an autonomous art, define some particular qualities of sculpture implied in Yeats's allusions to it and important to his poetry. Sculpture is, primarily, a tactual rather than a visual art.[34] By abstracting color, light, line, and texture from the solidity of objects, painting appeals mainly to the eye, while sculpture asks the viewer to touch it, to feel its forms as they curve out of sight, to explore the textures of its material.[35] "Since Rodin's time," commented Herbert Read in his pioneering work on the aesthetics of sculpture, *The Art of Sculpture,* "there has arisen a virtually new art—a concept of a piece of sculpture as a three-dimensional mass occupying space and only to be apprehended by senses that are alive to its volume and ponderability, as well as to its visual appearance."[36] Yeats, who participated as we have seen, in the general enthusiasm for sculpture Rodin spurred, does not seem to have anticipated the aesthetic theorists by explicitly identifying sculpture as a tactual art, but he did think of it as something molded by the hands—Callimachus "handled marble as if it were bronze" (*VP* 566)—and played with the literal as well as metaphorical hardness of stone, such as that Dante set his chisel to.[37] Increasing blindness may have made Yeats more aware of the tactual qualities of art in general; he praised the "roughened surface of the bricks" in the Stockholm Town Hall, thinking it helped take "away all sense of mechanical finish" (*Au* 555).

Unlike the space before a painting, the space around a sculpture contributes to the aesthetic experience. The space between a viewer and a painting is "inert"—the viewer must imaginatively overcome it to enter the space presented in the painting. The space between a sculpture and a viewer, on the other hand, is "enlivened."[38] It plays an active role in our experience of the sculpture; it is, in fact, an integral part of the art, not something to be "gotten over" that we may then perceive the work. Because of the nature of sculptural space, we do not actually have to touch a sculpture to experience it tactually. F. David Martin explains: "the space around a sculpture, although not a part of its material body, is still an essential part of the perceptible structure of that sculpture. And the perceptual forces in that surrounding space impact on our bodies directly, giving to that space a translucency, a thickness, that is largely missing from the space in front of a painting."[39]

Because of the role of its surrounding space, sculpture is more "immediate" than painting. "Sight-space," that in front of a painting, is, as Martin explains, "'distant-space'—our eyes must normally be some distance from the thing seen." In painting, there is always a subject-object dichotomy between both painter and painted, and viewer and painting. "Touch-space," that around a sculpture, "is 'near-space'—our skins directly touch the thing."[40] The subject-object dichotomy diminishes. Sculpture, thus, "gives us a sense of 'withness' that no other art achieves."[41] As we saw in chapter 4, Yeats recognized this difference in our experience of the two arts and related it to poetry when, in a 1904 *Samhain*, he distinguished pictorial poetry from dramatic, gestural (sculptural) poetry: "When the tide of life sinks low there are pictures, as in the *Ode on a Grecian Urn* and in Virgil at the plucking of the Golden Bough. The pictures make us sorrowful. We share the poet's separation from what he describes" (*Ex* 163). In 1917 the distinction resurfaced in Ille's (Willie's, said Ezra Pound) famous depiction of Keats, always for Yeats a pictorial poet:[42] "I see a schoolboy when I think of him,/With face and nose pressed to a sweet-shop window . . ./Shut out from all the luxury of the world" (*VP* 370). The opposite example for both Yeats and his father was Michelangelo, who did not "admire" life as Keats did when he gazed on the sweets, but "loved" it in its midst: "How Michel Angelo *loved* life," J. B. Yeats wrote his son in 1914, "is visible in his moulding and carving of the human body which palpitates with a too sentient life."[43] When Yeats, a year before, had explained his new poetic goals to his father, he expressed his desire for the immediacy sculpture can give: he wished his readers to "feel the presence of a man thinking and feeling" (*L* 583).

Sculpture, as Read points out in the passage already quoted, depends on the effects of its actual "volume and ponderability"—its three-dimensionality—effects that painting only hints at by illusion. Because of its literal presence as an object in this world—unlike an object in a painting which always belongs to the picture's world—sculpture remains tied to physical life. The idealized forms of a Greek sculpture may imply otherworldly perfection, but its solidity keeps it anchored to earth.[44] The very fact of its three-dimensional form, furthermore, endows sculpture with an illusion of movement that belies its status as a static work of art and puts it in harmony with the flux of the natural world. A painting remains fixed no matter where we stand to observe it; a sculpture changes and transforms as we move.[45] The painter must settle for the non-natural, artificial stasis that accompanies artifice; the sculptor can have both the motion of nature and the finality of art. As early as 1906, Yeats, not yet thinking much about sculpture, had realized the connection between movement, physical presence, and attachment to life. In the famous passage of a letter to Florence Farr, he explained that he had started Eastern meditation "with the object of trying to lay hands upon some *dynamic* and *substantializing* force as distinguished from the eastern quiescent and supersensualizing state of the soul—*a movement downwards upon life,* not upwards out of life."[46]

Sculpture could serve Yeats's purposes, however, precisely because it could be so worldly and otherworldly at the same time: Greek statues embody an ideal of perfection. They are present in three-dimensional space, inhabitors of our world, but they are also art, connected to a world beyond ours. The tension produced is precisely what made sculpture, as we have seen, a satisfying model for dramatic presentation. In the later poems, Yeats played with, as well as on, the paradox. His recognition that even images that "keep a marble or bronze repose" "break hearts" leads to "Among School Children"'s climactic apprehension of body united to soul (*VP* 445–446). In "A Bronze Head," Yeats immediately sees the sculpture of Maud Gonne as "Human, superhuman." The poem suggests that the bronze head—which triggers the meditation on Maud Gonne's dual nature—may itself express both her earthy "wildness" and her "supernatural" look (*VP* 618–619).

Yeats's sculptural references here and elsewhere point to one of the most striking facts about sculpture: that nine-tenths of it depicts the human body. Herbert Read speculates that this arises from man's need for a self-image.[47] Physically incapable of viewing himself whole, man creates a replica—a statue—which he can see. Painted images, because they cannot reproduce three-dimensional physical presence, may not satisfy as well as sculpted images. Yeats, looking from the beginning for a self-image, had always been interested in his own portraits. Several were sculpted: a bronze mask by Kathleen Bruce (1908; *L* 507), a bronze bust "mounted on a rough block of green mable" by Albert Power (1917; *L* 627), and "a fine bust" by Mary Klauder (1936; *L* 857). These sculpted portraits and Yeats's admiration for the last two in particular suggest that his desire for poetic self-portraiture may be a sculptural as well as a pictorial analogy. Furthermore, if Read's theory is correct, Yeats's desire for self-portraiture itself is a sculptural impulse in that it coincides with the fundamental need that prompted the creation of most of the world's sculpture.

Sculpture's traditional association with the human figure accorded in general with Yeats's interest in people as poetic subjects. Read claims that the image of the self the sculptor projects in his work is drawn in part from the images of those around him. The gaps in self-knowledge left by man's inability to see all of himself are filled by observation of others.[48] Yeats's poetic self-portraiture similarly depends on such observation for completeness. Maud Gonne, Lady Gregory, John Millington Synge, Lionel Johnson, Robert Gregory exist for their own sakes in the poems, but they also contribute to the image of Yeats that emerges. In addition, as portraits in their own right, Yeats's images of friends and acquaintances are connected to sculpture in their memorializing function. Yeats's awareness of statues as common forms of memorial and his concern that statues of Irish heroes be well executed encouraged his impulse to think of his own portraits as sculptural.[49]

Sculpted images of people also served a metaphysical purpose for Yeats. *A Vision* had taught him that "The first portraits were statues buried in tombs and buried there, as we believe, to assist the *Spirit* in its *Dreaming Back* (*AV-A* 240). Sculpture could, in other words, provide an image of the self after life, as in life. Sculpted portraits could give the spirit a model from which to fashion those bodies that appeared to Yeats as materializations. The soul possesses, he believed, "a plastic power," which allows it to "mould" the body "to any shape it will" (*Myth* 349). Yeats had "no doubt" that a sculpted portrait he had admired in the Egyptian Room of the British Museum had "helped a dead man to build out of his spirit-body a recognisable apparition" (*Ex* 69). Such a belief probably prompted part of Yeats's interest in the sculpted portraits of himself, and may have given extra significance to his own portraits of others.

Sculpture, finally, possesses an inherent unity that painting does not. The palpability of sculpture, Read argues, involves not only the surface touch, but the sense of holding the work in its entirety.[50] Sculpture is round, whole, of itself, independent. This explains why great sculpture, true to its medium, has a certain compactness.[51] Yeats found plasticity, as we have seen, a prerequisite for Unity of Being in general. He discovered such unity realized in "A Bronze Head" and in those images that "keep a marble or a bronze repose," forms molded or carved from plastic material according to the sculptor's will. The appeal of such unity to Yeats needs no explanation.

Yeats's later verse may be considered sculptural in that both the poetic images and the poems themselves possess the qualities of sculpture. They have "volume and ponderability," a weight, solidity, wholeness, and presence that distinguish them from the early pictorial images and poems.

Yeats endowed his images with sculptural qualities most explicitly by turning more often to sculpture for source, subject, and symbol than he had before. In his introduction to *The Words upon the Window-Pane,* he proclaimed:

> Let images of basalt, black, immovable,
> Chiselled in Egypt, or ovoids of bright steel
> Hammered and polished by Brancusi's hand,
> Represent spirits.
>
> (*Ex* 367)

The poems speak, as we have seen, of Phidias' statues, of Michelangelo's *Morning* and *Night,* and of Callimachus' "handiwork." Yeats meditated on Laurence Campbell's bronze-painted plaster head of Maud Gonne in the Dublin Municipal Gallery, envisioned himself as "A weather-worn, marble triton," and found poetic analogue in Raphael's statue of a dolphin (*VP* 329; *LTSM* 165). The overt references automatically call up sculptural images, and the sculptural sources perhaps suggest them. Furthermore, like the second musician in a draft of the opening lines of *The King of the Great Clock Tower,* Yeats sometimes turned to sculpture's hard materials, metal or stone, for imagery:

> I call to mind the iron of the bell
> And get from that my harsher imagery,
> All love is shackled to mortality,
> Love's image is a man-at-arms in steel;
> Love's image is a woman made of stone
>
> (*L* 817)

Yeats had heard from Pound about the "hard" in poetry and chose, as one of the three Pound selections for *The Oxford Book of Modern Verse,* Canto XVII, set in "the forest of marble."[52] Yeats's later poems are filled with the stones of the Irish countryside, the "bronze and marble" of its ancestral houses (*VP* 418), and the stones of Thoor Ballylee (e.g., *VP* 406, 419). "The Second Coming"'s "rough beast," which recalls Egypt's stone sphinx, emerges from "twenty centuries of stony sleep"; the fanaticism that Yeats thought heralded its coming "enchanted" the hearts of the 1916 revolutionaries "to a stone" (*VP* 402, 393). The poems sometimes speak, directly or indirectly, of the hardness of images: in "Ego Dominus Tuus" Ille argues that Dante "fashioned from his opposite/An image that might have been a stony face"; in "Byzantium," "golden smithies" and the "Marbles of the dancing floor" "Break bitter furies of complexity" transforming the unpurged images of life to the purged images of a metallic art; and "Old iron" is among the refuse of the heart's "rag-and-bone shop" where images begin (*VP* 368, 498, 630).

Such evocations of sculptural form and material, however, are relatively rare in Yeats's later verse. Sculpture as source and reference occurs no more often than painting, and stone and metal are almost as frequent in the early as in the later poetry. The images of the later poems are most often sculptural in a subtler way: they possess the qualities of sculpture without being linked directly to it. They have "volume and ponderability": they seem "solid" as critics frequently note;[53] they are tactual as much as visual; they seem to exist as three-dimensional forms in a space that we as readers share with them; and they appear to us as immediate and present.

"Ponderability and volume" also describe ordinary objects simply as they exist in the world. The sculptural analogy might thus seem unnecessary to explain the nature of Yeats's images. We could say, instead, that they are lifelike and point out that their special quality seems to have arisen from Yeats's sense of being in life as opposed to viewing it from a distance. But "lifelike" cannot account for the peculiar tension that exists between the images and the reader. As Richard Ellmann observes about the language of Yeats's middle and late poetry,[54] the poet advocates "The natural words in the natural order" (*LDW* 62), but rarely does the verse sound like normal speech, reminding us that while there is some relation to life, this is art. The poems may be peopled by familiar personages in familiar places, but both are, by various methods, heightened and transformed. We as readers never feel as comfortable with the images of Yeats's poems as with the objects of this world or of another poetic world, for instance, Robert Frost's. While we seem to share their space and perceive them as present and palpable, we are constantly aware that they belong to another realm. This tension is precisely that which defines the relation between viewer and sculpture and which Yeats exploited when he took sculpture as model for dramatic presentation.

Unlike Yeats the dramatist, however, Yeats the poet did not manipulate actual physical form. His poems create the illusion of sculpture. It might seem, then, that certain kinds of painting that also create the illusion of sculpture—such as the work of two artists Yeats especially admired in later life, Michelangelo and Poussin—might provide a more fitting analogy. That analogy, however, would still lead back to sculpture itself, and there seems no reason to take the circuitous route through sculptural painting, especially when Yeats suggests the direct route.[55]

Like sculpture, the images of Yeats's later poems seem immediate and present in a way that they do not in the early poems. The sense of immediacy derives first from Yeats's increased awareness of the reader in relation to the speaker and the poetic world. Rather than "eavesdropping" on the poet's contemplation, as Ellmann nicely explains the position of the reader in the early poems, the reader is now taken into the poetic world, often as audience to a speech addressed to another, sometimes as direct recipient of a speech.[56] The aesthetic distance that characterized the early verse and that marks the relation of viewer and painting diminishes; the reader apprehends the poetic world as here and now.

Yeats created temporal and spatial immediacy in a number of ways. The abrupt opening of many poems assumes the reader's presence in a common world. "Meditations in Time of Civil War" begins in the midst of a conversation between poet and reader: "Surely among a rich man's flowering lawns" (*VP* 417). At times, the speaker demands the reader's presence by opening with one of those questions so characteristic of the later Yeats ("Why should not old men be mad?"; "O what has made that sudden noise?" [*VP* 625, 583]), or asking a question in the midst of speech ("What can I but enumerate old themes?" [*VP* 629]). Both compel the reader to listen even when the question is not addressed to him, and even though it demands no answer. Sometimes, however, the speaker turns directly to the reader, asking, for example, "You ask what I have found" or commanding in the imperative: "Come let us mock at the great"; "Come, let me sing into your ear"; "Remember all those renowned generations"; "Get all the gold and silver that you can,/Satisfy ambition, animate/The trivial days and ram them with the sun,/And yet upon these maxims meditate" (*VP* 580, 432, 524, 613, 500).

In many poems the reader is not so abruptly summoned into the poetic world, but seduced by Yeats's use of the present tense: "I meditate upon a swallow's flight"; "I walk through the long schoolroom questioning"; "Picture and book remain,/An acre of green grass/For air and exercise,/Now strength of body goes" (*VP* 488, 443, 575). The action these first lines signal is happening now, and the reader witnesses it. Although the speaker may talk to himself, the reader is present as silent companion. The present tense functions similarly in poems where the speaker specifically addresses someone other than the reader. In "After Long Silence," it draws the reader into the room where speaker and lover talk: "Speech after long silence; it is right,/All other lovers being estranged or dead . . . That we descant and yet again descant/Upon the supreme theme of Art and Song" (*VP* 523).

Frequent "now"s create and reinforce temporal immediacy,[57] as in the passage quoted above from "An Acre of Grass." So, too, with: "Now days are dragon-ridden, the nightmare/Rides upon sleep"; and "Upon the border of that lake's a wood/Now all dry sticks under a wintry sun" (*VP* 429, 490).

Yeats creates spatial immediacy—makes the reader feel he inhabits a three-dimensional world that is here—by using the demonstrative adjectives "this" and "that" to indicate objects in a commonly shared space,[58] and by using adverbs to locate objects in a world with depth as well as height and breadth. When Yeats asks, "How can I, that girl standing there,/My attention fix/On Roman or on Russian/Or on Spanish politics?" (*VP* 631), we as readers are not only drawn into the world, but we perceive that world spatially. We and the reader stand here, that girl—the speaker points her out for us—is there. So, too, in "The Delphic Oracle upon Plotinus":

> Behold that great Plotinus swim,
> Buffetted by such seas . . .
> Scattered on the level grass
> Or winding through the grove
> Plato there and Minos pass,
> There stately Pythagoras
> And all the choir of Love.
> (*VP* 530–531)

Or the magnificent opening line of "A Bronze Head," which immediately establishes the presence of the object in three-dimensional space:

> Here at right of the entrance this bronze head,
> Human, superhuman, a bird's round eye
> (*VP* 618)

Or in "The Tower" where the poet gazes over the countryside and points out the places made famous by story:

> I pace upon the battlements and stare
> On the foundations of a house, or where
> Tree, like a sooty finger, starts from the earth . . .
> Beyond that ridge lived Mrs. French . . .
> Some few remembered still when I was young
> A peasant girl commended by a song,
> Who'd lived somewhere upon that rocky place
> (*VP* 409–410)

Or the opening line of the collection *The Tower,* "That is no country for old men" (*VP* 407).

Colloquial language, particularly as characterized by unexpectedly unpoetic diction and syntactic compression, furthers the sense of presence. As Ellmann has shown, Yeats's diction and syntax are far from those of normal speech, but they do, nevertheless, create the impression of a person speaking. Yeats, of course, aimed particularly for that and explained his goal in terms of presence: "I have tried to make my work con-

Figure 50. Nicolas Poussin, Acis and Galatea (formerly *The Marriage of Peleus and Thetis),* 1628–1630.
The National Gallery of Ireland, Dublin.

vincing with a speech so natural and dramatic that the hearer would feel the presence of a man thinking and feeling" (*L* 583). The much-discussed colloquial diction and the syntactic compression Yeats accomplished by dropping articles and verbs, as in "where/Tree, like a sooty finger, starts" or "Here at right of the entrance this bronze head," convey the presence not only of another human being, but of common space. The casualness of linguistic shortcuts and expression reduces the distance between reader and poetic world.

In "News for the Delphic Oracle" (1939; *VP* 611–612), we can see Yeats's techniques for creating spatial and temporal immediacy at work, transforming the pictorial scene of the opening section to the sculptural scene of the last part, making present and immediate the world of past heroes and past deeds depicted in section 3's source, Poussin's painting *The Marriage of Peleus and Thetis* (fig. 50).[59] The poem opens with a comic picture of the "golden codgers," "Man-picker Niamh," Oisin, "Tall Pythagoras," and Plotinus with "salt-flakes on his breast" lounging and sighing in the grass and silver dew.[60] The past tense removes the scene from us temporally, as the repeated "there" does spatially. We gaze across the "sight-space" and view the picture. The gold and silver in the first two lines alert us, as they do in other poems, that we look on the world of art.

But there is a discomforting paradox in the combination of past tense and "there." "There all the golden codgers lay, / There the silver dew" may create a picture separated from us by sight-space, but its abruptness as an opening and its "there" place us in the landscape the golden codgers once occupied. As in "The Tower," we stand with the speaker as he points out particular places where past events occurred. That sense of spatial relation is reinforced by "came," which suggests "here, to this place," not "there" ("Plotinus came and looked about"), and by the casual language that pervades the poem and allies us with the speaker ("Man-picker," "looked about," "pitch," and, of course, "belly," "brutal," and "bum").

Because part 1's spatial continuity jars with its temporal discontinuity, part 2's slip into the present tense seems somehow right—it resolves the discrepancy—and Yeats thus wins our willingness to believe in the temporal immediacy of the stanza's supernatural events. The scene remains at some distance, as "Those Innocents" and the vague "some cliff-sheltered bay" suggest, but the action is happening now as we watch: "Straddling each a dolphin's back / And steadied by a fin, / Those Innocents re-live their death, / Their wounds open again."

Suddenly, in part 3, the scene is here as well as now. We do not view a picture as we did in part 1 or as we might expect given the source of this section's images. The pointing speaker of the first two parts has vanished. No longer do we stand here while the scene occurs "there." Abruptly we are in the midst of it: "Slim adolescence that a nymph has stripped, / Peleus on Thetis stares." As at the sudden introduction of the Chinamen at the beginning of "Lapis Lazuli"'s last section ("Two Chinamen, behind them a third" [*VP* 566]), past and present, there and here conflate. We witness:

> Foul goat-head, brutal arm appear,
> Belly, shoulder, bum,
> Flash fishlike; nymphs and satyrs
> Copulate in the foam.

The copulating nymphs and satyrs appear not only immediate and present but disconcertingly palpable. They seem to be solid and round, to have volume and weight. They seem tactual. It is this tangibility, which critics often remark, combined with the presence and immediacy, that make the images of the later poems seem so sculptural. Here, as in much of the later poetry, Yeats relies on nonvisual senses to create his world. Yet the verse does not appeal to the senses through description. The adjectives so plentiful in the early poetry as carriers of sensual detail become secondary to nouns and verbs in the later poetry.[61] "Slim," "delicate as an eyelid," and "fishlike" convey some sensual qualities, but they are not especially strong. There is none of the early Niamh's visual brilliance, nor is there that hardness of the images "Chiselled in Egypt" or "polished by Brancusi's hand." Yeats does, however, appeal to the ear, both in his explicit reference to "Intolerable music" and, more important, through the verse itself. The palpable quality of Yeats's images comes not from the meanings of the words, but through their sounds and rhythms.

Perhaps because our perception of sound is based on a tactual response—waves literally hit the ear drum and set it vibrating—and our production of sound is accompanied by the tactile sensations of mouth and vocal cords, we describe the sounds of language, especially those made by consonants, as hard or soft (as in a hard or soft *c*). Although alliteration in general is not characteristic of Yeats's verse, the harder consonant sounds, the "stops" *b, t, d, k,* and *g,* repeated in succession, stand out from the generally neutral sound patterns of the later verse and endow the poetic world with a seemingly physical hardness and roundness.[62] These sounds in the context of the English language are characterized by a slight pause, then an abrupt "explosion"—an absence followed by a sudden presence.[63] One seems to run up against the sound as if it were solid. "Foul *g*oa*t*-hea*d*, *b*ru*t*al arm appear, / *B*elly, shoul*d*er, *b*um" thus conveys not only the energy associated with explosive sounds, but a palpable physicality.[64] The *b*s, furthermore, seem to create an effect of roundness,[65] in part because the shape the mouth makes in forming the sound suggests the roundness of objects.[66] These are not examples of what W. K. Wimsatt calls "verbal mimesis" in which the sounds imitate the sense.[67] Verbal mimesis, however, attests to language's power to convey, through its sounds, the effects of objects in the world.

Hard sounds reinforce what Yeats's poems constantly remind us, that mortal life is bound to a physically present world. Although the beggar may be touched with the supernatural, Yeats's sounds insist he is earthbound: *"Beggar to beggar cried, being frenzy struck"* (*VP* 299). The hard *d*s of "In Memory of Major Robert Gregory"'s lines,

> I am accustomed to their lack of breath,
> But not that my dear friend's dear son,
> Our Sidney and our perfect man,
> Could share in that discourtesy of death
> (*VP* 325)

help make present and palpable the image of one who is absent. So, too, the hard sounds of "The Second Coming" aid the materialization of the image out of *Spiritus Mundi:*

> A shape with lion body and the head of a man,
> A gaze blank and pitiless as the sun,
> Is moving its slow thighs, while all about it
> Reel shadows of the indignant desert birds.
> The darkness drops again
>
> (*VP* 402)

"Under bare Ben Bulben's head" conveys the solid roundness of the mountain, and the less obtrusive consonants of "Among School Children" help body forth Yeats's most famous romantic image:[68]

> Labour is blossoming or dancing where
> The body is not bruised to pleasure soul,
> Nor beauty born out of its own despair,
> Nor bleared-eyed wisdom out of midnight oil.
> O chestnut-tree, great-rooted blossomer,
> Are you the leaf, the blossom or the bole?
> O body swayed to music, O brightening glance,
> How can we know the dancer from the dance?
>
> (*VP* 445–446)

The hard sounds of these verses would not be as noticeable if they were not emphasized by the forceful rhythms Yeats sought in the later poems. The "wavering, meditative, organic, rhythms" Yeats cultivated in the early poems have been replaced by "a strong driving force" (*E&I* 163; *L* 845–846). His early fondness for the anapestic with its "lightness and lilt" gives way to a preference for iambic and trochaic meters.[69] The emphatic quality of the latter, which Yeats used more often than most poets,[70] and which he sometimes combined with spondees, conveys, like emphatic sound, the solidity of the world. Yeats had recognized as early as his 1902 essay on Spenser that modern poetry, in becoming more spiritual, had "broken up . . . those great rhythms which move, as it were, in masses of sound" (*E&I* 380). He now wanted for his poetry the weight and tangibility "masses" implies. In poems like "The Black Tower," with its extra load of stressed syllables, he achieved those qualities:

> Say that the men of the old black tower,
> Though they but feed as the goatherd feeds,
> Their money spent, their wine gone sour,
> Lack nothing that a soldier needs,

That all are oath-bound men:
Those banners come not in.
(*VP* 635)

Masculine rhyme had been characteristic of Yeats's verse from the beginning, but now its ability to produce "an effect of some force and weight"[71] contributes to the sense of a palpable world. Rather than allowing the end of the line to drift up as feminine rhyme tends to, the masculine ending forces it down, making the poetic world seem solid and earthy.

Yeats, however, never allows us to believe for a moment that we are in the world. The images may seem immediate and palpable, but Yeats reminds us at every step that they are not lifelike. They are artlike, sculptural. While he deploys devices for lessening aesthetic distance, for drawing the reader into the poetic world, for creating a sense of immediacy, he simultaneously asserts the artificial. The methods are those he used in the theater. As in the Noh plays where the musicians unfolded and folded the cloth, so there is a ritualistic element in many of the poems. "All Souls' Night," for example, opens with the setting out of glasses of muscatel. The language, too, for all its colloquial feel, has a persistent formality in diction and syntax. "Yeats treads gingerly, and marvellously," as Ellmann comments, "between a distant and a familiar tone."[72] Objects of the poetic world, which seem three-dimensional and palpable, function, the poems remind us, not as mere settings or props, but as symbols. The tower is a tower, and we may stand on its battlements, but both tower and battlement are more. The sound and rhythm, furthermore, speak, as we have seen in the early poems, of an order that does not exist in the natural world. They help create a solidity, but their very presence reminds us it is the solidity of art.

Yeats's view of his poems as monuments as well as his desire for unity in all things suggest that he, like other modern artists, conceived of his works as objects. His poems were to be like the sculptural monuments he so admired: round, whole, independent, of themselves, enduring.

As early as 1903 Yeats wrote AE:

> The close of the last century was full of a strange desire to get out of form, to get to some kind of disembodied beauty, and now it seems to me the contrary impulse has come. I feel about me and in me an impulse to create form, to carry the realization of beauty as far as possible. The Greeks said that the Dionysiac enthusiasm preceded the Apollonic and that the Dionysiac was sad and desirous, but that the Apollonic was joyful and self suf-

> ficient. Long ago I used to define to myself these two influences as the Transfiguration on the Mountain and the Incarnation.

Six years later he noted in his journal:

> The Incarnation involved modern science and modern efficiency and also modern lyric feeling which gives body to the most spiritual emotions. It produced a solidification of all things that grew from the individual will.[73]

These two passages not only indicate the change in Yeats's idea of images—he would body them forth in his later poetry—but suggest his emerging concept of poetic form. He saw the movement away from all that tries to escape form, to be disembodied, and toward all that seeks solidification, material form; away from the Dionysiac whose desire and sadness grow from incompleteness, and toward the Apollonic with its self-sufficiency. Yeats's own symbol for unity, the egg or sphere, which he acquired from Blake and the theosophists and developed in his own system,[74] more clearly defined the kind of poetic form he wanted. In *The Oxford Book of Modern Verse* he proclaimed, "form must be full, sphere-like, single" (xxv), and he associated the poet's ability to create such form with his "control of plastic material" (xxviii). For Yeats, poetic form was, in the broadest sense, sculptural rather than pictorial.

Yeats's later poems acquired the solidity and three-dimensionality implied in "full, sphere-like" in part from their images. The palpability, presence, and volume they convey lend the poem as a whole those qualities. But "full, sphere-like, single" suggests that, in addition, Yeats wanted for a poem the unity and independence of a complete geometrical shape in space and the counteracting fullness that threatens to burst the self-contained form.[75] "The nobleness of the arts," Yeats had written in 1907, "is in the mingling of contraries, the extremity of sorrow, the extremity of joy, perfection of personality, the perfection of its surrender, overflowing turbulent energy, and marmorean stillness" (*E&I* 255). As the last pair suggests, nobility for Yeats arose from formal as well as emotional contraries. The tension of unified, perfected form constraining what it contains allies Yeats's poems to sculpture in general and to the sculpture most admired in particular. It is what both Pater and Yeats saw as the genius of Greek and Renaissance art: the centrifugal pulling against the centripetal,[76] measurement disciplining chaotic emotion. As Ellmann has observed, the analogy between Yeats's own work and the Greek sculpture he praised in "The Statues" "was clear: it too concentrated system and number into what seemed like casual flesh."[77] The opposition of geometrically founded structure and living energy contributes to the sculptural quality of Yeats's poems as wholes.

Yeats acquired formal tension most often by opposing stanzaic regularity and metrical and linear variety. He turned to the measurement he urged on Irish artists in "The Statues" to control the violence of emotion and speech that characterize the later poems. As Parkinson has noted, "Stanzaic formality was necessary to him for many reasons, but chiefly he required it as discipline for the passionate syntax he accepted as a norm."[78] Yeats rejected the free verse with which Pound and other contemporaries were experimenting because he recognized that it would drain the intensity out of his passion by giving it nothing to resist.

"Her Vision in the Wood" (*VP* 536–537), a poem full of the bitterness of old age and the redeeming power of the imagination's images, illustrates the pressure of "passionate syntax" against containing form.[79] The large structure of the poem is measured, classical: four stanzas of eight rhymed lines each, each stanza break coinciding, like the stanzas, with syntactic units.[80] But the poem resists in several ways that measured, balanced form, giving it the fullness, the pressure of material about to break its bounds. The turn in the poem comes not where we might expect, between stanzas two and three, but in the fourth line of the second stanza ("But the dark changed to red"), disturbing the neat two-plus-two division and joining together the central stanzas despite the period that separates them.

Similarly, within stanza one, Yeats plays with the tension between sentence end and line end:

> Dry timber under that rich foliage,
> At wine-dark midnight in the sacred wood,
> Too old for a man's love I stood in rage
> Imagining men. Imagining that I could
> A greater with a lesser pang assuage
> Or but to find if withered vein ran blood,
> I tore my body that its wine might cover
> Whatever could recall the lip of lover.

"Imagining men" completes the stanza's first sentence, but the line break and the seeming finality of "I stood in rage" divide it from its syntactic unit. Yeats furthers the tensions by repeating "imagining." The ear—especially if it is schooled in Yeats's early practice of stringing repeated words together in apposition—may hear the period as a comma and expect "Imagining that" to amplify "Imagining men." Yeats reckons on that effect: the repetition holds the line together, as "Imagining men" precipitates "Imagining that I could / A greater with a lesser pang assuage" and the self-wounding that attends it. But the period and the difference in imaginings force the line apart, expressing and echoing the violence of "I tore my body."

The greatest tension, however, is created by the pressure of the rhythm. While each line contains usually ten syllables, five of them stressed, there is no regular rhythm. Heavy beats pile up against each other (as in the first line above: "Dry timber under that rich foliage") and create both the sense of solidity already discussed and the "driving force" Yeats deliberately sought. The feeling of movement, as of a living form, is restrained, as in the sculpture Yeats admired, by measurement, by well-defined structure. The poem seems to take on a solid shape of its own; it seems "full, sphere-like, single." It conveys its own presence as it asserts the presence of the vision:

> Those bodies from a picture or a coin
> Nor saw my body fall nor heard it shriek,
> Nor knew, drunken with singing as with wine,
> That they had brought no fabulous symbol there
> But my heart's victim and its torturer.

"I remember your once writing to me," Yeats had reminded his father in 1912, "that all good art is good just in so far as it is intimate" (*L* 568). Two years later, J. B. Yeats, writing his son about good art's most important quality—intensity—echoed and emended his previous opinion: intensity conveys itself, he said, through "a strangeness yet with something familiar—one's secret heart answers to it as to a language learned in one's infancy and then forgotten."[81] The combination of familiarity and strangeness moves Yeats's later poems. The tension it creates for the reader who feels at once both qualities never permits an easy response. One is conscious always of the doubleness, as was Yeats. The ability of his images and poems to seem present and palpable as though they might come over into life—the Pygmalion myth so popular in the late nineteenth century[82]—yet their firm assertion that they are art, dramatizes for the reader the theme of many of the late poems. Absence and presence dominate Yeats's later poetry, especially the two volumes that are perhaps his best, *The Tower* and *The Winding Stair.*[83] In poems such as "All Souls' Night," "The Tower," and "Her Vision in the Wood" Yeats deals directly with the imagination's ability to create presence, to summon images in response to decay, destruction, absence of all kinds. The poems themselves are Yeats's response, yet they assert constantly their own inadequacy. The images of dead friends or past beauty that the heart calls to ease its pain will never suffice. Absence cannot be filled by such presence. Even the images summoned and embodied in art—presences that "keep a marble or a bronze repose," Yeats's poems—will themselves become absences and the cause of pain: "Many ingenious lovely things are gone / That seemed sheer miracle to the multitude" (*VP* 428). Yet the poems, especially those of *The Tower* where the sculptural qualities of the poetic images are most evident, assert the sureness of such absence in words that create a powerful sense of presence. The poems' own defiance of what they take to be certain gives the volume its poignance. The creations of the mind are not life—they are strange—yet their presence, their intimacy, is man's compensation for loss.

Notes

Introduction

1. Quoted in Robert O'Driscoll, "Yeats on Personality: Three Unpublished Lectures," in *Yeats and the Theatre,* ed. Robert O'Driscoll and Lorna Reynolds (Canada: Macmillan, 1975), pp. 26–27.

2. Hazard Adams, *Blake and Yeats: The Contrary Vision* (New York: Cornell University Press, 1955), pp. 4–5.

3. Frank Kermode, *The Romantic Image* (New York: Random House, 1957), p. 136.

4. Jan Mukařovský, "Between Literature and the Visual Arts," in his *The Word and Verbal Art,* ed. John Burbank and Peter Steiner (New Haven: Yale University Press, 1977), p. 208.

Chapter 1. Yeats and the Pre-Raphaelites

1. Harold Bloom, *Yeats* (New York: Oxford University Press, 1970), p. 29; Richard Ellmann, *The Identity of Yeats* (New York: Oxford University Press, 1964), p. 117; Louis MacNeice, *The Poetry of W. B. Yeats* (1941; reprint, New York: Oxford University Press, 1969), p. 61. For other discussions of Yeats and Pre-Raphaelite poetry, see Dwight Eddins, *Yeats: The Nineteenth Century Matrix* (University, Ala.: University of Alabama Press, 1971); Peter Faulkner, *William Morris and W. B. Yeats* (Dublin: Dolmen Press, 1962); Alan Phil Pistorius, "D. G. Rossetti and Early Yeats," Ph.D. diss., University of California, 1973.

2. See, e.g., George Bornstein on Yeats's 1893 lecture to the National Literary Society in Dublin, in *Transformations of Romanticism in Yeats, Eliot and Stevens* (Chicago: University of Chicago Press, 1976), pp. 31–32.

3. James Sambrook, "Introduction," in *Pre-Raphaelitism: A Collection of Critical Essays* (Chicago: University of Chicago Press, 1974), p. 1.

4. Hunt, for example, painted *The Light of the World* outdoors at night in order to depict accurately such details as the stand of weeds at the Saviour's feet (Timothy Hilton, *The Pre-Raphaelites* [London: Thames and Hudson, 1970], pp. 89–90).

5. Quoted in Sambrook, "Introduction," p. 3.

6. William M. Murphy, *Prodigal Father: The Life of John Butler Yeats (1839–1922)* (Ithaca: Cornell University Press, 1978), p. 61.

7. Ibid., p. 74; *Au* 44. Rossetti may also have admired J. B. Yeats's picture of Job and his wife. See Richard Ellmann, *Yeats: The Man and the Masks* (New York: Macmillan, 1948), pp. 12–13.

8. Highlights include Hall Caine, *Recollections of Dante Gabriel Rossetti* (1883); Joseph Knight, *The Life of D. G. Rossetti* (1887); Esther Wood, *D. G. Rossetti* (1894); J. G. Millais, *Life and Letters of John Everett Millais* (1899); Lady Burne-Jones, *Memorials of Edward Burne-Jones* (1904); and William Holman Hunt, *Pre-Raphaelitism and the Pre-Raphaelite Brotherhood* (1905).

9. Pistorius, "D. G. Rossetti and Early Yeats," pp. 52–60, presents a useful survey of Pre-Raphaelite works appearing in periodicals of the 1890s.

10. "The Desire of Man and Woman" (no. 2, 1897); "Aodh to Dectora / Three Songs" (no. 5, 1898); "The Song of Mongan" and "A Symbolic Artist and the Coming of Symbolic Art" (n.s., vol. 1, 1898); "The Theatre: A Note" (n.s., vol. 3, 1899); "'Dust Hath Closed Helen's Eye'—A Note" (n.s., vol. 4, 1899); "The Irish Literary Theatre, 1900" and "Aodh to Dectora" set to music (n.s., vol. 5, 1899–1900); "Symbolism in Modern Poetry" (n.s., vol. 6, 1900); "The Philosophy of Shelley's Poetry" (n.s., vol. 7, 1900).

11. Now housed in the Tate. For a complete list, see *The Collections of the Tate Gallery* (London: Tate Gallery, 1967).

12. Oscar Wilde, "Lecture on the English Renaissance," in *The Writings of Oscar Wilde* (London: Keller-Farmer, 1907), 9:105, 116. Graham Hough, in *The Last Romantics* (London: Gerald Duckworth, 1949), p. 203, contends that Wilde's influence was not great and was never accepted by the younger men. Yeats's *Autobiographies* would argue otherwise. Robin Spencer has claimed that "to Wilde is owed the ultimate distinction of turning Pre-Raphaelitism into a fin-de-siècle movement" (*The Aesthetic Movement: Theory and Practice* [London: Studio Vista, 1972], p. 98).

13. "Two Poems Concerning Peasant Visionaries / A Cradle Song" (in *Collected Poems,* 1950; "The Unappeasable Host") and "The Valley of the Black Pigs"; "Two Poems / The Shadowy Horses" ("He bids His Beloved be at Peace") and "The Travail of Passion"; "Windle-Straws / I. O'Sullivan Rua to the Curlew" ("He reproves the Curlew") and "II. Out of the Old Days" ("To his Heart, bidding it have no Fear"); "O'Sullivan Rua to the Secret Rose" ("The Secret Rose"); and the short story, "The Binding of the Hair."

14. *The Letters of Ernest Dowson,* ed. Desmond Flower and Henry Maas (London: Cassell and Company, 1967), pp. 150, 197.

15. Murphy, *Prodigal Father,* pp. 83, 74.

16. Duran, like J. B. Yeats, was a portrait painter. Contemporary reviews, with which Yeats would have agreed, described his work as "precise, definite, absolute—true, even to cruelty" and as "all *en-façade,* his charms are exterior,—he attracts you, holds you not,—and has said all when he has called out to you" (quoted in Clara Clement and Lawrence Hutton, *Artists of the Nineteenth Century and Their Work: A Handbook* [St. Louis: North Point, 1969], p. 226). The entry in *Bryan's Dictionary of Painters and Engravers,* rev. ed. (London: George Bell and Son, 1909), p. 94, gave a similar account of Bastien-Lepage: his work was "actual and realistic." Yeats owned the revised and enlarged edition of 1919-

1921; *YL* 46. In the *Autobiographies* Yeats disparages Lepage's "clownish peasant staring with vacant eyes at her great boots" (*Au* 125).

17. Ellmann, *Man and Masks*, p. 22.

18. James White, *W. B. Yeats: A Centenary Exhibition* (Dublin: National Gallery of Ireland, 1965), p. 61.

19. An engraving of this picture made it a well-known image in the nineteenth century, as did the sermons and devotional poetry it inspired. See George P. Landow, *William Holman Hunt and Typological Symbolism* (New Haven: Yale University Press, 1979), p. 35.

20. *Au* 140. According to Virginia Surtees, *The Paintings and Drawings of Dante Gabriel Rossetti (1828–1882): A Catalogue Raisonné*, 2 vols. (Oxford: Clarendon Press, 1971), 1:131–134, none of the eight versions of *Proserpine* was ever owned by Morris. Yet, this is the only painting that Yeats could have misnamed *Pomegranate*. Jane Morris did own an 1871 pastel and black chalk study and an 1874 pen and ink study for *Proserpine*. Yeats possibly saw one of these two studies. He may also have seen the painting in a number of exhibitions during the 1880s and 1890s. After 1899 Yeats would also have known the painting from H. C. Marillier's account in *Dante Gabriel Rossetti: An Illustrated Memorial of His Art and Life* (London: George Bell and Sons, 1899).

21. Ellmann, *Man and Masks*, p. 12; and Murphy, *Prodigal Father*, pp. 68–69, 116.

22. See Ian Jack, *Keats and the Mirror of Art* (Oxford: Clarendon Press, 1967), pp. 53–57, for a discussion of how *Annals of the Fine Arts* promoted the affinity between literature and the visual arts.

23. Hough, *Last Romantics*, p. 135. Wilde had pointed out to the nineties that Keats was a forerunner of the Pre-Raphaelites (Wilde, "Lecture on the English Renaissance," 9:104).

24. Percy H. Bate, *The English Pre-Raphaelites, Their Associates and Successors*, rev. ed. (London: George Bell and Sons, 1905), pp. 67–68, includes a plate of *Asia*. Rossetti had also pictured the Belle Dame in 1848 and 1855 (Surtees, *Paintings and Drawings of Dante Gabriel Rossetti*, 1:7, 39–40).

25. Yeats recalled those faces in 1913 when he visited the Tate to see its Pre-Raphaelite pictures (*E&I* 346). The copy of Shelley's poems that Yeats probably first read is now in the Pforzheimer Library. George Bornstein discusses it and the Pre-Raphaelite sketches in "Yeats's Copy of Shelley at the Pforzheimer Library," *Bulletin of Research in the Humanities* (Spring 1979), 53–62.

26. *Au* 114–115. The painting Yeats saw is an 1871 oil replica that Rossetti did of an 1856 watercolor. It was acquired by the Liverpool Corporation (Walker Art Gallery) in 1881 (Surtees, *Paintings and Drawings of Dante Gabriel Rossetti*, 1:44). For a discussion of Yeats and Dante as a romantic legacy, see George Bornstein, "Yeats's Romantic Dante," *Colby Library Quarterly* 15, no. 2 (June 1979), 93–113.

27. He often complained when drawings were uncolored—e.g., *UP* 1:184 (Burne-Jones); *E&I* 124 (Blake)—and frequently judged works of art on the basis of their use of color—e.g., his comments on the Parnell banner in the 1890 Arts and Crafts Exhibition (*UP* 1:185).

28. For an account of Bedford Park's beginnings, see Ian Fletcher, "Bedford Park: Aesthete's Elysium?" in *Romantic Mythologies*, ed. Ian Fletcher (New York: Barnes and Noble, 1967), pp. 169–207.

29. Dante Gabriel Rossetti, John Everett Millais, William Holman Hunt, James Collinson, William Michael Rossetti, Frederick Stephens, and Thomas Woolner.

30. Yeats recalled in 1937 that when he was thirty he considered "four or five pictures by Madox Brown" and "four or five early Millais" among "the best of modern pictures" (*E&I* vii). An 1890 review Yeats wrote of the Arts and Crafts Exhibition confirms that early view of Brown: it singled out two of Brown's works for special notice (*UP* 1 : 185–186). But after one more passing reference in "The Theatre" (1899), Brown dropped out of Yeats's published writings. Millais had been a favorite of J. B. Yeats, and Yeats must have frequently seen the large number of Millais acquired by the Tate during the 1890s. He owned a reproduction of a sketch for the early *Christ in the House of His Parents* (1849) and recorded in 1891 his pleasure in the illustrations done by Rossetti and Millais for William Allingham's *The Music Master* (1855). Millais illustrated "The Fireside Story" (*UP* 1 : 209). But by 1902 Yeats considered Millais one "whose art is founded upon the current art of his time . . . upon observation rather than upon imagination" (*UP* 2 : 292), a sentiment that Symons had expressed in his 1896 obituary notice of Millais, reprinted as "The Lesson of Millais," in *Studies on Modern Painters* (New York: W. E. Rudge, 1925). According to Yeats and his friends, Millais had crossed to the other side, his treason rewarded by knighthood and the presidency of the Royal Academy.

31. Yeats's "Preface" to *Letters to the New Island*, ed. Horace Reynolds (Cambridge: Harvard University Press, 1934), p. x, explains in passing his distaste for Hunt: "I spent my life among painters who hated the Royal Academy, popular art, fashionable life. I could remember some painter saying in my childhood, 'Holman Hunt will never come to anything, I have just heard that he gets his dress clothes at Poole's'—Poole was the most fashionable of all tailors." Arthur Symons supported this view of Hunt. He accused Hunt of having "no imagination," but he did allow that he had some "fancy" ("Romance, Reality and Imagination," in *Studies on Modern Painters*, p. 57).

32. This view of the movement is still current, as William E. Fredeman points out in *Pre-Raphaelitism: A Biocritical Study* (Cambridge: Harvard University Press, 1965), p. 21.

33. J. B. Yeats, *Early Memories; Some Chapters of Autobiography* (Dundrum: Cuala Press, 1923), p. 27.

34. Quoted in Ellmann, *Man and Masks*, p. 12.

35. Quoted in Murphy, *Prodigal Father*, p. 76.

36. Fredeman, *Pre-Raphaelitism*, p. 24.

37. In 1868 Walter Pater first used the term "aesthetic poetry" in discussing the work of Rossetti and his circle. Walter Hamilton's 1882 *The Aesthetic Movement* furthered the identification of Pre-Raphaelitism and aestheticism. See Fredeman, *Pre-Raphaelitism*, pp. 16–17.

38. John Dixon Hunt, "A Moment's Monument: Reflections on Pre-Raphaelite Vision in Poetry and Painting," in *Pre-Raphaelitism*, ed. Sambrook, p. 245.

39. Surtees, *Paintings and Drawings of Dante Gabriel Rossetti*, 1:191, 173.

40. John K. M. Rothenstein, in his account of his father, the painter William Rothenstein, confirms that this vision of Rossetti was current during the 1890s (*The Pot of Paint: The Artists of the 1890s* [1929; reprint, Freeport, N.Y.: Books for Libraries Press, 1970], p. 67).

41. *E&I* 53. For a short and helpful discussion of the discrepancy between Rossetti's aims and the 1890s perception of them, see Karl Beckson, "Introduction," in *Aesthetes and Decadents of the 1890s: An Anthology of British Poetry and Prose* (New York: Vintage Books, 1966), pp. xii–xxii.

42. Ellmann, *Man and Masks*, p. 12.

43. For an account of Rossetti's women, especially this aspect of them, see David Sonstroem, *Rossetti and the Fair Lady* (Middletown, Conn.: Wesleyan University Press, 1970).

44. *L* 287. *Astarte Syriaca* was the only Rossetti the museum owned at the time (1897). This information is derived from index of works owned and shown in Manchester (Surtees, *Paintings and Drawings of Dante Gabriel Rossetti*, 1:255).

45. Yeats owned an unmounted reproduction of an engraving (or possibly an etching) after Moreau's *La Chimère* (1867), oil on inlaid panel, now in the Fogg Art Museum, Harvard University. He also owned a reproduction of *Les Licornes* (c. 1885), unfinished oil, tempera, and watercolor on canvas, now in the Musée Gustave Moreau, Paris. Moreau, like the Pre-Raphaelites, attended to decorative detail and literary subjects, among them Salome, a favorite with Yeats's friends. In 1893 *The Dial* carried a note praising Moreau's Helen, which Giorgio Melchiori suggests affected Yeats's concept of Helen (*The Whole Mystery of Art: Pattern into Poetry in the Work of W. B. Yeats* [London: Routledge and Kegan Paul, 1960], p. 115). Arthur Symons also wrote on Moreau in *Studies in Seven Arts* (London: Martin Secker, 1924). See D. G. Gordon and Ian Fletcher, *W. B. Yeats: Images of a Poet* (Manchester: University of Manchester, 1961), pp. 96–98, for an account of Moreau's reputation among Yeats and his friends.

46. Charles Ricketts, Yeats's friend and a Pre-Raphaelite follower, probably introduced both Moreau and Puvis to Yeats (Gordon and Fletcher, *Images*, p. 96). Ricketts praised Puvis's "simplicity" (*Pages on Art* [London: Constable and Company, 1913], p. 76); that, along with his mythological subjects, his interest in mural painting and his admiration for Giotto and Piero della Francesca would have recommended him to Yeats. W. C. Brownell, whose *French Art* Yeats owned (*YL* 44), declared Puvis "unreal beyond the verge of mysticism" (*French Art: Classic and Contemporary Painting and Sculpture* [New York: Charles Scribner's Sons, 1901], p. 84). Yeats owned the Westminster edition published by Archibald Constable, 1902. Yeats also owned the well-illustrated *Puvis de Chavannes*, intro. Arsène Alexandre (London: George Newnes, [1905]). See *YL* 217. See also Gordon and Fletcher, *Images*, pp. 96–98, for an account of Puvis and Yeats.

47. George Frederic Watts had influenced Burne-Jones, had been associated with him in Ruskin's "The Mythic Schools of Painting," had been proclaimed by Symons "an attentive host to dreams and interpreter of souls" ("Watts," in *Studies in Seven Arts,* p. 60), and had been linked to Brown, Hunt, and Rossetti as well as to Burne-Jones in the pages of *The Savoy* (October 1896). During the 1890s the National Gallery acquired a number of his pictures, including the portrait of Morris, a reproduction of which later hung over Yeats's mantel and provided inspiration for his description of Morris in the *Autobiographies* (141). J. B. Yeats had also admired Watts; he copied him as a student and in 1914 boasted that Robert Henri considered J. B. Yeats's pictures better than Sargent's or Watts's (*Letters to His Son W. B. Yeats and Others, 1869–1922,* ed. Joseph Hone [London: Faber, 1944], p. 184). Following his father's interests, Yeats thought Watts a better painter of portraits than of allegories because the latter showed moralist tendencies (*E&I* vii). In 1906 Yeats delivered a lecture on Watts, "The Ideal in Art," to accompany Hugh Lane's Watts exhibit at the Royal Hibernian Academy. The *Daily Express*'s account of the lecture is printed in *UP* 2:342–345.

48. Although Whistler attempted to dissociate himself from the aesthetic movement in the Ten O'Clock Lecture, his admiration for Rossetti argued a Pre-Raphaelite connection that a picture like *Symphony in White* confirmed. Yeats saw Wilde and Whistler as the commanders of the intellectual world, keeping "literary London continually agog to know what they will say next" (*UP* 1:205), and the Rhymers unquestioningly accepted Whistler's proclamation that Japanese art had no literary ideas (*E&I* 349). Arthur Symons admired the decorative quality of Whistler's pictures (e.g., "Whistler," in *Studies in Seven Arts,* p. 74) and found that *At the Piano* summed up "all that was most significant in the Pre-Raphaelite movement" ("A Second View of Whistler," in *Studies on Modern Painters,* p. 37). J. B. Yeats had derided Whistler's portrait of his mother (*Au* 82–83), but in 1914 wrote an introductory notice to a catalog for a New York show of Whistler's works, *Oils, Water Colors, Pastels and Drawings by James McNeill Whistler* (New York: Knoedler Co., 1914). The copy of the catalog in Yeats's library contains Lily Yeats's bookplate dated 1914.

49. Beardsley had begun under the influence of Burne-Jones. His first work to gain public attention, the illustrations for John Dent's *Morte D'Arthur* (1893), which Yeats owned (*YL* 164), connected him to Pre-Raphaelite medievalism and showed a curiously transformed combination of Morris's decorative borders, Japanese prints, and Burne-Jones's sinuous figures. Arthur Symons's 1898 "Aubrey Beardsley," which Yeats called "a masterpiece" (*L* 298), indirectly linked him to the Pre-Raphaelites by emphasizing the decorative qualities of his art (*Studies in Seven Arts,* p. 105). Yeats praised the "patterns and rhythms" of Beardsley's line (*UP* 2:134), which on another occasion he described as "clean" and "swift" (*Mem* 92). Beardsley's drawings hung on the walls of Woburn Buildings next to a Rossetti (Melchiori, *Whole Mystery of Art,* p. 238; Joseph M. Hone, *W. B. Yeats, 1865–1939,* 2d ed. [New York: St. Martin's, 1962], p. 178). Yeats commissioned him for the cover design of *The Land of Heart's Desire* (1894) and for six illustrations to *The Shadowy Waters* (1896) of which Beardsley completed only one, and that was apparently never published with Yeats's work (David R. Clark, "Aubrey

Beardsley's Drawing of the 'Shadows' in W. B. Yeats's *The Shadowy Waters,*" *Modern Drama* 7, no. 3 [December 1964], 267–272).

50. Yeats's relation to these last three is discussed at length in chapter 3.

51. In addition to his collaboration with Edwin Ellis on *The Works of William Blake: Poetic, Symbolic and Critical,* 3 vols. (London: Bernard Quaritch, 1893), Yeats's enthusiasm for Blake resulted during the 1890s in an edition of *The Poems of William Blake* (London: Lawrence and Bullen, 1893); a review of the Parchment Library edition of Blake (*The Bookman,* August 1893); a review of Richard Garnett's *William Blake* (*The Bookman,* April 1896); "William Blake and His Illustrations to the *Divine Comedy*" (*The Savoy,* July, August, September 1896); "William Blake and the Imagination" (*The Academy,* 19 June 1897); as well as numerous references to him in other essays.

52. A. Norman Jeffares, *W. B. Yeats: Man and Poet,* 2d ed. (New York: Barnes and Noble, 1966), p. 149. Yeats also had an engraving of Blake's head.

53. Quoted in W. J. T. Mitchell, *Blake's Composite Art: A Study of the Illuminated Poetry* (Princeton: Princeton University Press, 1978), p. 53. My discussion of Blake is indebted throughout to Mitchell's book.

54. *E&I* 120. *The Savoy* version of the essay was revised for publication in *Ideas of Good and Evil* (1903) and later printings. I quote from the *Savoy* version except where it coincides with the more accessible version published in *E&I.*

55. *The Savoy* (July 1896), 49. In later versions Yeats was more adament: Blake "refused to admit" (*E&I* 121). Edward Engelberg correctly sees that in Yeats's affection the lights and shadows of Pre-Raphaelitism (especially as seen in Rossetti's late paintings) won out over the "imperishable lineaments" of Blake, at least during the 1890s (*The Vast Design: Patterns in W. B. Yeats's Aesthetic* [Toronto: University of Toronto Press, 1964], p. 98). However, Yeats's love of Blake is not at odds with his desire for pattern or for "an art allied to poetry," as Engelberg contends.

56. In addition to the brothers' contributions to Gilchrist's *Life of Blake* (see below), William Michael Rossetti edited and wrote a "Prefatory Memoir" for *The Poetical Works of William Blake: Lyrical and Miscellaneous* (London: George Bell and Sons, 1874), and edited "*The Passions,* an Unpublished Poem by William Blake," *Review* 12 (August 1903), 123–129. The publication of Gilchrist's *Life of Blake* sparked interest in Blake, resulting in exhibitions of his paintings and drawings and a growing knowledge of his poetry (G. E. Bentley and Martin K. Nurmi, *A Blake Bibliography* [Minneapolis: University of Minnesota Press, 1964], pp. 15–16).

57. Quoted by Gordon and Fletcher in *Images,* p. 92, from an account in *Irish Times* (15 April 1918) of a lecture Yeats gave. They speculate that the pictures to which Yeats refers to are the illustrations to *Job.*

58. Dante Gabriel Rossetti wrote a "Supplementary" chapter (39), an account of the *Inventions to Job* (in 32), short descriptions of the illustrations to *Jerusalem* and *Milton* (in 21), and edited and wrote the headnotes for Blake's writings in volume 2. William Michael Rossetti wrote an interpretation of "The Mental Traveller" and a catalogue raisonné of Blake's writings and paintings for volume 2 and offered editorial advice. See Deborah Dorfman, *Blake in the Nine-*

teenth Century: His Reputation as a Poet from Gilchrist to Yeats (New Haven: Yale University Press, 1969), pp. 81, 102; and Bentley and Nurmi, *Blake Bibliography,* p. 14.

59. Dorfman, *Blake,* p. 6. He even suggested that Burne-Jones be hired as copyist for the Blake designs to be included in the book (Bentley and Nurmi, *Blake Bibliography,* p. 271).

60. Yeats owned the 1890 edition of William Michael Rossetti's *The Poetical Works of William Blake.* Although he considered William Michael the "dull brother" (*Au* 314), the notes on the inside cover of the book (eighteen biographical entries outlining Blake's life from 1757 to 1804) indicate that Yeats used the "Prefatory Memoir" as the basis for his biographical sketch in the Ellis-Yeats *Blake* and in his 1893 edition of the poems.

61. See, e.g., Yeats, "Introduction," in *The Poems of William Blake,* reprinted in *Nineteenth Century Accounts of William Blake,* ed. Joseph Anthony Wittreich (Gainesville, Fla.: Scholars' Facsimiles and Reprints, 1970), pp. 285, 286; also *E&I* 125–126.

62. J. B. Yeats, e.g., had painted a *Job* (Ellmann, *Man and Masks,* p. 12), and Rossetti had done a *Paolo and Francesca* (Surtees, *Paintings and Drawings of Dante Gabriel Rossetti,* 1:36–37).

63. See, for example, Pater's "Preface," in *The Renaissance: Studies in Art and Poetry,* ed. Donald L. Hill (Berkeley: University of California Press, 1980), p. xxi; and idem, "Dante Gabriel Rossetti," in *Appreciations: With an Essay on Style* (New York: Macmillan, 1906), pp. 213–227.

64. *Some Winchester Letters of Lionel Johnson* (London: George Allen and Unwin, 1919), p. 182.

65. Arthur Symons, *William Blake* (New York: E. P. Dutton, 1907), p. v.

66. Murphy, *Prodigal Father,* p. 65.

67. *Au* 157. The twelve "Blake Drawings," now owned by the University of Reading, were done around 1870. See Gordon and Fletcher, *Images,* plates 27 and 28, for reproductions of two of them, and Morton D. Paley, "John Trivett Nettleship and the 'Blake drawings,'" in *Blake: An Illustrated Quarterly* 14 (Spring 1981), 185–194, for a list of the drawings, additional reproductions, and a short discussion of Yeats's relationship with Nettleship. *Art Review* was discontinued before it could publish Yeats's essay. See *L* 150, 154; and Ian Fletcher, "The Ellis-Yeats-Blake Manuscript Cluster," *Book Collector* (Spring 1972), 75.

68. Northrop Frye, *Fearful Symmetry: A Study of William Blake* (Princeton: Princeton University Press, 1947), p. 8.

69. Yeats, "Introduction" to *Poems of William Blake* in *Nineteenth Century Accounts,* ed., Wittreich, pp. 283–284.

70. He took heart, for example, in the belief that "until the stream of the world has begun to flow in a different direction, a Rossetti will always draw worse than a Millais" (*UP* 2:292). It justified his own imperfect attempts at poems and plays.

71. *L* 35; *UP* 2:149. For a brief account of the Oxford Union project, see Hilton, *Pre-Raphaelites,* pp. 163–164. Although Yeats's belief in the Irishness of

Blake's ancestors is significant, it is not unprecedented. Hugh Kenner has discovered that the 1854 *Encyclopaedia Britannica* gave the same account of Blake's heritage (*A Colder Eye: The Modern Irish Writers* [New York: Alfred A. Knopf, 1983], p. 162).

72. The inscription in the copy of H. C. Marillier's *Dante Gabriel Rossetti,* which John Masefield gave to Yeats, illustrates this view of artists and their appreciators:

> There is delight in singing though none hear
> Beside the singer, and there is delight
> In praising though the praiser sit alone
> And set the praised far off him—far above.

For a discussion of the artist's isolation and its romantic roots, see Frank Kermode, *Romantic Image* (New York: Random House, 1957), pp. 1–29.

Chapter 2. Poems and Pictures

1. For example, in a 1906 lecture on the painter George Frederic Watts, Yeats told his audience that "all the arts were fundamentally one art, and that what was true of one art was, if properly understood, true of them all" (*UP* 2:343).

2. Robert O'Driscoll, "Yeats on Personality: Three Unpublished Lectures," in *Yeats and the Theatre,* ed. Robert O'Driscoll and Lorna Reynolds (Canada: Macmillan, 1975), pp. 26–27.

3. Quoted in Richard Ellmann, *Yeats: The Man and the Masks* (New York: Macmillan, 1948), p. 29.

4. Ibid., p. 35.

5. A sketch and description of the painting were published in *Royal Hibernian Academy, 1886,* the Illustrated Art Supplement to the *Dublin University Review* (March 1886). Yeats seems to have found inspiration not only in the picture but in the description of the "king of beasts": "the saliva drops from his mouth, and he is roaring—not as when he shakes the forest—but a low musical roar." For a reprint of the description, see W. B. Yeats, *The Poems, A New Edition,* ed. Richard J. Finneran (New York: Macmillan, 1983), p. 692.

6. *L* 122. It is unclear whether Yeats means "orthodox" here poetically or religiously. Considering Katharine Tynan's strong Christian views, with which Yeats later quarreled, the latter is probable.

7. Ian Jack, *Keats and the Mirror of Art* (Oxford: Clarendon Press, 1967), pp. 117, 122ff., 130ff.

8. Giorgio Melchiori, *The Whole Mystery of Art: Pattern into Poetry in the Work of W. B. Yeats* (London: Routledge and Kegan Paul, 1960); Edward Engelberg, *The Vast Design: Patterns in W. B. Yeats's Aesthetic* (Toronto: University of Toronto Press, 1964).

9. Yeats's poetry of vision can be set in the tradition of literary prophecy discussed by Joseph Wittreich in *Visionary Poetics: Milton's Tradition and His Legacy* (San Marino, Calif.: Huntington Library, 1979). In two ways that are important for our purposes here this poetry participates in the visionary poetics Wittreich describes: it attempts to combine word and picture, to resolve the controversy of the arts (p. 19); and, as we will see, the purpose of the resulting pictorialism is not simply to describe the visual but to "create visual impressions, or images, in order to render visual experiences" (p. 24), to induce vision in the reader. Yeats's poetry of vision, of course, also differs from Wittreich's visionary poetics in numerous ways, especially in its distance from explicit Christian concerns and in its overt ties to magic.

10. Ellmann, *Man and Masks,* pp. 62, 63–64.

11. The "Preliminary Examination of the Script of E. R.," completed in 1914, shows Yeats's continuing belief in the primacy of the images magic can invoke. There he describes the process by which "controls" communicate through automatic writing: "the controls claimed an elaborate system of communication, one to guide the hand, one to make mental pictures of the facts to be told, one to put these pictures into words." Here, as with Yeats's poetry, picture precedes the word. The "Preliminary Examination" has been edited by George Mills Harper and John S. Kelly in *Yeats and the Occult,* ed. George Mills Harper (Canada: Macmillan, 1975), quotation from p. 160.

12. *E&I* 28. M. C. Flannery points out that Yeats initially used magic and mysticism interchangeably, but magic is more what he means. A magician controls, the mystic does not. See Flannery, *Yeats and Magic: The Earlier Works* (New York: Barnes and Noble, 1978), p. 5.

13. Edwin John Ellis and William Butler Yeats, *The Works of William Blake: Poetic, Symbolic, and Critical,* 3 vols. (London: Bernard Quaritch, 1893), 1 : 239.

14. The commissioning of Pamela Colman Smith, an artist and friend of Yeats, to design a tarot pack for the Golden Dawn suggests the importance of getting the "right" picture.

15. Melchiori, in discussing the "visualness" of Yeats's poetry, makes the distinction between description and, quoting Donald Stauffer, "revelation through visual evocation" (*Whole Mystery of Art,* p. 9). This explains, in different terms, the difference between description of symbolic vision and the invocation of vision by symbol.

16. In some 1900 advice to AE, Yeats revealed his interest in calling up, rather than presenting, a picture. Recommending that AE avoid the word "vague," he explained, "I think I would myself avoid it in poetry for the same reason that I would avoid 'haunted' and because vague forms, pictures, scenes etc. are rather a modern idea of the poetic and I would not want to call up a modern kind of picture. . . . All ancient vision was definite and precise" (*L* 343). Again, the qualities he wants for his pictures are those so characteristic of early Pre-Raphaelite paintings.

17. *E&I* 49. Yeats implies at the end of his essay "Magic" that the "supreme Enchanter" speaks through the arts and that his language is that of the symbol (*E&I* 52). Suzanne Langer has expressed this view in less esoteric terms: "I also

believe that art is essentially one, that the symbolic function is the same in every kind of artistic expression" (*Feeling and Form* [New York: Charles Scribners' Sons, 1953], p. 103).

18. Engelberg has also noted that it is significant that "Symbolism in Painting" preceded "The Symbolism of Poetry" (*Vast Design,* p. 96).

19. Lessing's *Laocoön,* published in German in 1766, was first translated into English in 1836 (Jack, *Keats and the Mirror of Art,* p. 281) and was well-known in the latter half of the nineteenth century. For a discussion of Arnold and Lessing, see Alan Roper, *Arnold's Poetic Landscapes* (Baltimore: Johns Hopkins University Press, 1969), pp. 23–29. Although Yeats probably did not read *Laocoön,* he was most likely familiar with its stance on the arts. A. S. Murray's *A History of Greek Sculpture* (London: John Murray, 1880) in Yeats's library (*YL* 186) discusses Lessing (pp. 2–3, and in "The View of Lessing"). Yeats, however, may not have seen this book until the late 1910s or early 1920s.

20. Gotthold Lessing, *Laocoön: An Essay upon the Limits of Painting and Poetry,* tr. Ellen Frothingham (New York: Noonday Press, 1957), sec. xvi, pp. 91–92.

21. A picture's revelation cannot, for example, be instantaneous; the eye needs time to apprehend its forms in space. Space may be characteristic of the visual arts as time may be of the written arts, but space and time are never really separate. As Joseph Frank points out, and as Yeats's concept of a region as a place to "wander" (*L* 106) suggests, space implies time. See Frank, "Spatial Form in Modern Literature," in *The Widening Gyre* (New Brunswick, N.J.: Rutgers University Press, 1963), pp. 56–57. Similarly, it has been argued that we cannot perceive events temporally without placing them in space. See W. J. T. Mitchell's excellent rebuttal of Lessing in "Spatial Form in Literature: Toward a General Theory," in *The Language of Images,* ed. W. J. T. Mitchell (Chicago: University of Chicago Press, 1980), pp. 271–299, esp. 273–274.

22. Yeats would have found such be-pictured poetry among the romantics. Keats's narrative "Eve of St. Agnes," for example, can be viewed as a series of pictures.

23. *The Letters of John Keats,* ed. Hyder Edward Rollins, 2 vols. (Cambridge: Harvard University Press, 1958), 1:170.

24. Louis MacNeice, *The Poetry of W. B. Yeats* (1941; reprint, New York: Oxford University Press, 1969), p. 50.

25. John Butler Yeats, *Early Memories; Some Chapters of Autobiography* (Dundrum: Cuala Press, 1923), p. 20.

26. Ruskin appeared in Yeats's thought early in his life as the author of *Unto This Last,* which Yeats read in defiance of his father, and late in his life as the man who threw from a window "a tempting demon in the form of a cat," the subject of a lengthy debate with T. Sturge Moore (*LTSM* 63–114).

27. *Au* 28. For an account of the expedition, see William M. Murphy, *Prodigal Father: The Life of John Butler Yeats (1839–1922)* (Ithaca: Cornell University Press, 1978), p. 110.

Chapter 3. Poetry of Vision

1. Marshall McLuhan and Harley Parker point out that perspective makes the space of the picture seem continuous with that of the spectator; see *Through the Vanishing Point: Space in Poetry and Painting* (New York: Harper and Row, 1968), p. 12. See also Kenneth Clark, *Landscape into Art* (1949; reprint, Boston: Beacon Press, 1961), p. 17, on the "remarkable sense of our being *in* the modern landscape."

2. Clark, *Landscape into Art,* p. 54.

3. Yeats had read Alexander Gilchrist's *Life of William Blake, "Pictor Ignotus"* (London and Cambridge: Macmillan, 1863), which contains a short chapter on the illustrations (pp. 270–275) and reprints three of the designs (p. 271).

4. *Au* 81. The painting was on loan from the National Gallery, London; see James White, *W. B. Yeats: A Centenary Exhibition* (Dublin: National Gallery of Ireland, 1965), p. 61.

5. A fair copy of the poem in nearly final form appears in a notebook dated August 1884, although Yeats subsequently made minor changes, particularly in the last scene. A transcription of this manuscript will appear in *The Early Poems of W. B. Yeats,* vol. 1: *Mosada and The Island of Statues,* ed. George Bornstein (Ithaca: Cornell University Press, forthcoming). Yeats was enrolled in the art school from May 1884 to April 1886 (William M. Murphy, *Prodigal Father: The Life of John Butler Yeats (1839–1922)* [Ithaca: Cornell University Press, 1978], p. 139).

6. Richard Ellmann, *Yeats: The Man and the Masks* (New York: Macmillan, 1948), p. 36.

7. In fact, James Frazer, when he used this painting as the frontispiece to *The Golden Bough,* thought the location was Lake Nemi. See John Gage, "Turner and Stourhead: The Making of a Classicist?" *Art Quarterly* 37 (1974), 74.

8. Edward Engelberg, "'He Too Was in Arcadia': Yeats and the Paradox of the Fortunate Fall," in *In Excited Reverie: A Centenary Tribute to William Butler Yeats, 1865–1939,* ed. A. Norman Jeffares and K. G. W. Cross (New York: Macmillan, 1965), p. 80.

9. Yeats realized by 1902 that Turner's paintings reveal a modern restlessness. In an essay on Spenser, Yeats distinguished between the classic view of the world and the modern, using Claude and Turner to illustrate that the natural harmony and integration found in classic art does not exist in modern (*E&I* 377–378).

10. Gage, "Turner and Stourhead," p. 75. For its overview of critical discussions of *The Golden Bough,* I am indebted to Martin Butlin and Evelyn Joll's *The Paintings of J. M. W. Turner* (New Haven: Yale University Press, 1977), 1 : 186.

11. Engelberg, "'He Too Was in Arcadia,'" p. 85.

12. George Harper, for example, notes that "to a large degree, perhaps, Yeats's early failure may be attributed to the fact that although he imitated pastoral styles and structures he had not assimilated their fundamental assumptions" ("Yeats's Quest for Eden," in *The Dolmen Press Yeats Centenary Papers MCMLXV,* ed. Liam Miller [Dublin: Dolmen Press, 1968], p. 299).

13. "The Song of the Happy Shepherd" (*VP* 64–67); "The Cloak, the Boat, and the Shoes" (*VP* 69–70).

14. Michael J. Sidnell, "The Allegory of Yeats's 'The Wanderings of Oisin,'" *Colby Library Quarterly* 15, no. 2 (June 1979), 145.

15. E.g., T. S. Eliot, "Yeats," in *On Poetry and Poets* (New York: Farrar, Straus and Giroux, 1961), 300; Louis MacNeice, *The Poetry of W. B. Yeats* (1941; reprint, New York: Oxford University Press, 1969), p. 63; and Ellmann, *Man and Masks*, p. 51.

16. Richard Ellmann, *The Identity of Yeats* (New York: Oxford University Press, 1964), pp. 20–23.

17. Ellmann, *Man and Masks*, p. 50.

18. Yeats would have approved of the combination of poetry and the visual arts in the pieces Lilly helped embroider. Many, like the Kelmscott bed valence (fig. VIII), worked lines of poetry into their designs. Other pieces worked in part by Lilly Yeats were *Fruit Tree—Curtain* and a panel or cushion cover *Olive and Rose*, both displayed at the 1890 Arts and Crafts Exhibition which her brother reviewed, and the Kelmscott bed curtains (Oliver Fairclough and Emmeline Leary, *Textiles by William Morris and Morris & Co., 1861–1948* [London: Thames and Hudson, 1981], pp. 83–84).

19. See Harold Bloom, *Yeats* (New York: Oxford University Press, 1970), p. 294; Ellmann, *Identity of Yeats*, p. 117; and *Au* 141.

20. Fairclough and Leary, *Textiles by William Morris*, pp. 55, 42.

21. Ibid., p. 61.

22. Quoted in ibid., p. 55.

23. Ibid.

24. Ibid., p. 56.

25. Ellmann first noted the weaving images, including the tapestry in *The Countess Cathleen;* see Ellmann, *Man and Masks*, p. 21.

26. Peter Faulkner notes that "Yeats saw Morris's work in close relation to the Symbolist movement" ("W. B. Yeats and William Morris," *Threshold* 4, no. 1 [Spring–Summer 1960], 20).

27. Rudolph Arnheim claims that language is necessarily linear and that the images presented in language are an accretion of details (*Visual Thinking* [Berkeley: University of California Press, 1969], pp. 246–250). This suggests that language might most easily present details linearly and that in the absence of indicators that tell the reader to place figure A in some particular relation to figure B, he will place them side by side.

28. There are several possible interpretations of the poem's temporal structure. The most interesting posits that the events Oisin narrates all happen in one day and night, with three hundred-year time "loops" on each island (Sidnell, "Allegory of Yeats's 'Oisin'"). Within even this elaborate time scheme, however, Oisin's story follows chronological order.

29. Quoted in Fairclough and Leary, *Textiles by William Morris*, p. 55.

30. The idea of rhythm as connection between art and literature was not peculiar to Yeats. Laurence Binyon, Yeats's friend and the keeper of prints and draw-

ings at the British Museum, declared in a 1918 lecture: "The unifying principle of all the arts is rhythm; for the movement of life, unimpeded by circumstances, is naturally rhythmical, and art expresses life at its fullest and most intense" (*English Poetry and Its Relation to Painting and the Other Arts* [London: Oxford University Press, n.d.; reprinted from the *Proceedings of the British Academy,* vol. 8, 1918, pp. 381–402], p. 3). For an interesting aside on the origins of the word "rhythm" in the physical act of drawing, not in speech or music, see W. J. T. Mitchell, "Spatial Form in Literature: Toward a General Theory," in *The Language of Images,* ed. W. J. T. Mitchell (Chicago: University of Chicago Press, 1980), p. 280.

31. Critics have noted the hypnotic effect of "Oisin"'s meter, especially in book 3, the part that seemed to Yeats "a kind of vision" (*L* 87), so there is evidence that for some, rhythm does "enchant." See Daniel Albright, *The Myth Against Myth: A Study of Yeats's Imagination in Old Age* (London: Oxford University Press, 1972), p. 109.

32. Clark, *Landscape into Art,* p. 3. Robert Goldwater, examining the symbolist movement in art, also explores the coincidence of the symbolic and the decorative in *Symbolism* (New York: Harper and Row, 1979), p. 18.

33. Peter Bicknell, *Beauty, Horror and Immensity: Picturesque Landscape in Britain, 1750–1850* (Cambridge: Cambridge University Press, 1981), p. xii.

34. *The Savoy* (July 1896), 49.

35. Yeats could have gathered the details of his heroine from a number of works: Rossetti's *Dante's Dream* with Beatrice's red lips and white gown; his *Lucretia Borgia* with her flowing dress and citron hair; Morris's *Queen Guinevere* who buckles a cincture around her long embroidered gown; and numerous tapestries.

36. Sidnell, "Allegory of Yeats's 'Oisin'"; and Albright, *Myth Against Myth,* chap. 2.

37. See Ellmann, *Identity of Yeats,* pp. 27–37; and Allen R. Grossman, *Poetic Knowledge in the Early Yeats: A Study of "The Wind Among the Reeds"* (Charlottesville: University Press of Virginia, 1969), *passim.*

38. Gold (162 times), red and crimson (116), gray (102), and green (75); from Stephen Maxfield Parrish and James Allan Painter, *A Concordance to the Poems of W. B. Yeats* (Ithaca: Cornell University Press, 1963).

39. Edwin John Ellis and William Butler Yeats, *The Works of William Blake: Poetic, Symbolic, and Critical,* 3 vols. (London: Bernard Quaritch, 1893), 1: 309–314.

40. For an analysis of Yeats's rhythmic structure, see Adelyn Dougherty, *A Study of Rhythmic Structure in the Verse of William Butler Yeats* (The Hague: Mouton, 1973).

41. John Unterecker notes the abundance of hair in *The Wind Among the Reeds* (*A Reader's Guide to William Butler Yeats* [New York: Noonday Press, 1959], pp. 92–93), as do Frayne (*UP* 1 : 390) and Bloom (*Yeats,* p. 124).

42. See Goldwater, *Symbolism,* pp. 60–70. For a discussion of specifically golden hair in Victorian art and literature, see Elizabeth G. Gitter, "The Power of

Women's Hair in the Victorian Imagination," *PMLA* 99 (October 1984), 936–954, esp. 942 and 948 for brief comments on Yeats.

43. This same image of hair occurs in another work that influenced Yeats, Villiers de l'Isle Adam's *Axel*. There, Sara, having fled the nunnery just as she was to take the vows, shoots Count Axel who has discovered her in his basement. As William York Tindall explains, "Enchanted by her cruelty and her shape, he covers himself in her long hair and breathes the spirit of dead roses" ("The Symbolism of W. B. Yeats," in *Yeats: A Collection of Critical Essays*, ed. John Unterecker [Engelwood Cliffs, N.J.: Prentice-Hall, 1963], p. 47). Tindall discusses Yeats's debt to *Axel*'s symbolism, but does not mention the hair.

44. Yeats had described Maud's skin as like apple blossoms and remembered her standing, on the day they met, amidst a "heap" of those flowers (*Au* 123). Yeats's image of Maud recalls Rossetti's *A Vision of Fiammata* in which Fiammata is pictured against a background of carefully painted apple blossoms. The painting was frequently exhibited during Yeats's youth and young manhood (Virginia Surtees, *The Paintings and Drawings of Dante Gabriel Rossetti (1828–1882): A Catalogue Raisonné* [Oxford: Clarendon Press, 1971], p. 148).

45. The picture was reproduced in *The Pageant* in 1896, the year "Michael Robartes Remembers Forgotten Beauty" was published. In the Tate in 1913 Yeats saw and admired (*E&I* 346) another Rossetti painting of the same theme, *Mary Magdalene Leaving the House of Feasting* (1858), acquired by the Tate in 1911 (Surtees, *Paintings and Drawings of Dante Gabriel Rossetti*, p. 50).

46. Yeats disregarded Palmer's early sepia drawings done under Blake's direct influence—even though his friend Charles Ricketts had praised them (D. J. Gordon and Ian Fletcher, *W. B. Yeats: Images of a Poet* [Manchester: University of Manchester Press, 1961], p. 105)—perhaps because they were not prints like Blake's illustrations of Virgil. In later life, Yeats admired specifically Calvert's woodcuts (*Au* 550), but he probably did not, in fact, distinguish between them and the engravings because, as Raymond Lister has noted, "in Calvert's dextrous hands, the two techniques become almost interchangeable" (*Edward Calvert* [London: G. Bell and Sons, 1962], pp. 77–78). The slides of Blake's, Palmer's, and Calvert's work that Yeats collected for a 1918 lecture on Blake and his school include Calvert's engraving *The Sheep of His Pasture* as well as woodcuts. See T. R. Henn, *The Lonely Tower: Studies in the Poetry of W. B. Yeats* (London: Methuen, 1950), pp. 347–350, for a list of the slides.

47. Gordon and Fletcher, *Images*, p. 92. Gilchrist's *Life of William Blake* contains a chapter titled "Hampstead; and Youthful Disciples" (pp. 292–304).

48. Yeats owned a copy of *A Memoir*, signed by the author, as well as a copy of Calvert's *Ten Spiritual Designs* (Portland, Maine: Thomas Bird Mosher, 1913), which contains enlarged reproductions of Calvert's woodcuts, etchings, and lithographs (*YL* 51).

49. Gordon and Fletcher, *Images*, p. 106. See also the preface to Calvert's *Ten Spiritual Designs* for an account of this project and Thomas Bird Mosher's unsuccessful efforts to commission Yeats for an essay for this book (p. vii).

50. See Marion Witt, "The Making of an Elegy: Yeats's 'In Memory of Major

Robert Gregory,'" *Modern Philology* 48 (Nov. 1950), 112–121, for the influence of Palmer and Calvert on Yeats's elegy.

51. Gordon and Fletcher, *Images,* p. 105. See also Witt, "Making of an Elegy."

52. Thomas L. Dume, "William Butler Yeats: A Survey of His Reading," Ph.D. diss., Temple University, 1950, p. 277.

53. Much has been made in the critical literature of Palmer's visionary powers; see Geoffrey Grigson's *Samuel Palmer: The Visionary Years* (London: Kegan Paul, 1947), and idem, *Samuel Palmer's Valley of Vision* (London: Phoenix House, 1960).

54. Lister, *Edward Calvert,* pp. 100–101.

55. Herbert P. Horne, "A Brief Notice of Edward Calvert, Painter and Engraver," in *Ten Spiritual Designs,* p. 5.

56. Charles Ricketts, "A Note on Original Wood Engraving," *The Pageant* (1897), 263.

57. Lister, *Edward Calvert,* p. 94

58. Lister comments that "Calvert generally did not depict actual scenes" (ibid., p. 20).

59. F. A. C. Wilson notes, "In his translation of *Kabbala Unveiled,* [MacGregor] Mathers explains that the typical Kabbalistic tree of life is an *apple tree* which grows from earth to the apex of heaven and bears the sun and moon for fruit" (*Yeats's Iconography* [New York: Macmillan, 1960], p. 250).

60. *E&I* 125. Yeats misquotes from A. H. Palmer, *The Life and Letters of Samuel Palmer, Painter, and Etcher* (London: Seeley and Co., 1892), pp. 15–16. "Misty" should read "mystic."

61. For a discussion of Yeats's responses to Shelley's star, see George Bornstein, *Yeats and Shelley* (Chicago: University of Chicago Press, 1970), pp. 18–19, 48.

62. Clark, *Landscape into Art,* pp. 14–15 and *passim.*

63. For a survey of the contest between man and nature in Yeats's early verse, see David Daiches, "The Earlier Poems: Some Themes and Patterns," in *In Excited Reverie,* pp. 48–67.

64. Of course, observation of nature was prompted in part by the demands of his art—he literally had to picture a tree and must know what one looked like.

65. Yeats and Horton probably met in 1896, drawn together by a common interest in the occult. Although their attitudes toward religion and spiritual knowledge grew increasingly incompatible and strained their relationship, they remained friends until Horton's death in 1919. George Harper acutely suggests that Yeats valued Horton's friendship precisely because their views differed; see Harper, *W. B. Yeats and W. T. Horton: The Record of an Occult Friendship* (Atlantic Highlands, N.J.: Humanities Press, 1980), p. 3. Yeats had considered dedicating *A Vision* to Horton, though he knew Horton would disapprove (Harper, pp. 2–3), and he invoked him in that book's epilogue "All Souls' Night." Horton was a friend whose life seemed antithetical to Yeats's own, but full of a strange nobility (*VP* 471–472). Early in their friendship Yeats helped advance Horton's career as an artist by giving him generous advice and encouragement and show-

ing his work to Arthur Symons, who chose three drawings and a head and tail piece for the April 1896 *Savoy.* Horton's work appeared occasionally in subsequent issues of *The Savoy:* a head and tail piece to "The Song of the Women" by Ford Madox Hueffer in August 1896; *Ballade des Pendus* in October 1896; and a print after a pen and ink sketch in November 1896. For a brief and informative account of Horton and his friendship with Yeats, see Richard J. Finneran and George Mills Harper, "'He loved strange thought': W. B. Yeats and William Thomas Horton," in *Yeats and the Occult,* ed. George Mills Harper (Canada: Macmillan, 1975), pp. 190–203. They helpfully reprint the third part of Yeats's introduction to *A Book of Images,* the part Yeats excised when he republished the introduction as "Symbolism in Painting."

66. Yeats especially admired *The Magi* (fig. 26). Here, Yeats said, was Horton "at his best" ("Introduction," in *A Book of Images* [London: Unicorn Press, 1898], p. 14). T. R. Henn finds this picture "a bad piece of drawing that owes much to William Morris" (*Lonely Tower,* p. 96).

67. Yeats to W. T. Horton, 15 July 1900; manuscript at the Humanities Research Center, University of Texas at Austin. See also Harper, *Yeats and Horton,* pp. 26–27, for discussions of this and the following two letters; and pp. 114–115, for summaries of them.

68. Yeats to W. T. Horton, dated 29 July 1901; manuscript at the Humanities Research Center, University of Texas at Austin.

69. Yeats to W. T. Horton, dated 11 August 1901; manuscript with typescript at the Humanities Research Center, University of Texas at Austin.

70. Quoted by L. A. G. Strong, "Yeats at His Ease," in *W. B. Yeats: Interviews and Recollections,* 2 vols., ed. E. H. Mikhail (New York: Barnes and Noble, 1977), 1:149.

Chapter 4. From Painted Stage to Sculpted Image

1. Thomas Parkinson, *W. B. Yeats Self-Critic: A Study of His Early Verse* (Berkeley: University of California Press, 1971).

2. Quoted in Allan Wade, *A Bibliography of the Writings of W. B. Yeats* (London: Rupert Hart-Davis, 1968), p. 67. Leonard E. Nathan discusses Yeats's rejection of the "excesses of Pre-Raphaelitism" in the style and structure of the plays, in *The Tragic Drama of William Butler Yeats: Figures in a Dance* (New York: Columbia University Press, 1965), pp. 89–90.

3. Quoted in Ian Fletcher, "Rhythm and Pattern in *Autobiographies,*" in *An Honoured Guest,* ed. Denis Donoghue and J. R. Mulryne (London: Edward Arnold, 1965), p. 184.

4. *E&I* 99. Yeats was not alone in his belief. Arthur Symons wrote, "If we take drama with any seriousness, as an art as well as an improvisation, we shall realize that one of its main requirements is that it should make pictures." Quoted in Peter Ure, *Yeats the Playwright* (London: Routledge and Kegan Paul, 1963), p. 23.

5. Joan Coldwell, "'Images That Yet Fresh Images Beget': A Note on Book

Covers," in *The World of W. B. Yeats,* rev. ed., ed. Robin Skelton and Ann Saddlemyer (Seattle: University of Washington Press, 1967), pp. 134–139, offers a survey of Yeats's book covers and their meanings.

6. J. B. Yeats provided a portrait of the author for *Mosada* (1886) and *The Tables of the Law* (1897), and the frontispiece *The Last Gleeman* for *The Celtic Twilight* (1893); Ellis designed the frontispiece for the second issue of *The Wanderings of Oisin* (1892); Nettleship did the one for *The Countess Cathleen* (1892); Beardsley designed the cover for *The Land of Heart's Desire* (1894); and H. Granville Fell did the cover of *Poems* (1895). See Wade, *Bibliography,* pp. 19, 43, 27–28, 23, 25, 30, 37.

7. In 1904 Yeats inscribed in John Quinn's copy of *Mosada,* "There was to have been a picture of some incident in the play but my father was too much of a portrait painter not to do this instead." He thought Nettleship's *Cuchulain Fighting the Waves* for *The Countess Cathleen* (1892) a "rather disappointing picture" by one who "might have been a great imaginative artist" (written in 1904 in Quinn's copy). And he commented about Fell, "The man who made this cover made a beautiful design which I saw at an exhibition, but after I saw it Dent had spoilt him, with all kinds of odd jobs & when he did this the spirit had gone out of him. I hate this expressionless angel of his" (Wade, *Bibliography,* pp. 19, 27, 37). For an account of Althea Gyles, see Ian Fletcher's excellent "Poet and Designer: W. B. Yeats and Althea Gyles," *Yeats Studies* 1 (1971), 42–79. A less complete but helpful account can be found in D. J. Gordon and Ian Fletcher, *W. B. Yeats: Images of a Poet* (Manchester: University of Manchester Press, 1961), pp. 98–101.

8. William O'Donnell points out that the cover of *The Secret Rose* looks like the textbook of the magical order described in "Rosa Alchemica" ("Yeats as Adept and Artist: *The Speckled Bird, The Secret Rose* and *The Wind Among the Reeds,*" in *Yeats and the Occult,* ed. George Mills Harper [Canada: Macmillan, 1975], pp. 62–63). For a further account of Yeats's talismanic books, especially those designed by Althea Gyles, see Allen R. Grossman, *Poetic Knowledge in the Early Yeats: A Study of "The Wind Among the Reeds"* (Charlottesville: University Press of Virginia, 1969), pp. 46–48 and *passim.*

9. James W. Flannery, *W. B. Yeats and the Idea of a Theatre: The Early Abbey Theatre in Theory and Practice* (New Haven: Yale University Press, 1976), p. 146.

10. *E&I* 100. Yeats used "realistic" and "naturalistic" interchangeably.

11. James Flannery notes Yeats's use of "the focused compositional technique of portrait painting" ("W. B. Yeats, Gordon Craig and the Visual Arts of the Theatre," in *Yeats and the Theatre,* ed. Robert O'Driscoll and Lorna Reynolds [Canada: Macmillan, 1975], p. 87).

12. In Robert O'Driscoll, "Yeats on Personality: Three Unpublished Lectures," in *Yeats and the Theatre,* p. 22. The lobby of the Abbey Theater symbolized Yeats's continuing alliance to Pre-Raphaelite decoration: its stained-glass window, which Yeats commissioned from Sarah Purser, echoes in the color and pattern of its interwoven branches the art of Yeats's favorite Pre-Raphaelites. Yeats to Sarah Purser, MS 15781, National Library of Ireland, Dublin. See also *Ex* 124. Yeats was contemplating an essay on Sarah Purser's windows in the nuns' chapel.

13. *Ex* 220; *VP* 849. Hazard Adams has claimed that "Sloughing off the imagery of withdrawal and dream, Yeats began to champion Blakean action." See Adams, *Blake and Yeats: The Contrary Vision* (Ithaca: Cornell University Press, 1955), p. 149.

14. Quoted in Robert Hogan and James Kilroy, *The Abbey Theatre: The Years of Synge, 1905–1909* (Dublin: Dolmen Press, 1978), p. 69.

15. Ann Saddlemyer, "'The Heroic Discipline of the Looking-Glass': W. B. Yeats's Search for Dramatic Design," in *World of W. B. Yeats*, p. 67.

16. *L* 371. For discussions of Yeats and Craig, see Karen Dorn, "Dialogue into Movement: W. B. Yeats's Theatre Collaboration with Gordon Craig," in *Yeats and the Theatre*, pp. 109–136; Flannery, *W. B. Yeats and the Idea of a Theatre;* idem, "W. B. Yeats, Gordon Craig, and the Visual Arts of the Theatre," in *Yeats and the Theatre*, pp. 82–108; Liam Miller, *The Noble Drama of W. B. Yeats* (Dublin: Dolmen Press, 1976); idem, "W. B. Yeats and Stage Design at the Abbey Theatre," *Malahat Review* 16 (1970), 50–64; Reg Skene, *The Cuchulain Plays of W. B. Yeats: A Study* (New York: Columbia University Press, 1974); and Alan Tomlinson, "Yeats and Gordon Craig," *Ariel: A Review of International English Literature* 3 (July 1972), 48–57.

17. Flannery, *W. B. Yeats and the Idea of a Theatre*, p. 264.

18. Ibid., p. 269, n. 91.

19. Ibid., p. 272.

20. Yeats tried to circumvent that difficulty by designing his own version of Craig's invention (ibid., p. 277).

21. See Peter Alderson Smith, "'Grown to Heaven Like a Tree': The Scenery of *The Countess Cathleen*," *Eire-Ireland* 14, no. 3 (Fall 1979), 65–82, for a discussion of the symbolic significance of the scenery and its relation to the play. Smith deals primarily with those versions of the play prior to the revisions made for and immediately following the 1911 production.

22. Richard Ellmann, *Eminent Domain: Yeats among Wilde, Joyce, Pound, Eliot and Auden* (New York: Oxford University Press, 1967), p. 66.

23. *The Letters of Ezra Pound, 1907–1941*, ed. D. D. Paige (New York: Harcourt, Brace and World, 1950), pp. 25, 27.

24. Ibid., p. 27.

25. *E&I* 166. Arthur Symons probably contributed to Yeats's interest in Rodin. His statement in a 1902 essay that "Rodin is a visionary, to whom art has no meaning apart from truth" demonstrates the perspective that allowed Yeats to link Rodin to Rossetti (*Studies in Seven Arts* [1906; reprint, London: Martin Secker, 1924], p. 5). Yeats knew Symons's essay well enough to quote from it (p. 9) in *A Vision* (*AV-A* 211).

26. *Letters of Ezra Pound*, p. 45.

27. Roger Cole, *Burning to Speak: The Life and Art of Henri Gaudier Brzeska* (Oxford: Phaidon, 1978), provides a helpful account of Gaudier-Brzeska and a catalog of his work.

28. *Letters of Ezra Pound*, p. 45.

29. Ibid., p. 26.

30. Ibid., pp. 26–27. The two statuettes were probably *The Embracers* (marble, 1913) and *Small Fawn* (brownstone, 1913), both listed in Horace

on other artists. He had read Adolf Furtwangler's *Masterpieces of Greek Sculpture* (see *Self-Portrait,* p. 86) and is perhaps the source of Yeats's interest in that book, which provided information recorded in "Dove or Swan" (*AV-A* 182).

7. Daracott, *All for Art,* p. 41.

8. Ibid., p. 24 and plate 4.

9. The collection included 426 drawings and watercolors and 68 engravings by all the major European artists, 41 Japanese drawings, paintings of the Italian, French, Flemish and English schools, and a collection of Egyptian, Greek, and Roman antiquities, including red and black figure vases and 47 classical gems. Much of the Ricketts-Shannon collection of Western art was left to the Fitzwilliam Museum, Cambridge. I am grateful to that museum for allowing me to look at their list of the collection's contents. See also ibid., pp. 17–86.

10. MS 58106, British Library, London; *The Senate Speeches of W. B. Yeats,* ed. Donald R. Pearce (Bloomington: Indiana University Press, 1960), p. 163.

11. *L* 595–596. Typically, Yeats explained Cole's work in terms of literature: "He is a thorn in the Futurist and Cubist flesh for he draws incomparably in the style of Michael Angelo. If his sculpture, which no one seems to have seen, is as fine as his drawings, it will be like the publication of *Paradise Lost* in the very year when Dryden announced the final disappearance of blank verse."

12. L. A. G. Strong, "Yeats at His Ease," in *W. B. Yeats: Interviews and Recollections,* ed. E. H. Mikhail, 2 vols. (New York: Barnes and Noble, 1977), 1:150.

13. *L* 451, 837, 901. William O'Donnell has identified the Rossetti drawing as *Cat's Cradle.* See O'Donnell, "The Art of Yeats's 'Lapis Lazuli,'" *Massachusetts Review* 23 (Summer 1982), 355.

14. *L* 682. Several years later his enthusiasm for Pre-Raphaelite blue found further expression in the study of his Merrion Square house: it was decorated entirely in that "certain shade of blue," which Yeats said always affected him. See Nancy Pyper, "Four O'Clock Tea with W. B. Yeats," in *Interviews and Recollections,* 1:161.

15. *L* 683. For a discussion of Thoor Ballylee and its renovations, see Mary Hanley, *Thoor Ballylee: Home of William Butler Yeats* (Dublin: Dolmen Press, 1965).

16. Which, Gordon and Fletcher note, Yeats read in preparation for writing *A Vision* (*W. B. Yeats: Images of a Poet* [Manchester: University of Manchester Press, 1961], p. 82). In her introduction to *Apotheosis and After Life* (New York: Dutton, 1916), Strong, arguing against the dogmatism of one of Yeats's other sources, Josef Strzygowski, calls for a balanced view of Roman art, one that accords it the respect and dignity it deserves without overstating its achievements.

17. Thomas Whitaker, *Swan and Shadow: Yeats's Dialogue with History* (Chapel Hill: University of North Carolina Press, 1964), p. 78. See also Bloom, *Yeats,* chap. 14, for a discussion of *A Vision*'s sources in Yeats's concept of the romantics, especially Blake. Bloom treats Yeats's debt to Blake's pictures as well as poems.

18. Thomas Parkinson, "Yeats and the Limits of Modernity," in *Yeats: An Annual of Critical and Textual Studies,* ed. Richard J. Finneran, vol. 3 (Ithaca:

Cornell University Press, 1985), p. 64. Parkinson attributes the confusion to Yeats's desire "to accommodate realities that were superficially incompatible."

19. Complete integration is impossible, in part because desire, which does not exist at phase 15, always remains. Yeats explained of Rossetti's women that "desire becomes wisdom without ceasing to be desire" (*E&I* 53).

20. See Mario Praz, *Mnemosyne: The Parallel between Literature and the Visual Arts* (Princeton: Princeton University Press, 1970), chap. 2.

21. George Harper and Walter Hood, "Notes," in *AV-A* 21.

22. Flinders Petrie, *The Revolutions of Civilisation* (London: Harper and Brothers, 1911), p. 2.

23. See, for example, John Orchard writing in *The Germ,* no. 4, quoted by David Masson, "Pre-Raphaelitism in Art and Literature" (1852), in *Pre-Raphaelitism: A Collection of Critical Essays,* ed. James Sambrook (Chicago: University of Chicago Press, 1974), p. 83.

24. Whitaker, *Swan and Shadow,* p. 86. See Walter Pater, *Greek Studies* (London: Macmillan, 1910), pp. 252–253.

25. Pater, *Greek Studies,* pp. 252, 253; *AV-A* 182.

26. Thomas L. Dume, "William Butler Yeats: A Survey of His Reading," Ph.D. diss., Temple University, 1950, p. 173. See also *AV-A* 182.

27. George Redford, *Sculpture: Egyptian—Assyrian—Greek—Roman* (London: Sampson Low, Marston, Searle and Rivington, 1886).

28. *AV-A* 182. Bloom notes that, in describing phases 13 and 14, Yeats is "still a good Pre-Raphaelite" (*Yeats,* p. 281).

29. It is unclear where Yeats got the idea that the chair was marble since his sources do not mention this. See Harper and Hood, "Notes," in *AV-A* 47.

30. *The Literary Works of Leonardo da Vinci,* comp. and ed. by Jean Paul Richter, 2 vols. (London: S. Low, Marston, Searle and Rivington, 1883). See Dume, "Yeats: Survey of His Reading," p. 291.

31. *AV-A* 200; Pater, *The Renaissance: Studies in Art and Poetry,* ed. Donald L. Hill (Berkeley: University of California Press, 1980), pp. 41–42.

32. See Holman Hunt, "Pre-Raphaelitism and the Pre-Raphaelite Brotherhood" (1905), in *Pre-Raphaelitism,* pp. 31–32.

33. See Giorgio Melchiori, *The Whole Mystery of Art: Pattern into Poetry in the Work of W. B. Yeats* (London: Routledge and Kegan Paul, 1960), p. 160.

34. See Martin Harrison and Bill Waters, *Burne-Jones* (New York: G. P. Putnams' Sons, 1973), p. 116.

35. "The re-evaluation of Byzantine art had been due, after all, to the aesthetes of the Beardsley period," Melchiori reminds us (*Whole Mystery of Art,* p. 216). There is some debate about when Yeats became interested in Byzantium. Melchiori suggests that Yeats's interest was not aroused until he visited Stockholm—whose Stadhaus he saw as a triumph of the Byzantine sort—to collect the Nobel Prize in 1924 (pp. 214–218). In 1903 Yeats had, however, asked Sir Eric Maclagan, director of the Victoria and Albert Museum, to look up some information on banners which turned out, as Maclagan reported, to have been "in very early use in Byzantium (under Constantine)" (*LTWBY* 127). According to his son, Maclagan loaned "Yeats a copy of *Luitprand of Cremona,* who is the prime

source for the trees and birds of the Byzantine court" (headnote, *LTWBY* 126). Presumably, this also happened around 1903.

36. Gordon and Fletcher, *Images,* pp. 83–85.

37. Herbert J. Levine, "Yeats's Ruskinian Byzantium," in *Yeats Annual No.* 2, ed. Richard J. Finneran (Atlantic Highlands, N.J.: Humanities Press, 1983), pp. 25–34.

38. Thomas McAlindon, "The Idea of Byzantium in William Morris and W. B. Yeats," *Modern Philology* 64 (May 1967), 314. Cf. *AV-A* 192.

39. McAlindon, "Idea of Byzantium," p. 312.

40. *"The Secret Rose," Stories by W. B. Yeats: A Variorum Edition,* ed. Phillip L. Marcus, Warwick Gould, and Michael J. Sidnell (Ithaca: Cornell University Press, 1981), pp. 144–145. Melchiori has shown the relation of this story to the imagery of the Byzantium poems (*Whole Mystery of Art,* pp. 218–224).

Chapter 6. Picture and Book Remain

1. See, for example, David R. Clark, *Yeats at Songs and Choruses* (Amherst: University of Massachusetts Press, 1983), pp. 90–136, on "Her Triumph"; Curtis Bradford, "Yeats's Byzantium Poems: A Study of Their Development," in *Yeats: A Collection of Critical Essays,* ed. John Unterecker (Englewood Cliffs, N.J.: Prentice-Hall, 1963). pp. 93–130; and idem, *Yeats at Work* (Carbondale: Southern Illinois University Press, 1965), esp. pp. 87–88.

2. The principal studies of visual sources are: T. R. Henn, *The Lonely Tower: Studies in the Poetry of W. B. Yeats* (London: Methuen, 1950); idem, "Yeats and the Picture Galleries," *Southern Review* 1 (January 1965), 57–75; Giorgio Melchiori, *The Whole Mystery of Art: Pattern into Poetry in the Work of W. B. Yeats* (London: Routledge and Kegan Paul, 1960); Edward Engelberg, *The Vast Design: Patterns in W. B. Yeats's Aesthetic* (Toronto: University of Toronto Press, 1964); and Clark, *Yeats at Songs and Choruses.*

3. For the debate over the source of "Astraddle on the dolphin's mire and blood, / Spirit after spirit!" see Edgar Wind, "Raphael: The Dead Child on a Dolphin," *TLS,* 25 October 1963, 847; and replies by Margaret Whinney, 7 November 1963, 907, and James Tudor-Craig, 21 November 1963, 956.

4. Ian Fletcher, in the process of offering a few more, reviews the proposed visual sources of "Leda and the Swan," in "'Leda and the Swan' as Iconic Poem," *Yeats Annual No. 1,* ed. Richard J. Finneran (Atlantic Highlands, N.J.: Humanities Press, 1982), pp. 82–113.

5. See David R. Clark, "Poussin and Yeats's 'News for the Delphic Oracle,'" *Wascana Review* 2, no. 1 (1967), 33–44.

6. Clark, *Yeats at Songs and Choruses,* chap. 4, esp. pp. 94–136.

7. See ibid. for a clear summary of previous suggestions for sources.

8. *LTWBY* 353. See Colin White, *Edmund Dulac* (New York: Charles Scribners' Sons, 1976), p. 97. Hugh Ross Williamson in a letter to *TLS,* 31 August 1962, 657 mentions a "small Dulac centaur," which he owns, as a possible source. This picture, however, was done in 1923, the poem written in 1920.

9. White, *Edmund Dulac*, p. 92.

10. Ibid., p. 92; *LTWBY* 344. Yeats's reply praises one picture for the *Tanglewood Tales* especially, *Europa and Zeus*. See Diana Poteat Hobby, "William Butler Yeats and Edmund Dulac: A Correspondence, 1916–1938," Ph.D. diss., Rice University, 1981, p. 109.

11. See Salkeld's account, "Memories of W. B. Yeats," in Hobby, "Yeats and Dulac," pp. 146–152, excerpted in Joseph M. Hone, *W. B. Yeats, 1865–1939* (New York: Macmillan, 1943), pp. 326–329. Salkeld's painting was a "watercolour picture of a weird centaur at the edge of a dark wood: in the foreground, in the shade of the wood, lay the nine [corrected in pencil: seven] Ephesian 'topers' in a drunken stupor, while far behind on a sunny distant desert plain Elephants and the glory of a great army passed away into the infinitesimal distance" (in Hobby, "Yeats and Dulac," p. 150). The picture may coincide with the details of Yeats's poem because Salkeld painted it after he had seen a draft (although he said it was "impossible" to read) and heard Yeats talk of Ephesian topers and "eternity." Despite William O'Donnell's extensive efforts to track it down, Salkeld's picture remains lost. A third visual source is suggested by a passage from "Four Years" often quoted in connection with this poem. Speaking of cultural Unity of Being, Yeats wrote, "I knew no mediaeval cathedral, and Westminster, being a part of abhorred London, did not interest me, but I thought constantly of Homer and Dante, and the tombs of Mausolus and Artemisia, the great figures of King and Queen and the lesser figures of Greek and Amazon, Centaur and Greek. I thought that all art should be a Centaur finding in the popular lore its back and its strong legs" (*Au* 191). When C. T. Newton excavated the site of Mausolus' tomb for the British government in 1856, he discovered, in addition to the statues of Mausolus and Artemisia, three sculptural freizes. Two of them contain the "lesser figures" to which Yeats refers: a battle of Greeks and Amazons, and a battle of Lapiths and Centaurs. Yeats had seen Newton's finds in the British Museum, but the freize containing the centaurs is very fragmented and only one slab exists whole. This shows two Lapith women, but just the rear end of a centaur. The freize is, in addition, "undistinguished," according to Bernard Ashmole. Given the condition and quality of the freize, it is likely that Yeats had fused it in his mind with the more memorable and famous freize from the Parthenon of Lapiths and Centaurs, also in the British Museum. See Ashmole, *Architect and Sculptor in Classical Greece* (New York: New York University Press, 1972), pp. 162–164; and B. F. Cook, *Greek and Roman Art in the British Museum* (London: British Museum Publications, 1976), esp. p. 139.

12. Cleanth Brooks is only partly right in seeing the centaur as simply the animal side of man, in "Three Revolutions in Poetry: III, Metaphysical Poetry and the Ivory Tower," *Southern Review* 1, no. 3 (Winter 1935–1936), 581.

13. White, *Edmund Dulac*, p. 93.

14. John Unterecker, *A Reader's Guide to William Butler Yeats* (New York: Noonday Press, 1959), pp. 189–191; Richard Ellmann, *The Identity of Yeats* (New York: Oxford University Press, 1964), pp. 264–266; and Margaret E. Nielsen, "A Reading of W. B. Yeats's Poem 'On a Picture of a Black Centaur by Edmund Dulac,'" *Thoth* 4, no. 2 (Spring 1963), 67–73.

15. White, *Edmund Dulac,* p. 97. In a note to the archer vision episode in "The Trembling of the Veil," Yeats further reveals a possible connection between Greek pots and "On a Picture of a Black Centaur by Edmund Dulac." He refers the reader to Salzmann, *Nècropole de Camires,* plate 39, and quotes "a man learned in East Mediterranean antiquities" (*Au* 576): "'There is a fragment of a very early Greek pot showing two roughly drawn centaurs with long thin legs, one of the centaurs touching with his hand a tree which has long leaves and what seems to be a round fruit. Above the centaurs, but apparently separate from the tree, a bird perches on a twig'" (*Au* 579). Here, again, is the poem's combination of centaur and bird. The man has been identified as Vacher Burch. See Richard J. Finneran, "Explanatory Notes," in W. B. Yeats, *The Poems, A New Edition,* ed. R. Finneran (New York: Macmillan, 1983), p. 664.

16. Nielsen, "W. B. Yeats's Poem," p. 70.

17. See, e.g., Gibbon, *Decline and Fall of the Roman Empire* and Ruskin, *St. Mark's Rest*—a condensed version of *Stones of Venice*—which Yeats owned and perhaps bought for his 1907 trip, and which is subtitled *Written for the help of those few travellers who still care for its monuments.* See Herbert J. Levine, "Yeats's Ruskinian Byzantium," *Yeats Annual No.* 2, ed. Richard J. Finneran (Atlantic Highlands, N.J.: Humanities Press, 1983, p. 28. Castiglione had also used the term in one of Yeats's favorite books, *The Courtier,* in a passage Yeats quoted in his 1909 journal and in *A Vision* (*Mem* 157; *AV-A* 203). But Castiglione's notion of beauty as the "true monument and spoile of the victory of the soul" suggests a less corporeal notion of monument than Yeats's.

18. Joseph Daracott, ed., *All for Art: The Ricketts and Shannon Collection* (Cambridge: Cambridge University Press, 1979), p. 89.

19. Yeats's Senate speeches show his commitment to issues ranging from the National Gallery and Art School's governance to the protection of Irish manuscripts, the inspection of "Ancient Monuments" and the well-being of Ireland's stained-glass industry. See *The Senate Speeches of W. B. Yeats,* ed. Donald R. Pearce (Bloomington: Indiana University Press, 1960).

20. White, *Edmund Dulac,* pp. 130, 115, 173.

21. See, e.g., the Malatesta Cantos (8–11) for Pound's use of Renaissance medals.

22. Meštrović's designs arrived too late to be considered. The final designs chosen were by the young English sculptor Percy Metcalf. See Yeats's "What We Did or Tried to Do," in *W. B. Yeats and the Designing of Ireland's Coinage,* ed. Brian Cleeve (Dublin: Dolmen Press, 1972), pp. 12, 13, 20. Cleeve, in his introduction, points out the function of coins as monuments to a nation: "Of all a nation's monuments, the most enduring is its coinage" (p. 5).

23. In 1912–1913 Yeats unsuccessfully lobbied the Irish government to allocate funds to build a gallery for the collection that Lady Gregory's nephew Hugh Lane had promised to give Ireland if it could be properly housed (*L* 573–574). When Lane died in the sinking of the *Lusitania* in 1915, Yeats joined Lady Gregory's efforts to demonstrate that Lane had meant to leave the pictures to Ireland even though the codicil to his will doing so had never been witnessed. See *UP* 2:415–429, 431–432; *L* 616–623; Lady Augusta Gregory, *Case for the Return*

of Sir Hugh Lane's Pictures to Dublin (Dublin: Talbot Press, 1926); and *Senate Speeches of W. B. Yeats,* pp. 46–49, 118–124.

24. James White, *W. B. Yeats: A Centenary Exhibition* (Dublin: National Gallery of Ireland, 1965), p. 5.

25. Yeats could have found precedent in Rossetti, whose first poem for *The House of Life* talks of the sonnet as a "moment's monument."

26. Daniel A. Harris points out that "Yeats's historical myths of self-exploration were also myths of possession," a prime possession being Thoor Ballylee. See Harris, *Yeats: Coole Park and Ballylee* (Baltimore: Johns Hopkins University Press, 1974), p. 9. See also pp. 87–113 on Yeats's relation to Thoor Ballylee. Harris specifically notes that Yeats sought the right (his own) background for his portrait and found it in Ballylee.

27. *VP* 373. Yeats read *The Shorter Poems of John Milton* (London: Seeley and Compay, 1889), illustrated by Samuel Palmer. *The Lonely Tower* printed there differs from the picture usually shown—the 1879 version in the Victoria and Albert Museum. See the frontispiece for Henn, *Lonely Tower.*

28. "The word, which I had not thought of myself, is a word I want" (*L* 908–909).

29. For Yeats's use of portraits as points of departure, see Elizabeth W. Bergmann, "Yeats's Gallery," *Colby Library Quarterly* 15 (June 1979), 127–136.

30. Yeats, "William Blake and His Illustrations to the *Divine Comedy,*" *The Savoy,* 3 (July 1896), pp. 46–49.

31. My discussion of "Lapis Lazuli" is indebted throughout to William H. O'Donnell, "The Art of Yeats's 'Lapis Lazuli,'" *Massachusetts Review* 23 (Summer 1982), 353–367. For the origins and composition of the poem, see Jon Stallworthy, *Vision and Revision in Yeats's 'Last Poems'* (Oxford: Clarendon Press, 1969), pp. 43–59.

32. *VP* 566. Harold Bloom, countering the general admiration for this poem, warns that "we might be a little wary of 'the mesage of affirmation' Yeats is bringing to us." See Bloom, *Yeats* (New York: Oxford University Press, 1970), p. 438.

33. For a discussion of the kinds of gaiety in Yeats's poem and their relation to Indian philosophy, see Engelberg, *Vast Design,* pp. 170–172.

34. Dulac offered to translate the Chinese poem, but that was never done. See O'Donnell, "'Lapis Lazuli,'" pp. 354–355.

35. "Mountains," like Yeats's lapis lazuli, were traditionally used as objects of meditation. See ibid., p. 355.

36. Yeats resolves the Keatsian dilemma by making the picture's static figures move. See Unterecker, *Reader's Guide,* pp. 259–260.

37. Unterecker notes that the poem itself requires the reader to assemble its parts (ibid., p. 258). Yeats, thus, forces us into imaginative activity as we contemplate *his* work of art.

38. Bloom, *Yeats,* p. 286. See also Thomas Whitaker, *Swan and Shadow: Yeats's Dialogue with History* (Chapel Hill: University of North Carolina Press, 1964), p. 90.

39. *UP* 2:479. Yeats often fought censorship by recalling responses to Mi-

chelangelo's art. Frank O'Connor remembered an incident before a meeting with the Minister of Justice over the banning of George Bernard Shaw's "The Adventures of a Black Girl in Her Search for God." Yeats pulled out "a roll of stiff paper"—"a reproduction of the Sistine Chapel Roof," and "Higgins and I got no chance for our 'mechanical logic,' and the morning was wasted with a dissertation on Michaelangelo and the Pope." See O'Connor, "Yeats's Phantasmagoria," in *W. B. Yeats: Interviews and Recollections,* ed. E. H. Mikhail, 2 vols. (New York: Barnes and Noble, 1977), 2:268.

40. See Whitaker, *Swan and Shadow,* pp. 88–90, for a discussion of how Yeats qualifies his praise for Byzantium in *A Vision.*

41. Yeats's references to the four figures on the tombs of Giuliano and Lorenzo de'Medici are inaccurate, so it is difficult to know precisely which he has in mind. "Morning" and "Night" probably refer to *Day* and *Night* on Giuliano de'Medici's tomb: there *Night*'s sinew is "pulled tight," *Day*'s is "loosed," perhaps in repose (Michelangelo's figure depicts a middle-aged man, so Yeats may be playing here on the various associations of "repose"). But Yeats could also have in mind the two female figures, *Night* and *Dawn,* the latter on Lorenzo's tomb. Yeats explicitly mentions *Dawn* and *Night* elsewhere, but describes them as "vast forms shadowing the strength of antideluvian Patriarchs and the lust of the goat" (*UP* 2:438); this suggests, perhaps, that he is thinking of the two male figures *Day* and *Dusk.*

42. See Clark, *Yeats at Songs and Choruses,* chap. 4, for a discussion of the painting's identity. Yeats located the story of St. George and the dragon in phase 16, a phase "of physical life for its own sake": "What but a dragon could dream of thwarting a St. George" (*AV-A* 72, 73).

43. For a discussion of Yeats's antipathy to Modernism in general, see Thomas Parkinson, "Yeats and the Limits of Modernity," in *Yeats: An Annual of Critical and Textual Studies,* vol. 3, ed. Richard J. Finneran (Ithaca: Cornell University Press, 1985), pp. 60–71.

44. *VP* 610; *AV-A* 203. Engelberg attributes Yeats's desire for movement in art to the visual arts, especially to Pater's emphasis on movement as a characteristic of Greek art (*Vast Design,* p. 70).

45. *LTSM* 165. See also note 3, above. References to Renaissance and Greek art were revised out of "Sailing to Byzantium," perhaps because they seem less representative "monuments of unaging intellect." For transcriptions and a discussion of the poem's drafts, see Bradford, "Yeats's Byzantium Poems," pp. 96–116.

46. For a discussion of Michelangelo as "the presiding mind," see Melchiori, *Whole Mystery of Art,* pp. 242–243.

47. *AV-A* 73. In the 1925 *A Vision,* Yeats had also named Blake among those "begotten in the Sistine Chapel" (*AV-A* 209), and indeed Blake had admired Michelangelo. See Melchiori, *Whole Mystery of Art,* pp. 235–242, for Yeats's association of Michelangelo and Blake.

48. As Hazard Adams points out, however, "Blake beat on no walls." Yeats's idea of Blake's creative mind comes from observing the energy of the works themselves. See Adams, *Blake and Yeats: The Contrary Vision* (New York: Cornell University Press, 1955), p. 194.

49. J. B. Yeats, *Letters to His Son W. B. Yeats and Others, 1869–1922,* ed. Joseph Hone (London: Faber, 1944), pp. 193–194.

50. See Stallworthy, *Vision and Revision,* p. 122.

51. *VP* 438. Pater had distinguished between Michelangelo and Phidias along similar lines: Phidias purged his figures of the particulars of personality and circumstance to achieve universality, but at the expense of expression; Michelangelo, with his sense of the personal and peculiar, achieved "not vitality merely, but a wonderful force, of expression." See Pater, *The Renaissance: Studies in Art and Poetry,* ed. Donald L. Hill (Berkeley: University of California Press, 1980), pp. 51–53.

52. For a discussion of the sources of Yeats's knowledge of mathematics and its relation to his vision of history, see Whitaker, *Swan and Shadow,* pp. 235–245. For Yeats and mathematics, see also Melchiori, *Whole Mystery of Art,* pp. 254–258; Edward Engelberg, *Vast Design,* pp. 186–187, 189–191; Hazard Adams, *The Philosophy of the Literary Symbolic* (Tallahassee: Florida State University Press, 1983), pp. 300–312; and Daniel Albright, *The Myth Against Myth: A Study of Yeats's Imagination in Old Age* (London: Oxford University Press, 1972), pp. 126–131, who distinguishes usefully between proportional mathematics, of which Yeats approved, and Cartesian, of which he disapproved. All discuss mathematics in relation to "The Statues."

53. See Whitaker, *Swan and Shadow,* p. 236.

54. Yeats's bookplate on the inside title page is inscribed "Aberdeen May 19, 1923." On the verso is pasted an article "Mathematics of B.C. / Ancient Egyptian Papyrus Deciphered," marked in Yeats's hand, "Observer, Sept. 23, 1928." On p. 226 a marginal stroke runs along sections 170–185 about the remains of Empedocles, and in the margin is drawn the scheme of Yeats's gyres.

55. Yeats finished "Under Ben Bulben" in September 1938. See Unterecker, *Reader's Guide,* p. 293.

56. Yeats's new respect for mathematics helped him appreciate Robert Gregory's paintings—which at first "perplexed" him (*UP* 2:430)—with their underpinnings of geometrical shapes and to admire the mathematically founded art of Poussin, whose *Peleus and Thetis* (fig. 50) probably inspired the images in the last part of "News for the Delphic Oracle." For a discussion of the "Pythagorean landscape" of Poussin—temperamentally opposite to Yeats's early hero Claude—see Kenneth Clark, *Landscape into Art* (1949; reprint, Boston: Beacon Press, 1961), p. 67. For Poussin and the literary tradition, including Yeats, see D. S. Bland's fine "Poussin and English Literature," *Cambridge Journal* 6, no. 2 (Nov. 1952), 102–122. For a thorough discussion of Yeats's debt to Poussin in "News for the Delphic Oracle," see Clark, "Poussin and Yeats's 'News for the Delphic Oracle.'"

57. Mario Praz makes this point in "Sameness of Structure in a Variety of Media," in *Mnemosyne: The Parallel between Literature and the Visual Arts* (Princeton: Princeton University Press, 1970), pp. 60–64. Yeats pointed out the early connection between Pythagorean numbers and music: "Pythagoras made some measurement of the intervals between notes on a stretched string" (*L* 719). Those intervals became the basis of Pythagoras's numerical theories.

58. As shown, for example, in Yeats's revisions of "To Ireland in the Coming Times" for the 1925 *Early Poems and Stories,* where he uses "measure" to tie together the first creation with music, dance, and his own art. He originally justified his pursuit of the "red-rose-bordered hem" (which itself evokes the paintings and embroidery of the Pre-Raphaelites):

For in the world's first blossoming age
The light fall of her flying feet
Made Ireland's heart begin to beat;
And still the starry candles flare
To help her light foot here and there

In revision, these lines became:

When Time began to rant and rage
The measure of her flying feet
Made Ireland's heart begin to beat;
And Time bade all his candles flare
To light a measure here and there
(*VP* 138)

She of the "red-rose-bordered hem" is both the principle of order in the world and the muse of all the arts. As both, her measures make hearts beat. The artist, here specifically Yeats, "treads in measured ways," the next stanza tells us, and may "barter gaze for gaze" with those "elementary creatures" "that hurry from unmeasured mind." Yeats had thought of using the same opposition of measured and unmeasured in "Byzantium." In one draft "changeless metal" had been "measured metal" (although Bradford has some question about his reading of the words); the "mire and blood" had been described as "measureless"; and the "agony of trance" had been "a measured dance." See Bradford, "Yeats's Byzantium Poems," pp. 122–123.

59. E.g., Ellmann, *Identity of Yeats,* p. 156; and Melchiori, *Whole Mystery of Art,* p. 261.

60. See Ezra Pound, *Gaudier-Brzeska: A Memoir,* rev. ed. (New York: New Directions, 1970), pp. 91–92.

61. See Stallworthy, *Vision and Revision,* pp. 134, 141.

62. For discussions of this poem that treat some of the issues raised here but reach different conclusions, see Bloom, *Yeats,* pp. 441–445; Engelberg, *Vast Design,* pp. 180–204; Helen Vendler, *Yeats's "Vision" and the Later Plays* (Cambridge: Harvard University Press, 1963), pp. 112–113; Whitaker, *Swan and Shadow,* pp. 235–245; and F. A. C. Wilson, *Yeats's Iconography* (New York: Macmillan, 1960), pp. 290–303.

63. See p. 46 of George Harper and Walter Hood's "Notes," in *AV-A:* "Yeats liked to think that the Irish belonged to the Greek tradition: 'Not only Achilles but our own Cuchulain also, as competent men have thought, coming from that tribal fermentation' (rejected typescript)."

64. Yeats to William Rothenstein. Quoted in *Scattering Branches,* ed. Stephen Gwynn (New York: Macmillan, 1940), p. 52.

65. Most pages of Yeats's copy of A. Foucher's *The Beginnings of Buddhist*

Art and Other Essays in Indian and Central-Asian Archaeology (London: Humphry Mulford, 1917) are uncut (*YL* 98). Pages 111–115, however, are cut and contain a discussion of the Greek origins of the Buddha image. My thanks to Anne Yeats for pointing out this passage.

66. Whitaker, *Swan and Shadow*, p. 241. This view is opposed to Engelberg's argument that Yeats urges the Irish "to grow round and slow" like the Buddha (*Vast Design*, p. 204). The poem, it seems to me, calls for measurement to counter Eastern formlessness.

67. Buddha is a dreamer "of" the Middle Ages in that the rise of his image as depicted by Gandhara sculptors was contemporary with the development of medieval mysticism (Whitaker, *Swan and Shadow*, p. 241). Morris, of course, dreamed of the Middle Ages.

68. As Sarah Youngblood has pointed out in making an interesting distinction between Greek statues and the "Buddha-idol": "The active and passive distinction between statue and idol is implicit in the image of the mirror: Phidias gave women dreams through art; Buddha himself is the dreamer." See Youngblood, "The Structure of Yeats's Longer Poems," *Criticism* 5 (Fall 1963), 326.

Chapter 7. Yeats's Sculptural Poetry

1. Richard Ellmann, among others, comments on this change and attributes it primarily to Yeats's marriage. Ellmann, *Yeats: The Man and the Masks* (New York: Macmillan, 1948), p. 239.

2. For a discussion of Yeats's interest in materializations, see Kathleen Raine, "Hades Wrapped in Cloud," in *Yeats and the Occult*, ed. George Mills Harper (Canada: Macmillan, 1975), pp. 97–101.

3. *Ex* 53. As evidence of their presence, the materializations would sometimes "imprint their powerful faces upon paraffin wax [and] leave there sculpture that would have taken a good artist, making and imagining, many hours" (*Myth* 350).

4. As Robert Beum notes in *The Poetic Art of William Butler Yeats* (New York: Frederick Ungar, 1969), p. 44. Both Thomas Parkinson and Richard Ellmann note in particular a change between *The Winding Stair* and *Last Poems*. See Parkinson, *The Later Poetry* (1964: reprint, Berkeley: University of California Press, 1971), pp. 178–179; and Ellmann *The Identity of Yeats*, 2d ed. (New York: Oxford University Press, 1964), pp. 190–201.

5. Daniel Albright, *The Myth Against Myth* (London: Oxford University Press, 1972), p. 134; Frank Kermode, *Romantic Image* (New York: Random House, 1957), p. 36; Edward Engelberg, "Space, Time and History: Towards the Discrimination of Modernisms," *Modernist Studies* 1 (1974), 15; and Ellmann, *Man and Masks*, p. 275. See also F. A. C. Wilson's comment that "The Statues" is "one of the most monumental of *Last Poems*" (*Yeats's Iconography* [New York: Macmillan, 1960], p. 291), and Giorgio Melchiori's note that the later verse conveys "the feeling of concreteness" (*The Whole Mystery of Art: Pattern into Poetry in the Work of W. B. Yeats* [London: Routledge and Kegan Paul, 1960], p. 235).

6. *L* 605. C.f., Wordsworth's less domestic comparison of his canon to a

Gothic church in the preface to *The Excursion*. See *The Prose Works of William Wordsworth*, ed. W. J. B. Owen and Jane Worthington Smyser, 3 vols. (Oxford: Clarendon Press, 1973), 3:5–6.

7. *Au* 554–556. In December 1926 Yeats entertained the architect of Sweden's Staudhaus, Ragnar Östberg (*L* 720).

8. *Literary Essays of Ezra Pound* (New York: New Directions, 1968), p. 219; *UP* 2:435.

9. Yeats seems to have admired sculpture still part of its original stone, a taste he may have acquired from Pater who praised the incompleteness of Michelangelo's statues. See Pater, *The Renaissance*, ed. Donald L. Hill (Berkeley: University of California Press, 1980), p. 53. The reasons for their admiration, however, differ; Pater saw Michelangelo "etherealizing pure form"; Yeats saw form emerging from the formless.

10. *E&I* 477. In the prefatory poem to the early play *Vivien and Time*, Yeats had envisioned the dreamer gathering together statues to make his dreamland, but he had conceived of those sculptures as partaking of the evanescence of the dream. See Michael North, *The Final Sculpture: Public Monuments and Modern Poets* (Ithaca: Cornell University Press, 1985), p. 45.

11. *VP* 369. Dante's notion of "visible speech" and the sculpture of the Annunciation and statues of David and Tragan in canto 10 of the *Purgatorio* may have suggested Yeats's metaphor.

12. Quoted in Ann Saddlemyer, "'The Heroic Discipline of the Looking Glass': W. B. Yeats's Search for Dramatic Design," in *The World of W. B. Yeats*, rev. ed., ed. Robin Skelton and Ann Saddlemyer (Seattle: University of Washington Press, 1967), p. 63.

13. A. W. Schlegel, *A Course of Lectures on Dramatic Arts and Literature*, tr. John Black, 2 vols. (London: Baldwin, Cradock, and Joy, 1815), 1:9. This passage is pointed out in Nancy Goslee, "Plastic to Picturesque: Schlegel's Analogy and Keats's *Hyperion* Poems," *Keats-Shelley Journal* 30 (1981), 119.

14. See *Coleridge's Shakespeare Criticism*, ed. Thomas Raysor (Cambridge: Harvard University Press, 1930), 2:159–160.

15. Murray Krieger, in his examination of the *ekphrastic* principle in nineteenth- and twentieth-century poetry, adopts the romantic view and claims stillness the most significant quality of sculpture. See Krieger, "The Ekphrastic Principle and the Still Movement of Poetry, or *Laokoön* Revisited," in *The Play and Place of Criticism* (Baltimore: Johns Hopkins University Press, 1967), pp. 105–128.

16. Pater, *Renaissance*, p. 216. For Coleridge, see Goslee, "Plastic to Picturesque," p. 119. Keats's use of classical stillness, especially in *Hyperion*, is discussed in Ian Jack, *Keats and the Mirror of Art* (Oxford: Clarendon Press, 1967), pp. 162–163; and in Goslee, "Phidian Lore: Sculpture and Personification in Keats's Odes," *Studies in Romanticism* 21 (Spring 1982), 73–85.

17. For a discussion of sculpture in "The Island of Statues," see North, "The Paradox of the Mausoleum," in *The Final Sculpture*.

18. Thomas Whitaker, *Swan and Shadow: Yeats's Dialogue with History* (Chapel Hill: University of North Carolina Press, 1964), p. 237.

19. Ezra Pound, *Guide to Kulchur* (New York: New Directions, 1970), p. 49; and Donald Hall, Interview with Ezra Pound, in *Writers at Work: Second Series* (New York: Viking, 1963), p. 44.

20. Donald Davie's *Ezra Pound: Poet as Sculptor* (New York: Oxford University Press, 1964), p. 55 esp., argues the relationship between Pound's art and sculpture.

21. *AV-B* 29 and *OBMV* xxvi with some reservations.

22. Ezra Pound, *Gaudier-Brzeska: A Memoir* (New York: New Directions, 1970), pp. 85, 82; *The Letters of Ezra Pound, 1907–1941,* ed. D. D. Paige (New York: Harcourt, Brace and World, 1950), p. 91. Donald Davie notes Pound's fondness for the word "cut," in *Poet as Sculptor,* p. 122.

23. Karl Beckson, "Introduction," in *Aesthetes and Decadents of the 1890's: An Anthology of British Poetry and Prose* (New York: Random House, 1966), p. xix.

24. In "The Statues," the lines "And pressed at midnight in some public place / Live lips upon a plummet-measured face" (*VP* 610) seem to echo one of Olive Custance's (Lady Alfred Douglas's) poems on statues: "I yearn / To press warm lips against your cold white mouth" ("The White Statue," in *Aesthetes and Decadents,* ed. Beckson, p. 76).

25. *Literay Essays of Ezra Pound,* p. 363; *Au* 223.

26. Jerome H. Buckley, ed., *The Pre-Raphaelites* (New York: Random House, 1968), p. 96.

27. Pound spoke explicitly of *The Cantos'* material as stone. See Hall, *Writers at Work,* p. 39.

28. *Au* 150. George Redford's *A Manual of Ancient Sculpture: Egyptian—Assyrian—Greek—Roman* (London: Sampson Low, Marston, Searle and Rivington, 1886), which Yeats owned (*YL* 223), described the tomb as so surpassing "all others that it was named amongst the seven wonders of the world" (p. 157).

29. *Selected Poems of Ezra Pound* (New York: New Directions, 1957), p. 80.

30. *Au* 283. Characteristically, he links the sculpture to literature, George Bernard Shaw's *Arms and the Man.*

31. Austin Warren and René Wellek, *Theory of Literature,* 3d ed. (New York: Harcourt, Brace and World, 1956), p. 126.

32. Stephen A. Larrabee usefully distinguishes between "sculptural" and "sculpturesque." "Sculptural" means, he says, "Possessing, or suggesting the qualities of sculpture. 'Sculptural' is a general word and, when applied to poetry, refers to the suggestion of any work of sculpture or of the materials, instruments, or distinctive manner of expression belonging to the art." "Sculpturesque," on the other hand, "refers to any impression of sculpture, but primarily to suggestions of relief, vases, carving, etc.—that is, to sculpture which tends in the direction of the linear and pictorial rather than the 'statuesque.'" See Larrabee, *English Bards and Grecian Marbles: The Relationship between Sculpture and Poetry Especially in the Romantic Period* (1943; reprint, Port Washington, N.Y.: Kennikat Press, 1964), p. 290. Warren and Wellek, as well as Yeats's critics, seem to mean "sculptural" even when using the term "sculpturesque." I am primarily concerned here with the sculptural, not sculpturesque, qualities of Yeats's poetry.

33. F. David Martin, *Sculpture and Enlivened Space: Aesthetics and History* (Lexington: University of Kentucky Press, 1981), p. 1.

34. I follow Martin's terminology (ibid., p. 10): Tactual includes "both tactile perceptions, i.e., feelings of things and events outside the skin, and haptic perceptions, i.e., feelings of things and events inside the skin."

35. Ibid., p. 67: "The power and glory of painting is founded on the ability of the painter to abstract sensa—color, light, line, and texture—from the weight of things."

36. Herbert Read, *The Art of Sculpture* (Princeton: Princeton University Press, 1956), p. ix.

37. *VP* 369. Pound, of course, was also interested in the "hardness" of poetry and approvingly detected it in the poems of *Responsibilities* (*Literary Essays of Ezra Pound,* p. 379).

38. Martin, *Sculpture and Enlivened Space,* p. 62.

39. So Martin argues against Read's contention that sculpture must be touched to be properly perceived and that the Do Not Touch signs in museums rob us of an essential aesthetic experience (*Art of Sculpture,* p. 50). See F. David Martin, "The Autonomy of Sculpture," *Journal of Aesthetics and Art Criticism* 34 (1976), 282.

40. Martin, "Autonomy of Sculpture," p. 283. See also Read, *Art of Sculpture,* p. 48. Yeats may have encountered the distinction between touch and sight in Berkeley. See Berkeley, *Essay towards a New Theory of Vision,* in *The Works of George Berkeley,* rev. ed., ed. A. C. Fraser, 4 vols. (Oxford: Oxford University Press, 1901), 1:93–210. Yeats certainly admired Berkeley for indicting the prevailing "conception of a physical world without colour, sound, taste, tangibility" (*E&I* 401) and for describing "in his youth" "the *summum bonum* and the reality of Heaven as physical pleasure" (*E&I* 410).

41. Martin, "Autonomy of Sculpture," p. 283.

42. Despite Keats's interest in sculptural images. See Jack, *Keats and the Mirror of Art,* pp. 162–163; and Goslee, "Phidian Lore," pp. 73–85.

43. J. B. Yeats, *Letters to His Son W. B. Yeats and Others, 1869–1922,* ed. Joseph Hone (London: Faber, 1944), p. 190.

44. Because of sculpture's materiality, "abstract sculpture can never reach the abstractness of abstract painting" (Martin, "Autonomy of Sculpture," p. 285).

45. For a full discussion of "The Illusion of Movement in Sculpture," see Read, *Art of Sculpture,* pp. 88–104.

46. Emphasis mine. Quoted in Ellmann, *Man and Masks,* pp. 187–188.

47. Read, *Art of Sculpture,* p. 29.

48. Ibid., p. 32.

49. As early as 1900 Yeats had pleaded, unsuccessfully, that Parnell's memorial be well sculpted (*L* 333).

50. Read, *Art of Sculpture,* p. 74.

51. Ibid., p. 75.

52. *OBMV* 243–246. Pound's "hard," of course, implies much more than images of hard objects.

53. Ellmann comments on the solidity of Yeats's later poems in *The Identity of Yeats,* p. 146; Parkinson remarks, in particular, that "The solidity of *The Tower* has often been noted" (*Later Poetry,* p. 56).

54. Ellmann, *Identity of Yeats,* pp. 130–137.

55. D. S. Bland, in discussing Yeats's debt to Poussin, notices an analogy between the painter's and the poet's works: both are "hard" and "spare." Poussin got his effects, as Bland shows, from ancient sculpture. See Bland, "Poussin and English Literature," *Cambridge Journal* 6 (Nov. 1952), 122.

56. Ellmann, *Identity of Yeats,* p. 130. Parkinson, correctly I think, points out that the speakers of the later poems seem "indifferent to our presence" (*Later Poetry,* p. 66). As his comment indicates, however, we are present in a way that we were not in the early poems. The speaker recognizes that presence, if only with indifference.

57. Ellmann, *Identity of Yeats,* p. 137.

58. Ibid.

59. The picture was part of the Lane collection and has been renamed *Acis and Galatea.* See Anthony Blunt, *The Paintings of Nicolas Poussin: A Critical Catalogue* (London: Phaidon, 1966), p. 89. Edward Engelberg notes about Yeats in general: "The unmediated presence of the Yeatsian past as it makes us its virtual witness brings an uncanny familiarity." See Engelberg, "Space, Time and History," p. 16.

60. For a discussion of the significance of these sighs and their relation to the picture, see David R. Clark, "Poussin and 'News for the Delphic Oracle,'" in *Lyric Resonance: Glosses on Some Poems by Yeats, Frost, Crane, Cummings, and Others* (Amherst: University of Massachusetts Press, 1972), pp. 39–54. Daniel Albright treats the poem at length, focusing on its sources, especially "The Wanderings of Oisin" (*Myth Against Myth,* chap. 3).

61. See Ellmann, *Identity of Yeats,* p. 200.

62. Robert Beum calls the later verse "phonologically neutral" (*Poetic Art of William Butler Yeats,* p. 53).

63. See David Masson's discussion of sound production in "Word and Sound in Yeats's 'Byzantium,'" *English Literary History* 20 (June 1953), 144.

64. Perhaps reinforced by the especially forceful physical contact of various parts of the mouth required to produce these sounds.

65. Sounds, in general, are, according to John Dewey (invoking William James), "spatially voluminous." See Dewey, *Art as Experience* (New York: G. P. Putnam's Sons, 1934), p. 207.

66. See Richard Paget's discussion of "gestural language" in his standard work, *Human Speech* (London: Kegan Paul, Trench, Trubner and Co., 1930), p. 157.

67. W. K. Wimsatt, "In Search of Verbal Mimesis," in *Day of the Leopards* (New Haven: Yale University Press, 1976).

68. Frank Kermode notes that "concreteness" is one of the characteristics of the romantic image and observes that it need not be visual, but he does not discuss how that concreteness is conveyed. See Kermode, *Romantic Image,* p. 46.

69. Beum, *Poetic Art of William Butler Yeats,* p. 51.

70. Ibid.

71. *Princeton Encyclopedia of Poetry and Poetics,* rev. ed., ed. Alex Preminger (Princeton: Princeton University Press, 1974), p. 450.

72. Ellmann, *Identity of Yeats,* p. 140.

73. *L* 402; *Mem* 166. Phillip Marcus's "Incarnation in 'Middle Yeats,'" in *Yeats Annual No. 1,* ed. Richard J. Finneran (Atlantic Highlands, N.J.: Humanities Press, 1982), pp. 68–81, brought these two passages to my attention, although he puts them to different use.

74. See Melchiori, *Whole Mystery of Art,* chap. 5.

75. Yeats in later years consistently associated unity with three-dimensional form. While the circle served to symbolize the approach to and falling away from unity, Yeats used the sphere when speaking of perfect Unity of Being in the Thirteenth Cycle (*AV-A* 170). Thus, in "Chosen" the wheel of the zodiac resolves into a sphere when "his heart my heart did seem" (*VP* 535).

76. Walter Pater, *Greek Studies* (London: Macmillan, 1910), pp. 252–253.

77. Ellmann, *Identity of Yeats,* p. 188.

78. Parkinson, *Later Poetry,* p. 201. See also Adelyn Dougherty, *A Study of Rhythmic Structure in the Verse of William Butler Yeats* (The Hague: Mouton, 1973), p. 56.

79. For readings of the poem, see John Unterecker, *A Reader's Guide to William Butler Yeats* (New York: Noonday, 1959), pp. 238–240; and James L. Allen's less convincing "Yeats' 'Her Vision in the Wood,'" *Explicator* 18 (May 1960), no. 45.

80. William York Tindall notes the "classical surface" of Yeats's later poetry. See Tindall, "The Symbolism of W. B. Yeats," in *Yeats: A Collection of Critical Essays,* ed. John Unterecker (Englewood Cliffs, N.J.: Prentice-Hall, 1963), p. 51.

81. J. B. Yeats, *Letters to His Son and Others,* p. 193.

82. Michelangelo, too, had toyed with this idea in a less radical way. In a sonnet he wrote, in response to G. B. Strozzi's praise of *Night,* the statue speaks to her admirer. See Jean Hagstrum, *The Sister Arts: The Tradition of Literary Pictorialism and English Poetry from Dryden to Gray* (Chicago: University of Chicago Press, 1958), p. 74.

83. See Edward Engelberg, "Absence and Presence in Yeats's Poetry," in *Yeats Annual No. 1,* pp. 48–67. Although different in approach, the following discussion is indebted to Engelberg's observations.

Index